© Max Lamirande, 2024
Published by Max Lamirande
Edited by Kevin Plaisance, MD

© 2024 Saguenay, Quebec, Canada

All rights reserved. No part of this book may be reproduced or modified in any form, including photocopying, recording, or by any information storage and retrieval system, without permission in writing from the publisher.

Cover image copyrights:
Alamy C4614A – Standard Image license
Order OY96234509

Cover image copyrights:
Alamy – TY7TRD - Standard Image license
Order OY96234390

Dear reader,

The first installment of the WW1 Alternate series was a lot of research before and during writing because I am less knowledgeable about the First World War.

But in doing so, I have discovered an entirely new world, and let me tell you, it will make for a very interesting book series. Just the naval aspects, which were not that exciting in the real war, will be very cool to write about since you know me, I love big gun ships and big gun battles. And this time around, there are no annoying planes or aircraft carriers to steal the show :).

We pick up the story right after the German conquest of Paris and as the Russians are still on the offensive in the East.

A plethora of new strategic and diplomatic possibilities open up with the fall of Paris. The Italians reconsider their potential involvement with the Entente, the Greek King, already a Germanophile, starts getting some support, and the German High Seas Fleet might just find a way to break the British blockade with all those nice and tidy French ports rip for the taking.

I hope you enjoy the reading!

PROLOGUE
Politics and Diplomacy

Rome, Italy, Palazzo Montecitorio
Seven days after the German victory at the Marne, September 19th, 1914

The history of Palazzo di Montecitorio, one of the most symbolic places of Italian politics, began in 1653 when Pope Innocent X ordered it to be built. It remained a papal building until the unification of Italy, when the building was chosen as the seat of the Chamber of Deputies. It was thus the logical place for a meeting for the Italian leadership to decide on its next moves following the major German victory at the Marne River a week before.

Italian Prime Minister Antonio Salandra took a sip of his grappa as dinner was being concluded with some dessert. A glass of grappa was a traditional Italian after-dinner drink. It packed a fiery punch and was believed in Italian culture to help digest big meals. He felt his throat light with fire, and it warmed his stomach as it settled down. He took a deep breath. Life was good.

Around the table with him, also enjoying their own glasses of grappa, sat Foreign Minister Antonio di San Giuliano, an experienced diplomat, cynical and cautious. The man was pale and sick but had been brought to this important discussion as it was about the future direction of Italy in the developing world war. His replacement in waiting, another career diplomat, was Sidney Sonnino, a shrewd man that Salandra liked very much because they saw things the same way. Tommaso Tittoni, the ambassador to France, was also there to report on the French mood and what they would do next. And, of course, the chief of the general staff, General Luigi Cadorna, was invited to the discussion. The only noticeable absentee for the critical talks was King Victor Emmanuel III, who had severe psychiatric problems and thus could not attend.

Antonio Salandra and the Italian cabinet were confronted with a critical decision on the outbreak of World War One in July. Despite the generation-old Triple Alliance of Germany, Austria-Hungary, and Italy,

Salandra (and the rest of the group assembled before him that day in the Roman Palace) had chosen neutrality, taking for legal ground the failure of the Austrians to consult the Italian government before they attacked Serbia as was mandatory by Article 7 of the Triple Entente.

Before events forced them to meet over the matter that day, Italy had been heading toward joining the Entente or, at the very least, supporting them in some way. With the exception of a few people in the Italian High Command, no one considered the possibility of Italy joining the side of the Central Powers as a serious eventuality. And that included the Germans and Austrians, who had a clear understanding of the situation of the Triple Alliance.

The Alliance that Italy had joined in 1882 was defensive in nature. Signed at a time when Italo-French relations were comparatively tense, the country had looked for friends then. But none of the men deciding in this room had been around at the time of the agreement with the Germans, so no one really cared. The central problem with the German alliance was the inclusion of Austria, Italy's nemesis. The damned Austrians had invaded Italy many times, and it had taken a herculean effort to oust them. Even then, in 1914, they still held Italian territories. This had been and was still a very hard thing to accept to secure the German friendship that, anyway, not many Italian politicians felt they still needed.

The relationship between Italy and Austria was not only difficult due to the long history of war, Austrian occupation, and rivalries between the two countries (three wars were fought between 1848 and 1866, and before that, Austria had just occupied most of Northern Italy) but by the unfinished settling of the issue of the "unredeemed lands."

Since the Italian unification, nationalists wailed for a return of Trento's large port cities like Trieste and Fiume, the province of Istria, and parts of the Adriatic coast. At the same time, Austria-Hungary couldn't comply with Italian demands. These cities and areas were critical to the Navy and the economy. Also, giving in to any national demands was tantamount to suicide for an Empire that had many other nationalities claiming their own country or being permitted to join nations where their brethren lived, like the Romanians in Transylvania or the Poles and Ukrainians in Galicia.

By 1914, when the war came barging in because of the European system of alliances, Germany was no longer that of Bismarck, and Italy was no longer mad at France. It was the opposite: Italy viewed Germany as a distant ally, Austria-Hungary as an enemy, and France as a friend. The idea of joining the Central Powers when the Austrians decided to go to war against the Serbians and the Germans proclaimed their unconditional support was never really discussed by the Italians – who instead proclaimed their neutrality.

But that was then, and now the situation had changed yet again. The German Army had won an unequivocal battle and occupied Paris. Hell, it wasn't even certain that the French would continue to fight. They had sued for peace in 1871 during the Franco-Prussian War. Notwithstanding their good feelings toward France and the Entente in general, it wouldn't be good for Italy if Germany and Austria won the war. Then Rome would be truly isolated.

Once his grappa was completely settled and he felt his companion glasses were done with theirs as well, the Prime Minister spoke. *"Well, gentlemen. As we have discussed over this excellent dinner, the situation is now a lot different than a month ago when we contemplated the possibility of either staying neutral or else joining the Entente against our old enemy, the Austrians."* He paused, joining his hands on the table and outing his elbows on the table. The room they were in was richly decorated, with expensive rugs on the floor, draperies on the walls and windows, and painting from well-known artists like Leonardo Davinci.

"*Indeed,*" answered Sydney Sonnino, the future Foreign Minister. The man worked under the current (and very sick) Antonio di San Giuliano, the ever-cautious one. Sonnino continued. *"The situation has changed* so much that we must decide on a new course of action since it could be that the Central Powers win the war." An uneasy silence installed itself in the room. It was dispelled a few moments later once everyone refilled their grappa glasses. *"Why don't we just stay neutral and sit this one out,"* countered the real Foreign-affairs minister Antonio di San Giuliano. *"Caution is often the best of options."*

"Well, we finally get to the essence of the matter and the reason I have all called you to dine with me tonight," said Salandra. *"We have discussed all of it during dinner, now we must decide on a course to follow. I know the German ambassador is waiting to hear news from us, as well as the French one,"* he continued, giving a head nod to Tommaso Tittoni, the ambassador to France.

"While we all want the return of our countrymen from Austria into the fold," began the Italian chief of the general staff, General Luigi Cadorna, *"There are other interesting territories we could gain from considering the Central Powers option."* Salandra smiled, as well as Sonnino. While the two men had wanted to stay neutral and negotiate a good deal to get Austro-Hungarian territory if they decided to join the Entente, this train of thoughts and intentions appeared to be an unlikely scenario after the German victory at the Marne and the occupation of Paris. The Kaiser held the trump card now.

If the French sued for peace or were defeated, there would be no victory for the Entente in the West as the British didn't have a big enough standing army. Things looked good for the Allies in the East, with Russia pushing for Berlin and occupying all of Galicia, but overall, without France and its millions of soldiers, Salandra didn't see how they could win. Thus, why join the losing side?

"What do you have in mind, General," asked Sonnino. *"Well, gentlemen, we all know that our Irredentism movement wants territory from France and England. These national territories in Austria are, of course, critical to our national objectives, but there are others. We have been claiming for the return of Nice and Monaco, Corsica,*

and Malta, amongst others. Why don't we join the winning side and just grab them?" The Military man paused to gently hit the table with his fist. *"While we are at it, there are always some nice lands in North Africa, like Tunisia, that we could claim."*

Sonnino nodded silently with his head while the ever-cautions Foreign Minister Antonio di San Giuliano kept a neutral face; the sick and cautious man was clearly not happy and then spoke again. *"You all should be wary of taking any rash decision. I understand that the situation has changed and that the better option might be NOT to join the Entente, but I believe we should simply stay out and continue to stay neutral. We do not know what the British will do if we enter the war."* Everyone around the table knew what Sonnonio proposed, and that was to intervene on the side of the Central Powers and honor the Triple Alliance treaty. But things could go awry if they challenged the Franco-British, and Giuliano had just issued a warning. While his words were from the mouth of a cautious, old, and hesitant man, they nonetheless sounded plausible. Tittoni, the ambassador to France, remained obviously lukewarm about the idea and nodded to the Foreign Minister's words. "Indeed, Mr. Giuliano."

Salandra was a seasoned politician and knew that it wouldn't be good to do something without all of these men in agreement and obviously, the men of power in Rome were not all of the same mind. San Giuliano and Tittoni were not excited, and perhaps even downright completely against the idea of a Central Powers alliance; thus, he would have to work on swaying them to his side or get rid of them. The Prime Minister had already decided that Italy would go to war on the side of the Central Powers. *"Let's see what the German ambassador has for us, and then we will reconvene. Do we all agree?"*

Wilhelm II in Paris,
September 21ˢᵗ, 1914

Following the German victory at the Battle of the Marne and the subsequent occupation of Paris, Kaiser Wilhelm II, the German Emperor, decided to pay a visit to the French capital and to his victorious troops. He came along with a delegation of military officers, including his chief of staff, von Moltke the Younger, and his Minister of war, von Falkenhayn.

The first stop was near Versailles in order to get a chance to visit the troops still facing the enemies of Germany. Wilhelm had walked amongst his soldiers, shaking hands, giving some medals, and personally congratulating them. The entire affair was far from the front, where the fighting was sort of mellowed out because the French had dug in trench lines from the Atlantic Ocean to Verdun and taken the high ground. The German forces dug as well and, in a sense, were quite content to stay on their side of the no man's land because they were exhausted.

The battle of the Marne had been a near run thing. The difference between the victory they now enjoyed and utter, abject defeat had been the timely arrival of 180,000 reinforcements that were never sent to the East. The situation there was now dire and even Berlin was threatened, with the Russian forces now almost on the Vistula River. It didn't look like it would take much for the Tsarist forces to push Ludendorff and Hindenburg's forces further into Germany.

The day after the Kaiser visited the frontlines, the tour itself began early in the morning. The streets were empty, every Frenchmen still wary of what the German occupier could do to them; they all stayed at home, window shutters closed. The normally bustling and noisy city was thus dominated by an eerie silence, and the entire scene was almost creepy, with the morning mist enveloping the central parts of the city.

They then moved toward the Place de la Concorde and spent some time on the Champ Elysés, where Wilhelm was able to contemplate the famous Arc de Triomphe and under where his troops had paraded a few days earlier. "*Well, Falkenhayn,*" he said to the Minister of War, riding the black car with an open top just beside him. Von Moltke was in the car behind them. "*It appears we are now masters of this place, just like my father before me.*" Kaiser Wilhelm the 1st had indeed conquered Paris with his troops in 1871 during the Franco-Prussian War and toppled the then-French Emperor, Napoleon III. "*Indeed, your Majesty,*" answered Falkenhayn with a broad smile.

The German leader looked at the engravings commemorating the victories of the Great Napoleon Bonaparte, commenting on some of them and what he knew of the battles commemorated in the markings. For a moment, Wilhelm felt like the conqueror of old and decided that the world would be his.

Half an hour later, they arrived at the magnificent view of the *Trocadéro*, a large plateau-like square facing the Eiffel Tower, just on the other side of the River Seine. There, the group admired the view of the tower, and several photographs were taken as propaganda material for the German Press and the rest of the world. The shot of a German Emperor with the symbol of France behind him was striking and would shock the entire world in the next few days as they made their way to newspapers worldwide.

Afterward, they went to the Eiffel Tower and visited the Champ de Mars. The Hôtel des Invalides was the third monument that the Kaiser felt he had to see, to spend some time looking at the Great Napoleon Bonaparte's tomb, a character that he admired for his military and strategic talents.

After passing in front of the now closed-down Assemblée Nationale building (all the French politicians had left for Bordeaux to organize a temporary capital), the convoy headed toward the Panthéon. Wilhelm was again impressed by the grandeur of it all, and he commented that the building reminded him of the Befreiungshalle monument, a large structure just like the pantheon, built by an old Bavarian King to commemorate the victory against Napoleonic France.

The final stop of the day was reserved for the famous Sacré-Cœur Basilica on Montmartre (a hill with a magnificent view of all of Paris). The Kaiser did not like the church at all, but he and his men enjoyed the view and bathed in the glory of it all. The view of Paris was magnificent from there, and Wilhelm wondered how things could get better.

That very evening, as Wilhelm II sat in the luxurious coach in his special diplomatic train, he felt as if he was finally fulfilling his destiny, and pulling all of Germany with him toward the world domination he so wanted. Falkenhayn and Moltke, both with him in the coach, were sound asleep, but he was not able to. He was dead tired but couldn't stop his mind from swirling with the myriad of possibilities now offering themselves to the German Empire. France might sue for peace, and if it did not do that, well, he felt (along with his generals) that they would just have to finish the job and completely beat the Anglo-French.

The occupation of the French Channel and Atlantic ports was the priority to have bases for the High Seas Fleet. With Brest, Le Havre, and Cherbourg in German hands, all was possible for his precious navy. He was thus confident it could break the naval blockade that England was imposing on Germany.

The situation in the East was worrisome, with the Russian hordes already at the Vistula, something his generals had said could not happen as the decision was taken not to send any reinforcements to the East. But be as it may with their wishes, the new commander they'd named a few weeks ago (Hindenburg) did not have the men to contend with so many Russian soldiers. Things would soon be rectified, as General von Moltke had told him they were railing hundreds of thousands of soldiers now that things were settling down somewhat in the West.

The Austro-Hungarians were struggling mightily against the powerful Russian offensive, which booted them out of Galicia altogether, and there again von Moltke had told him that the German Army was sending reinforcement to stiffen the K.u.K. Army's spine (name of the armed forces meaning in German: *"kaiserlich und königlich,"* and in Hungarian: *"csaszari es kiralyi"*).

On the diplomatic front, the Italians were now wavering and looking to meet up with his ambassador as the great victory at the Marne seemed to have changed their mind about their neutrality or even the possibility of joining the Entente powers. He also knew that the smaller powers of Europe would now look favorably on Germany or, at the very least, stay neutral. Romania, Greece, and Bulgaria would either likely stay out or join.

The Ottomans were doing all right in the Black Sea, although they seemed to be floundering badly in the Caucasus. He took a mental note to ask von Moltke about what could be done to help there since Germany did not have a land link (yet) with Turkey, as the rail lines cut through enemy Serbia and neutral Bulgaria.

As his eyes closed slowly, the German Emperor decided that things were looking up and that the war was going well for the Central Powers. Now, he just needed to get his army to smash the Tsarist forces, and all would be well.

Meeting in the new War Office building
Whitehall, London, September 22nd, 1914

France was in trouble, and things were not looking good for the future and the successful prosecution of the war. It was why the President of the French Republic, Raymond Nicolas Landry Poincaré, and its Prime Minister, Rene Viviani, were on a visit to London. Both men were flanked by their newly-named commander-in-chief, General Ferdinand Foch, and the top men in the Navy, Admiral Augustin Boue de Lapeyrere. The idea of the meeting with the British was to discuss what was next as to the continuation of the war. They were also accompanied by several lower-ranking politicians, military officers, and their aides.

Facing them were the leaders of Great Britain and the British Empire. First and foremost, the British Prime Minister, Herbert Henry Asquith, flanked by Herbert Kitchener, 1st Earl Kitchener, the Secretary of State for War. Beside them sat Winston Churchill, the First Lord of the Admiralty (head of the Navy), and British Foreign Secretary Sir Edward Grey.

The area at the west end of that day's meeting in Whitehall was called, in older times, the Royal Palace of Westminster, close by the Abbey. This Palace was an uncoordinated collection of buildings, many virtually unchanged for well over 100 years, cold, draughty, and uncomfortable. Over time, the area transformed into the center of British imperial power, with all its ministries housed in the area.

It was where the new War Office Building was located. Its construction was finished in 1906. The look of the all-white front of the building was grandiose-looking. Starting from the 2nd floor and up, were furbished by rows of columns. On the rooftop sides were placed stone statues showing Peace and War, Truth and Justice, Fame, and Victory, and on top of each of the four corner towers, a decorative dome was put in order to mask the irregularity of the building's shape.

The Main Entrance, Grand Hall, and Staircase were placed in the center of the west front, with the principal rooms on the second floor. The Secretary of State for War (Kitchener) occupied a suite above the main entrance, while the Parliamentary Under Secretary of State occupied the room across the main staircases. The Chief of the Imperial General Staff had his office in a large room in the center of the southern side. The circular tower rooms at the corners were for other members of the Army Council, and the Army Council Room was in the center of the north side. The more important rooms and office suites were decorated with great care, and a few were adorned with oak paneling.

The room that surrounded them and their meeting was intricately decorated with wood paneling, an old but expensive-looking rug, and a chandelier above. In the back of the room sat a fireplace, but the day was hot enough, and there was no fire burning in it. A large central table with twelve chairs sat right in the middle, where the group of Frenchmen and Englishmen were having their discussions.

The discouraged mood in the room was palpable as these proud men met to discuss defeat, its aftermath, and what should be done next. Following the fall of Paris, there had been a couple of days of instability within the French government as some elements sought to open peace talks with the Germans. But the President of the Republic, Raymond Poincarré, soon clamped down the political dissent and reaffirmed France's commitment to final victory.

After all, the French longed for revenge following their humiliation in 1871, and there was no way they would just stop fighting only because they lost Paris. The majority of the French territory was still free, all its colonies were yet to bring their contributions to Europe, and the French had the backing of the might of the British Empire. The fleets of the Entente were intact and still dominated the seas, so there was still hope.

"Gentlemen," started British Prime Minister Herbert Henry Asquith. "Thank you for coming to meet with us on so short notice," he continued, looking at one of the two translators standing erect beside the table to convey his words to the Frenchmen. Poincarré smiled at his British counterpart. The French delegation had come by ships via Brest and the dreadnought battleship France (a symbolic choice given the situation) had sailed right up to London to be in time for the discussions. He continued speaking. "Well, circumstances dictated that we... How should I put it... Meet urgently." "Indeed, Mr. President," answered Asquith as affably as possible. "First and foremost, I would like to reaffirm the British Empire's commitment to France and to the final victory."

The Frenchmen on the other side of the table visibly relaxed. They could not accept another defeat at the hands of the hated German enemy and knew that without Britain, the struggle would be pointless. The English didn't have the biggest army in the world, but it was growing and besides, what they had was proficient enough. Their fleets were powerful as well, and could bring the goods and soldiers to prosecute the war to France.

"Mr. Prime Minister, this is much appreciated," answered the President of the French Republic. "So, how do we do this," continued Pointcarré. The frontline was finally fixating on a rough line from the Atlantic Ocean to Verdun and down the Vosges. The French and British forces were busily digging trench lines to stop the Germans from advancing any further. So far, it had been working. The combination of artillery, trench, and machine guns had stopped all enemy assault and now the Kaiser's forces seemed to be content to stay on their side of no man's land.

While the main French concerns were to stop the Germans from advancing south, the British were greatly worried that the Germans would take over the French Channel and Atlantic coast harbors. "His Majesty's Government is concerned by the German seizure of all

French lands and port facilities north of Paris. What can be done about it?"

The French had been expecting these questions from the British. While they didn't want to give any more French land to the hated Huns, some things were not possible. Ferdinand Foch, the man now in command of the French Army since General Joffre was sacked, was a believer in defense first and then offense. He intervened following a nod from his President. *"We understand your concerns, Mr. Prime Minister, but as of this moment, there isn't much the French Army south of Paris can do about the enemy wanting to conquer these lands. We have garrisons in every important city, and they will defend them. Apart from having more British or other Allied troops land in the harbors we want to defend, there isn't much we can do since the main German armies are between us and Northern France."*

While the British knew of this, they had expected such an answer, and Churchill was ready for it. *"The Royal Navy would be in a position to transport troops from Southern France to the northern harbors by way of our numerous transport and commandeered cruise line ships. We propose to fortify the main cities of Brest, le Havre, and Calais. We have secured several British units for this and believe that if France supplies enough troops, we can hold them from the sea by using the fleet to supply the garrisons."* French Navy commander Admiral Augustin Boue de Lapeyrere pinched in. *"My ships could also participate in the operation, and I believe what Lord Churchill is proposing is possible."* Half an hour later, it was decided the Allies would fight for the three harbors, send troops, and position the fleets to supply them.

For the next few hours, the subject then moved to several economic and logistical matters before coming back to the military and diplomatic. The hot subject of the day was Italy. *"What news from Rome,"* asked the French Prime Minister, Rene Viviani. Before the Marne debacle, talks between the British and the Italians had started over the possibility that they would join the war on the side of the

Entente. The talks had been going in the right direction, albeit they had still been far from an agreement. Now that Paris was occupied and the Central Powers appeared to have the upper hand in the West, having Italy on the side of the Entente wasn't a safe bet anymore.

This question was for British Foreign Secretary Sir Edward Grey, thus he took the reigns for the discussion. "*Honestly, gentlemen,*" he paused to make his words more dramatic and waited for the translator to say his words in French. "*I cannot say what the Italians will do; however, they have started to dither and stall in our talks. The German ambassador has been received in Rome a few times already, which doesn't indicate anything positive. I have it from some sources that Prime Minister Antonio Salandra was there during the talks.*"

Everyone around the table stayed silent for a moment. They all knew the Italian government was trying to play its cards opportunistically. That state of affairs had suited them fine when Rome had declared itself neutral and started to talk with the Entente, but now it was the opposite situation. If the Italians joined the Central Powers, things would get very dicey very fast. *"That cannot be good,"* grunted Churchill, mirrored in his reaction by Kitchener and General Ferdinand Foch.

The Italian involvement would bind troops in the south at the border between the two countries. While the Nice and Monaco areas were well-fortified, the French "*Armee des Alpes*" had already been disbanded on the 17th of August for it to be incorporated into the Armée d' Alsace by Joffre as he tried to master the German onslaught.

It didn't take a military genius to see that Italy would attack the French alongside their border with five to eight corps in the event of war. This, in turn, would tie down troops that were dearly needed to contain the Germans south of Paris and at the eastern border.

With the inclusion of Italy, the Mediterranean Sea would be a contested one because the Italian fleet sported several dreadnought battleships. The French Navy was roughly its equal, but in an Italy-joining-the-Central-Powers scenario, the combination of the Austro-Hungarians and Italian navies would spell real trouble for the Entente. The British would thus have to send ships from their Grand Fleet in the North Sea (dearly needed to contain the powerful German fleet), and that wasn't good either.

Altogether, it was clear to the men in the war room that the addition of Italy would have a significant impact on the war and its outcome, regardless of Italian military performance. *"We need to find a way to sway the Italians to our side or, at the very least, keep them out of the conflict." "Or,"* Churchill made a contorted face while everyone turned their heads toward him, *"if it looks like they will join Germany, we attack them first."*

White House, Oval Office
September 24th, 1914

28th U.S. President Woodrow Wilson shook his head in disgusted amusement. There it was on the day's newspaper's front page: a picture of the boastful and ridiculous German Kaiser in front of the Eiffel Tower. Damn Europeans and their wars. They couldn't agree on anything, and if he had anything to say about it, he would keep America out of the war.

He was sitting alone in the Oval Office on that beautiful morning in September as the bright light of the sun entered the windows, giving way to the Rose Garden. He felt pretty good, and looked forward to his day, as he had to meet with a few of his people on important internal matters.

Wilson did not have a great deal of experience dealing with foreign affairs, and was not interested in bringing his country into the war. He had even promised it to his people. He was hell bent on peace and finding a way to get the leaders on the old continent to talk and figure things out. He also didn't want to deal with what he considered a stupid and childish German leader. The Central Powers did not correspond to his idea of a good political system, nor did the Russian Empire, for that matter. He bent the newspaper in two, his mind dwelling for a moment on a world where that stupid German Emperor was victorious in Europe and having to deal with the bastard. He didn't like the train of thought it created. Unfolding the newspaper again, he continued reading about the Kaiser's visit to Paris and tried to find some sense in the man and was surprised to find himself rooting for the Brits and the French for a change.

Then, for a flicker of a moment, he wondered if there was something he could do about it. Of course, he could, but he knew the country was not ready nor interested in war.

St Petersburg, Imperial Russia
Alexander Palace, September 22nd, 1914

Tsar Nicolas II, Emperor of all the Russians, sat below the great chandelier in the portrait hall of the Alexander Palace, the magnificent castle where he and his family resided. The room he was in got its name from a large number of portraits of the Romanov family members, including Nicholas I, his four sons, Alexander I, and Catherine the Great. This was also the ceremonial room, decorated with French Jacobean furniture, grand bronze chandeliers dating back to Catherine the Great, and exclusive parquetry in a diamond pattern.

He was reading yet another glowingly positive report from the front and smiled. While he knew that things were always embellished for him and had to read between the lines, this report was even more positive than what he was used to. And there was good cause for it. Following a few successful battles in East Prussia, his brave forces had almost reached the Vistula River, deep in German territory. The enemy armies were reeling back in disarray before his glorious soldiers. He fancied himself a great war leader and took a mental note to congratulate his uncle, Supreme Russian Commander in Chief, Grand Duke Nikolai Nikolaevich.

Nicolas was fascinated by the account of the advances across the German Empire and even more excited at the ton of victories over the Austro-Hungarians in Galicia. There, his armies had achieved an unheard of level of success, conquering most of the province, including its capital, Lemberg. There was only one area where the enemy resisted, and it was at the fortress of Przemysl.

The Tsar disregarded the not-so-stellar reports on the supply situation of his forces, nor on the logistical problems to bring them supplies to the frontlines. It seemed that his generals and brave soldiers overcame these details, but that was not the case.

The only reason the Russian armies were so successful was because the Germans had not yet transferred enough troops to attack and because of Austria's military weakness. That the Tsar didn't know or didn't want to know, but would soon get a taste of what the German Army could really do.

From Nicolas' point of view, the war was going well. While he worried somewhat at the German conquest of Paris and the unfolding disaster in the West, for him, these events were far away and as long as Russia was faring well, the rest would figure itself out. The Serbs had repulsed two Austro-Hungarian offensives, and looked like they would resist still for a while. With his troops advancing in Galicia and soon in Hungary proper, there was a good chance the war could be brought to a successful conclusion and that he could save the Serbs.

He disregarded the bad news out of the Black Sea as a mere sideshow theater. Yes, his pre-dreadnought fleet was gone, but there were two dreadnoughts in the last building stages that would be launched not so far in the future, and then he intended to get his admirals to even the scores with the Turks. At the same time, he read wolfishly about his troops' successes against the Turks in the Caucasus. The Battle of Sarikamish looked like it would be a landslide, the Ottomans had attacked in bad weather and with not enough troops to defeat his Caucasus forces.

The Tsar was happy, and his Empire was doing stellar. Clouds were gathering above, and the sky was darkening, but he didn't care for now.

Hofburg Imperial Palace
Vienna, September 24th, 1914

Franz Joseph was a monarch from a bygone era. In 1914, he had been the ruler of Austria-Hungary for sixty-six years. He was a conservative, a reactionary, and a nationalist. He was certainly no lover of democracy, didn't like too much liberty for the people, and was in favor of monarchist rule across the world.

His first goal was to ensure his empire survived the troubled times it was in by the early 19th Century. The man was ready for anything to keep it alive. Before the war, his empire was falling apart and nothing that he did or had done seemed to have slowed down the descent into the abyss. It was a patchwork of different ethnic groups, languages, religions, and cultures. It had been constantly threatened by nationalism, separatism, and revolution. It was also surrounded by enemies: Russia, Serbia, Italy, France, and Britain. In reaction, Franz Joseph tried to hold on to his power by suppressing dissent, strengthening the army, and forming alliances.

While he was all of these things and not willing to compromise in anyway, he could see the writing on the wall and had decided to seek the solution to all his empire's problems in war. The assassination of his nephew and heir, Archduke Franz Ferdinand, in Sarajevo on June 28, 1914, had given him the pretext, along with the full backing of the German Kaiser, to attack Serbia. Franz Joseph hated Serbia with a passion and saw it as a threat to his empire. And so, he declared war on it to finish the Serbs once and for all.

But he didn't realize or didn't want to accept that this would trigger a chain reaction of war declarations across Europe. Russia backed up Serbia; Germany backed up Austria-Hungary; France backed up Russia; Britain backed up France. Then, war exploded everywhere, and so far, Austria-Hungary was not doing very well.

First and foremost, it had failed in two offensives against its original objective, to conquer Serbia. The Austrian military had been humiliated by the small Slavic army, and that stung his imperial pride.

But the worst of it was that the Russians had slammed his forces hard in Galicia. His troops were so soundly defeated that the entire province was lost except for the powerful fortress of Przemysl. This was a disaster on an epic scale for the Dual Monarchy and his personal prestige.

The Emperor was sitting in his personal study inside the Hofburg Palace. Vienna was a prominent power in Europe, and nothing represented the city's prominence quite like the Hofburg. With origins that dated back to the 13th century, the Hofburg held over 700 years of history between its walls. It wasn't just one palace, but rather a complex of buildings being the primary residence of the Habsburg dynasty.

The Imperial Apartments, where he lived, worked, and held court, was housed in the Amalia Residence in the Imperial Chancellery Wing. The place was an impressive succession of glorious and magnificent rooms, including the Dining Room, both the Emperor and Empress' saloons used for entertaining, their bedrooms as well as the Audience Chamber, where Franz Joseph held a number of important meetings.

The leader of Austria was sitting at his desk, busy signing one edict or another, absently reading what was on the paper before him. He knew his underlings would do what was necessary and that they needed his signature, so he signed. But he didn't care for what, for at this moment, the only matter that was relevant to him was the news from the frontline and the conduct of the war.

As he tried to make sense out of the last month and a half of fighting, he wondered how things could have turned out differently. He shook his head in bewilderment, still stunned by the enormity of the problems he now faced. His country had been defeated, and soundly at that.

On paper, things had looked a lot better when he signed the official declaration of war on Serbia. His country had millions of soldiers under arms, a potent fleet, and a solid ally in Germany.

Furthermore, it had seemed well-prepared by the Chief of the General staff, Conrad von Hotzendorf. Austria-Hungary had two different plans prepared in 1914 for the event of a war with Serbia: Plan R (Russland) and Plan B (Balkan). Plan R was built around the eventuality of Russian intervention in case of war with Serbia. Four of the Austrian field armies were planned to be deployed into Galicia for an offensive into Poland and the Ukraine.

Plan B assumed that Russia wouldn't move a finger in a war with the Serbs, giving Austria-Hungary the opportunity to smash Serbia in a rapid campaign. For this plan, three armies were to be mobilized and moved to the border with Serbia. The only problem was that both plans used two of the same armies. After all, the Habsburg Empire did not have an infinite number of military forces at its disposal.

In early July 1914, as Austria-Hungary secretly prepared for war with Serbia, the commander of their army, Field Marshal Franz Conrad von Hotzendorf, ordered to execute Plan B, incorrectly assuming the Russians would not attack or at the very least not attack before he was done with Serbia. Only three armies would thus be mobilized in the north instead of four, and three (including the 2nd already near Serbia) would invade and attack south. Mobilization was deliberately handled slowly to avoid alerting the other Great Powers. It was also due to Austria-Hungary's farmers being needed to bring in the harvest first before they could be spared for a military campaign.

In the last week of July and as events careened out of control (leading to general war in Europe), Conrad realized that Russia was going ahead with its threats and mobilized at the border with Austria-

Hungary. No amount of German intimidation would work to keep them out of the war. He consequently saw that he would have to plan for a fight both against Russia and Serbia. He accordingly gave the orders to switch to Plan R with all the consequences that that would entail (confusion, problems of logistics, and others).

These problems were, of course, due to the Austrian Army having already begun mobilization. Hotzendorf's change of plan right in the middle of the execution of a plan putting the troops in a different theater, threw everything into chaos. The 2nd Army ended up having to deploy southwards to the border with Serbia, then get back into its trains to be shipped back north to the border with Russia, 2nd Army would consequently spend all of August 1914 being shuffled East and then West and then East, ending up missing both the fight against Russia and against Serbia. They were, of course, dearly missed.

Austria-Hungary was, therefore, stuck during the month of August with a defensive deployment against both Serbia (with only two armies instead of the three judged necessary to attack) and Russia (with only three armies instead of the four judged necessary to attack). In an astonishing display of over-confidence, Field Marshal Conrad nevertheless gave the order to both his groups of forces to attack immediately, despite both of them being understrength. Franz Joseph still fumed at the man's sheer boldness and audacity.

The result, predictably to everyone except Conrad and his many admirers, was a defeat of epic and humiliating proportions for Austria-Hungary — a defeat from which the Emperor feared it would never recover.

The defeat in the north against Russia cost the K.u.K. army about a third of its entire strength in less than a month of fighting. Lemberg and most of Galicia were under the Russian heel, and the rest of the Austrian forces were reeling backward into Hungary and the Carpathian Mountains. The defeat against Serbia in the south was slightly less devastating but even more humiliating given that Serbia had a population of only 5 million people and no indigenous arms industry, while Austria-Hungary was a modern industrial power with 50 million population.

The Austrian leader felt that he had lost control over events, and his only way out was the German Kaiser and his powerful armies. He took a deep breath and resolved to send his Foreign Affair Minister, Count Berchtold, to Berlin to urgently request help, because he didn't believe von Hotzendorf's assurances anymore.

Athens, Greece
What will the Greeks do? End of September 24th, 1914

Extract from Letter from King Constantine the 1st of Greece to his brother-in-law, Wilhelm the 2nd of Germany (German National archives):

(...) My dear Wilhelm, I must congratulate you on your stellar victory at the Battle of the Marne and your subsequent occupation of Paris. This is great news and a glorious moment for the German nation (...)

(...) I am writing to you today to answer your last letter on the matter of Greece's stand in the current conflict. As I have stated before, my sympathies lie with you and the German people (...)

(...) I can, for now, only answer the same as the week before. Greece is in no position to face Britain's naval might in the Eastern Mediterranean. The Ottoman victory against the Russians is fine and well, but you also know of my people's dispositions toward the Turks. We just cannot imagine an alliance with them. I also face mounting opposition within my own country on this matter, as many want the country to join the Entente (...)

(...) What I can tell you now is that your victory has given the proponents of a German alliance hope. If the naval situation in the Mediterranean can be reversed to the Central Powers advantage, like, for example if Italy joins you in your war, then I might be able to do something about it. But for now, I must regrettably answer no again at your pleas of support (...)

The outbreak of WWI in August 1914 added fuel to an existing rivalry between Greece's king, Constantine I, and prime Minister, Eleftherios Venizelos. Both leaders publicly shared credit for the country's victories over the Ottomans and Bulgarians in the Balkan Wars of 1912-1913. But behind the scenes, personalities clashed, and the relationship between the nationalist politician and the country's monarch steadily deteriorated.

The conflict also challenged Greece's relations with European powers like Britain, France, and Germany. Along with Russia, Greece maintained strong cultural, economic, and political ties with these European powers. However, the Greek political leaders and public opinion were split over the matter of what to do between joining the Central Powers, the Entente, or staying neutral.

For Venizelos (the elected Greek Prime Minister), the choice was obvious. He considered the British and French to be supportive of Greek expansion. Thus, joining the Entente offered the promise of territorial conquest that could fulfill the Greek nationalist goal of a Mediterranean empire modeled on Byzantium. A desire for Ottoman and Bulgarian land ruled out alignment with the Central Powers. His position was recently weakened by the German victory, giving credence to the people in favor of an alignment with the Central Powers.

On the other hand, King Constantine favored neutrality. As Kaiser Wilhelm's brother-in-law, Constantine would have been inclined to support Germany had it not been for British naval superiority in the Mediterranean. Moreover, members of the king's inner circle, like one of its most important military commanders, General Ioannis Metaxas, had strong ties to Germany but supported neutrality. The recent conquest of Paris emboldened the *"support Germany camp,"* but something needed to be done about British naval power before anything was decided.

On that beautiful fall day, King Constantine was hopeful that the matter would resolve itself soon. The leader of the Kingdom was walking his summer palace estate in the wooded foothills of Mount Parnitha in Attica.

As he walked a nicely chiseled path through the magnificent greenery, he was surrounded by dense forests overgrown with Aleppo pine trees, tall cypresses, poplars, plane trees, beech trees, Greek strawberry trees, olive trees, and citrus trees. Beside him walked his trusted advisor, Androlos Kostapukis, while some ten royal guards flanked them from behind and another ten in front.

Of the 4,200 hectares of forest belonging to the royal family of Greece, 1,400 hectares were conceded by the Greek State to the Greek King in the year 1877. The rest were gradually purchased by the royal family under various contracts. When the royal family bought the estate (Constantine's father), it was a very modest place with small houses and a few roads. Over the years, a variety of buildings were added, such as a garage, winery, cemetery, stables, and a magnificent swimming pool his children loved to play in.

The two men were busy discussing what they should do next, as the news of the victory at the Marne was still sending diplomatic shockwaves throughout Europe. "Androlos," started Constantine, "What do you think the Italians will do now?" "Your Majesty, I do not know for certain but I hear that they are now considerably colder to the idea of joining the Entente Powers."

"Well, I can understand why. They do not want to be on the losing side, just like me." "Indeed, Your Majesty," said the first royal councillor. "My dear Kostapukis, have you looked into the matter I asked you about concerning naval strength in the Mediterranean?"

The councillor fished a thick report from his pouch. "Yes, Your Majesty. It has been very complicated to get because of Prime Minister Venizelos' men and his control over many military leaders, but here it is." The King picked up the envelope. "Thank you. In essence, what does it say of Italian, Ottoman and Austro-Hungarian combined naval strength?"

"It says, your majesty," started Kostapukis with a wolfish smile, "that if Italy were to join the Central Powers, the naval strength in the Mediterranean would be evenly matched. With the British busy facing the German High Seas Fleet in the North Sea, we could very well see a Central Power naval dominance, at least in the Central and Eastern Mediterranean, making Greece's position secure." He paused. "Well, secure if we join the Central Powers, and difficult if we don't."

Constantine crossed his arms behind his back, still holding the report, and felt content. "*Very well, Councillor Kostapukis. We will await further developments with Italy before deciding anything else.*" "*As you command, Your Majesty.*"

Both men continued their walk amongst the greenery and flowers of the Royal estate and discussed some more over the matter and then some more.

Bucharest, Romania
Peles Palace, September 24th, 1914

We have secured clear benefits from this alliance in the last couple of decades; to leave it today would mean losing the benefits of 30 years of hard work",
King Carol at the Council of Sinaia, August 3rd, 1914

King Carol the 1st of Romania was deep in thought as he sat beside the large window in his beautiful castle. The double doors giving way to his suspended balcony were open, and a gentle fall breeze whistled in, warming his skin. Located at the foot of the Bucegi mountains, alongside the Peles River, and up from the Sinaia Monastery, the wild but picturesque palace was located in the Piatra Arsa massif. All around the castle, roads, paths, and lanes were built that passed through the forest in the most beautiful spots, beneath centuries-old fir trees and ancient beech trees covered in moss. The castle was his favorite because first of the spot and also because he closely oversaw all of the building works until its completion in the Spring of 1914.

Beside him on his work desk lay a newspaper describing the latest developments on the Western Front in France and then in the East. The war between the Central Powers and the Entente was a month and a half old.

The outbreak of the First World War caught Romania in a tough spot. It was reluctantly bound by a defensive treaty to the Triple Alliance (Germany, Austria-Hungary, and Italy) and, implicitly, to the Habsburg Monarchy that occupied Transylvania and Bukovina, two provinces mainly inhabited by Romanians. This was a major issue for most within the country as there was no love lost between Romanians and Hungarians.

Furthermore, the Entente wanted Romania to join their coalition opposing the Triple Alliance, but that meant the country would be coerced to ally itself with Russia, its traditional enemy, which was also occupying an old Romanian province, Bessarabia.

In essence, if Romania entered the war, it would be forced to choose which territories inhabited by fellow Romanians it was going to surrender to one side or the other.

Romania joined the Triple Alliance in 1883 to protect the independence it had proclaimed in 1877, and to defend itself against Russia's expansionist intentions. However, the events leading up to the outbreak of World War I highlighted the contradictions between the national aspirations of the Romanians, and the treaty with the Central Powers. Some within the country argued that the distancing from the Triple Alliance was normal because of the anti-Romanian policy of the Hungarian authorities in Transylvania.

King Carol the 1st was of the mind to join the Central Powers, even if the Kingdom's alliance with them was a defensive one, but the monarch's intentions were impossible to execute in August 1914 as long as anti-Austrian feelings dominated public opinion and the army. The majority of politicians were also in favor of maintaining a position of neutrality in the war between Austria and Serbia.

Carol thus called a council (the Council of Sinaia, named after the monastery right beside his beloved castle) to discuss and decide on the matter. It took place on August 3rd, the day when Italy's neutrality was announced, a country that was bound to Austro-Hungary through the same defensive treaty as Romania. During the discussion, the King claimed the need and obligation to enter the war alongside the Central Powers. Despite the tenacious appeal of the King, almost all those who participated in the Crown Council supported neutrality.

The discussion and the proclamation of neutrality had been barely two months ago, and the decision still stung Carol. He didn't have a lot of power as he was a constitutional monarch but had wanted his country to abide by the treaty with Germany and Austria-Hungary. He'd thought the matter solved for a while, but it was not anymore.

Things change quickly in war, as the strategic and diplomatic situations edged on one big victory or disastrous defeat. The German conquest and occupation of Paris, and what now increasingly looked like a Central Powers victory in the West changed the situation greatly. He knew that several voices were now being heard in the National parliament. But his country was not yet ready, as Russia was on the offensive and beating Germans and Austro-Hungarians alike.

However, if the Germans and or the Austrians managed to find a way to defeat the for now nearly unstoppable Russian offensive both in East Prussia and Galicia; he clearly saw his country in a position to join the Central Powers.

He sat up, walking the distance from his desk to the window. The room was richly decorated with wood paneling, golden gildings, several marble statues (even one of the former Roman Emperor Trojan), and expensive tapestries. The balcony gave way to one hell of a magnificent view of the Bucegi Mountains. He liked the view and took a deep breath of autumn fresh air.

Yes, he would wait for his moment, but by God, Romania would be on the right side of history.

Vrana, Bulgaria
The King ponders from his castle, September 26th, 1914

The Vrana Royal Palace sat southeast of Sofia, the Bulgarian capital. Surrounded by a magnificent park, it was one of the most amazing and beautiful places in all of the country. Much like that of its Romanian neighbor, it was created by its ruler, King Ferdinand I, in the period 1899-1912. It covered an area of over nine hundred hectares and was the private estate of the Bulgarian ruler. There were many trees, planted by Ferdinand himself that he hoped one day would grow to a large size and live to hundreds of years.

The Palace was a two-story building. On the ground floor, there was a large study, a dining room, a very large library, and a large veranda covered in windows. On the second floor were located the chambers for the Royal Family and guests. The royal palace was beautifully decorated with art and paintings. The southern facade was covered with lacquered wood. The tiles on the roof were a bright red, making the sun shine on them at sundown.

King Ferdinand I, ruler of Bulgaria, was busy watching a few bird specimens he'd spotted in the morning. The man was passionate about birds. The land was a great place for a castle, but there were many such places around Sofia. The King had chosen Vrana due to his ornithological passion, as there was no lacking of them. Binoculars in hand, he took some note of their colors and decided with confidence they were a male and female. He hoped they would still be in the area for the next season to see their offspring.

He was preoccupied with many things these days. Thus, it felt great to spend some time in his mansion away from the capital, Sofia. The affairs of the state were taking all of his time. The developing World War was not something he felt Bulgaria could avoid.

In fact, it was quite the opposite. He believed that his country needed to participate in order to be on the winning side of history to gain the territories it sought. He had both ambassadors from Germany, and France trying to woe him to their side, and he had not yet decided what he would do about it.

To King Ferdinand, who had not accepted the defeat in the Second Balkan War of 1912-1913 (like most Bulgarians), the unfolding events and the war in Europe were simply a continuation of that conflict. As with his Balkan neighbors, he was paying a lot of attention to the unfolding events in France and was impressed by the German victory at the Marne. Did this mean that it was now time to jump in and support the Central Powers? He certainly thought so and needed to discuss this with his people.

Bulgaria had a beef with Greece on the matter of the Bulgarian minority in Macedon Province near its border. He knew of the Greek king's Germanophile tendencies and wondered what would happen to his country if Athens joined the Central Powers before Bulgaria did. Would the Germans still have enough flexibility to have Bulgaria as well?

He also knew his northern neighbor was neutral, and the same scenario played in his mind. That left one interesting option open if he joined the Austrians and the Germans: Serbia, where a lot of "lost" territories could be conquered or liberated.

While he advocated for more of a wait-and-see attitude in order to see the result of the battle between the German Army and the Entente forces in France, he now thought differently since the Kaiser's forces were in Paris, and it looked like France could unravel and sue for peace. What then? Would the Germans even be interested in having a small country like Bulgaria as an ally?

He decided that they wouldn't. *"Call for the Foreign Minister; I would like to see him here at the earliest possible moment,"* he said, turning his head toward one of the Royal Majordomo waiting by the side of the door leading to the windowed veranda he was watching his birds from. "*Yes, your Majesty.*"

CHAPTER 1
THE WAR IN THE WEST

2nd German Army, approaching Calais
14th Imperial Division, Infanterie-Regiment Graf Schwerin

Private soldier Oskar Dantz, a member of the 14th Imperial Division, was in a foul mood like most of his comrades in the unit. His feet were blistered, and they hurt like hell. He dreaded to remove the boots and see the bloody things. Foot problems were the bane of soldiers. With the continuous marching of the last two months to attack and campaign through France added to the incessant rains, not one of the German soldiers could say they were doing good in that category.

The German 2nd Army had not stayed long in Paris. While the 1st German Army was sent toward Brest and the Atlantic Ocean to seize the ports there, the 2nd was marched up north to seize the Channel ports. The 3rd, 4th, and 5th stayed along the frontlines and were busy building up trench lines facing the ones the new French commander, General Ferdinand Foch, had ordered dug to stop the German advance. The 6th Army had drawn the short stick and was being railed East to help bolster the defenses against the Russian Juggernaut threatening the center of Germany, and even Berlin itself.

Calais was in sight, and he could see the towering columns of smoke since the German artillery was already at work, along with a thin line of infantry rushed to the area to encircle the town to begin the siege.

The town housed one of the main ports for British travelers to Europe. In the summer of 1914 (not even two months before), the British Expeditionary Force, or BEF, had landed at Calais harbor to make its way to the frontlines south of the Channel. Calais was a critical port for the British to send their armies, and for the French to receive supplies from them. Hence, it needed to be taken.

He could hear the loud rumbling of the guns, seemingly distant from where he was. But he knew better since he now had experience in gauging where and what guns were firing. The campaign in the fall had been quite an eye-opening experience for his military skills.

"We're about three miles out of the frontline near the city," claimed Florian Storch. Dantz grunted an answer. "That's about right." Both men were from the small Bavarian town of Kelheim, and were part of the Royal Bavarian Army, now integrated into the German Imperial Army.

"Sergeant Wilhelm," started Storch in as nice a voice as possible since their NCO was one hell of a difficult personality. "Do you know where the Infanterie-Regiment will be on the frontline?" The Sergeant looked at both Dantz and Stoch for a moment with a bland look. *"Just shut up, Storch; you will know when you need to. Now, march straight and be sharp,"* he answered, and the two men made sure they obeyed.

A couple of hours later, the German soldiers of the 14th Imperial Division were finally in view of the harbor and the city. The entire scene was surreal. British ships were sailing into the protected area, under fire from the German artillery in the rear. The entire city itself was ringed with Allied trenches, and they could see the tracer bullets racing from one side to the other while mounds of earth were catapulted in the air all around the perimeter by blasts from explosive shells. One of the enemy transport vessels was half-sunken into the harbor channel, probably hit by a German shell.

"Surprising how many guns they have been able to bring for the attack," commented Storch, while Dantz kept focusing on the enemy ships entering and exiting the harbor. *"Yeah, well, the bastards are bringing in more troops; this isn't going to be an easy siege."* Florian laughed out loud. *"Well, Oskar, it can't be worse than the Battle of the Marne,"* he finished by slapping Dantz on the shoulder. *"You worry too much."*

The military situation in the West
End of September 1914 – The entrenching and the race to the northern harbors

Following the Battle of the Marne, the two opposing armies were exhausted after a full month of fighting. Thus, an implicit pause was undertaken almost simultaneously, with the Germans not pushing further south than Paris and the Entente forces content to dig in and prepare their defenses. A few days following the Anglo-French move, the Germans followed suit and started to make their holes as well.

Ferdinand Foch, the new French commander, was made of a different cloth than his former superior, General Joseph Joffre. Following the string of disasters with the attack and "elan" mentality, he had come to realize (a lot sooner than Joffre, for that matter) that the French Army was better off facing the Germans on the defense than trying to attack it.

Something major had changed in military affairs, and it was the machine gun and the artillery. No longer could infantry use its will and push through an attack, as well-prepared troops behind defenses and with machine guns could stop any charge thrown at it.

Foch was a proponent of the defense, yes, but he was also a realist. With the heavy losses of August and September, the fall of Paris, and the general damage done to the French and English armed forces, defense was his only option.

The French were already entrenched from Versailles to Verdun in Alsace to Beford in the Vosges. The goal was to stop giving ground to the Germans. He put his troops hard at word to dig in west of Versailles on a proposed defensive line that ran almost horizontally to the Atlantic Ocean.

Foch would have loved to bar the enemy's way north and swing his frontline on the Seine River, but he didn't have the time nor the troops to do so. It was not ideal, as the North of France was where most of the industrial capability was located, but it was what it was. The Kaiser's armies had defeated the Entente, and there was a price to pay if he wanted to continue to prosecute the war.

Foch could not stop the Germans because of a lack of troops, but also because they didn't give him the opportunity. Starting about five days after the occupation of Paris, the German 1st and 2nd Armies, the very same ones that so brilliantly executed the offensive and the hook north that ended in the storming of the French capital, were ordered to conquer the north of France and particularly the major harbors of Brest, Le Havre, Cherbourg, and Calais.

The Allies, while not in a position to establish a coherent frontline to stop the Germans, still decided to garrison the main harbors as much as possible. Several French units from the local and nearby garrisons were recalled to Brest, Cherbourg, Le Havre, and Calais, while the British, under the dynamic leadership of the First Lord of the Admiralty, landed troops and supplies. The four cities were soon ringed with trenches and gun batteries, promising the German troops a hefty price to pay if they wanted the harbors.

Both sides knew the stakes. With these harbors, the German High Seas Fleet could rebase its units there, and potentially break the British blockade. The result of having such a powerful fleet able to deploy in the Atlantic could even be the disruption of convoy supplies to the British Home Islands.

With the transfer of the entire German 6th Army to the East to try and stop the Russian steamroller, this enabled the Allies to have rough parity with the German troops (German 3rd, 4th, and 5th Armies), thus establishing the perfect condition for a stalemate and what would soon be known as trench warfare.

French 14th Division
Versailles, September 25th, 1914

Private soldiers Philippe Cren and Armand Bonnier were sweating like pigs as they toiled to dig under the watchful eye of their NCOs. Armand was glistening with sweat and smelled even worse than normal, as they had been doing this for days on end following the defeat in Paris. It was a hot fall day, but at least rain had not come for the last few days, making their life a little better for a change.

The French 14th Division, or at least what was left of it after the terrible losses at the Battle of the Marne, was just north of the small city of Versailles, the very same place where the famous castle built by Louis XIV was. The French troops had retreated south following the end of the Battle at the Marne River. Most soldiers were not in a great mood, as they felt the sting of failure, a result of their inability to defend Paris. Many men were wondering if peace would soon ensue, but none of them were ready to accept that. The French had been beaten but not defeated, and they had no intention of surrendering like their grandfathers in 1871.

The entire French Army was digging in on a direct horizontal line from the south of the now-occupied capital to Verdun Fortress. The goal of their new commander, General Ferdinand Foch, was to stop the enemy from advancing. Both soldiers were happy that the offensive talks were over, as they'd experienced its failure from a front-row seat.

The typical trench was dug around twelve feet deep into the ground. They had also made an embankment at the top of the trench and other men were laying barbed wire fencing.

In some areas, Armand and Philippe had heard trenches were built with wood beams or sandbags. The bottom of their trench was being covered with wooden boards called duckboards by another batch of soldiers. The duckboard's purpose was to maintain the men's boots over the pooling water collecting at ground level.

"Did you notice we're not digging in one long straight line," said Philippe, as he stood straight for a moment, looking in the distance. *"No, why,"* grumbled Armand as he struggled with a rock stuck in the hard clay he was attempting to shovel into. Cren pretended as if Armand was interested, so he kept talking. *"Yeah, I heard we're making them in a zigzag pattern to have interlaying fields of fire."* Cren dropped his shovel on the ground, fished out a pack of cigarettes from his pocket, and offered one to his friend.

Armand decided that it was time for a smoke. He climbed out of the shallow trench and picked up the cigarette his friend offered him. They both turned their gaze toward the north. *"The Germans will be here by tomorrow,"* said Cren in between two puffs. The billowing smoke ran through his long mustache as he spoke. Armand didn't answer, instead taking yet another drag.

Trenches had a long history in warfare, going back in time to Antiquity. The Romans had protected their camps with trenches with wooden spikes to impede and defeat ambush or night enemy attacks. Trenches also made a name for themselves in the 17th Century by helping the besiegers during an attack on a fortress. In the 18th and 19th Centuries, defensive trenches were built to block enemy lines of advance amidst the Napoleonic Wars to conduct during siege operations).

In the American Civil War (1861–65), better weapons and precise firearms forced the warring sides to dig and defend. The trend increased during the Boer War (1899–1902) and became prevalent during the siege of Port Arthur in the Russo-Japanese War of 1904–05.

If one thing had become clear for both sides in the first month and a half of fighting, it would be that the developing conflict would bring the art of digging to a new level.

The rise of the machine gun and the incredible lethality of the artillery made trenches mandatory, and the first month and a half of fighting had made the necessity very clear to both the Entente and the Central Powers.

"Well, it looks like we'll be in the thick of it again soon, my friend," finally answered Armand, dropping his cigarette on the ground and smashing it with his feet. The butt smoked for a moment, a tiny veil of smoke rising.

"You two," said yet another crusty corporal walking by. *"Get back to work; the Huns are coming; we have to be ready."*

Command
German and Allied commanders planning, September 25th, 1914

(..) Oberste Heeresleitung (OHL), Louvres Castle (...)

The German Army High Command was meeting that day to discuss the new strategic and tactical options offered to Germany by the victory at the Battle of the Marne and the subsequent conquest of Paris.

The people present were Ludwig von Moltke, the Chief of the General Staff and commander of the OHL. Also present were his two deputies in most operational matters, the chiefs of the Operations Division, Colonel Gerhard Tappen, and the Information Division commander, Lieutenant Colonel Richard Hentsch.

The rest were the men responsible for the recent victory in France and the continuing campaign: 1st Army commander General Alexander von Kluck, 2nd Army commander General Karl von Bülow, and 3rd Army commander General Max von Haussen. The 5th Army commander, Wilhelm Kronprinz von Preußen (the crown prince Wilhelm, heir to the Imperial Throne), the 7th Army commander, General Josias von Heeringen, and the 4th Army commander, General Albrecht Herzog von Württemberg.

The 6th Army commander, Rupprecht Kronprinz von Bayern, and General von Hindenburg (8th Army) were absent because the first was in the process of transferring his army to East Prussia, and the second had its hands full trying to contain the Russian hordes.

The German HQ had been, during the entire campaign in France, located in Luxemburg, but it had just moved to the Louvres Palace, a sprawling and magnificent building located in the heart of Paris.

The Louvre was an iconic French palace located on the right bank of the Seine in Paris, near the Tuileries Garden. It had been built eons ago and even used by Napoleon and other important state officials like Napoleon III. The Germans had decided to use it as much because it was a large castle, well-located and big enough to house the officers of the OHL, as to make a statement they had again won over the French. The Louvres was an important place for Frenchmen and had been occupied, amongst others, by the Bonapartes. The fact that Germany had defeated them both times was not lost on everyone, and since they occupied the palace, they wanted to make it clear to France that they were the masters.

"Gentlemen, thank you for being here," started von Moltke. *"We are gathered today in this magnificent place to discuss the next phase in the campaign."* He signaled to his Information Division commander, Lieutenant Colonel Richard Hentsch, to bring over the map on the wooden board they'd prepared. The man's job was to get operational maps and other reports done for the top brass to decide the course to follow.

After moving right beside it and picking up a small wooden stick, he started. *"As per your orders and the instructions we have given you in the last few days, the French are not inclined to discuss a cease-fire like their grandfathers did in 1871. They want to continue to fight."* The assembled group seemed uncomfortable at the words since several chairs moved, and ruffling sounds were heard. It would have been too easy if the French had thrown the towel in and surrendered. Alas, it was not to be, and they would still have to fight and send men to their deaths. *"And by the Emperor, since they want a fight, we will give them one,"* continued Moltke, to which the other officers smiled and laughed softly.

"As you all know, the 1st and the 3rd Armies have already been sent north with the objectives of taking all of France's Northern coast and its Atlantic coast to as south as possible before the French put up too much resistance. The job of the 3rd, 4th, 5th, and 7th armies will be to first defend and then eventually break through the line of defense the Entente forces are working on building up as we speak. While we

cannot launch an offensive south in light of the current state of our forces," Moltke said in reference to the general exhaustion of the German armies, much like the Anglo-French, we eventually will be in a position to do so. "The offensive northward is possible because we removed elements of all the other armies to bolster supplies and numbers of soldiers to the 1st and 2nd, but our numbers are not infinite."

He paused to point at the harbors of Calais, Le Havre, Cherbourg, and Brest. *"We estimate that by snowfall this year, we should be in control of much of the north part of France, enabling us to negate most of the enemy's capability for war production."* In this, the German commander-in-chief was referring to the fact that most of the French factories were located in the north and the northwest of the country, in addition to the Parisian region, which was about 40% of all the country's production. The western coast and the south of the country were mostly rural.

The Kronprinz (5th Army commander) spoke up by raising his hand slightly. The man was carrying a lot of influence in the OHL in his capacity as the heir to the imperial throne. *"So, sir, our objectives are simply to hold the French while our other armies attack to the North?"* *"Yes, Kronzprinz, that is the essence of it. We are railing the 6th Army eastward and we think we might have to send more troops there to try and throw the Russians out of Eastern Prussia. If we achieve that, we will also have to help the Austro-Hungarians who are being seriously mauled in Galicia. For these reasons, I do not expect any of the armies holding the frontlines nor the ones attacking north to get the harbors to get any reinforcements before 1915 or whenever we can make the situation better in the East."*

The 3rd Army commander, General Max von Haussen, followed with his own question. *"How are things now in the East? I have seen in the official reports that Hindenburg has retreated behind the Vistula. Are we planning any counter-offensives, and how what is the situation in Koenigsberg?"*

"Yes, General Hindenburg is in the last few details of a general attack, now that his ranks have been bolstered by 6th Army's 400,000 men. In Koenigsberg, things are holding and the fortress city is so far defending quite well."

"General von Bulow, General von Kluck," continued von Moltke as he gestured the two men to sit up and come by the map. *"Would you be so kind as to give us the general outlines of your situation and timetable..."*

(...) Chateau de Versailles, French High Command (...)

"In short, gentlemen, the situation is nothing short of a disaster," continued General Ferdinand Foch, the new commander-in-chief of all French forces. General Lanzerac, who had just been rehabilitated by Foch following his dismissal by Joffre for *"not attacking enough,"* spoke up as he grumbled. *"If only we had listened to what was obvious and set ourselves up like we are now on the defensive."*

"Indeed, there is no other way to describe the problem we are in," said his replacement as commander of the French 5th Army, Commanding General - Général d'Armée Louis Franchet d'Espèrey. Lanzerac, for his part, had been Foch's first order of business, and he named the dismissed commander to his spot on the 9th Army as he moved up to overall command. Everyone around the table nodded in silent agreement with the stupidity of Joffre's *"offensive à outrance"* strategy. The other two men present in the four-generals meeting were the commander of the French 6th (Général Joseph Maunoury) and 10th (General Louis Ernest Maud'huy's) Armies.

The meeting of the temporary front HQ was held in the incredible Hall of Mirrors in Louis XIV's former royal palace, Versailles. The palace was quite close to the front, and the generals could hear the sounds of distant battle since the door giving way to the superb garden view was open, and a gentle fall breeze brought it in. The Hall of Mirrors was designed to symbolically represent the power and glory of the King of France.

The opulence and grandeur of the furnishings and art in the space illustrated France's achievements in politics, economic achievement, and artistic advancement. The Hall of Mirrors was 240 feet long and 34 feet wide located on the back of the Palace at Versailles facing the gardens. One wall of the Hall of Mirrors had 17 large arched windows opening into the gardens. Directly opposite these windows were arched mirrors the same size as the windows. It was one hell of a magnificent room for a meeting, and Foch hoped it would instill some spine into his discouraged generals.

The Palace of Versailles was a few miles outside Paris and quite close to the frontlines. The original buildings had been a hunting lodge for Louis XIII but Louis XIV wanted it converted into a palace. This was the greatest architectural project of its time -- involving a large number of architects, landscape architects, and interior designers. The scale of the place was enormous, with a huge park, gardens, sculptural fountains, and a large number of buildings for government officials, military guards, and servants. While it was too close for a permanent HQ building, it was fitting for the message Foch wanted to convey: *"This is where we defend, and we will not give another inch of French ground without a fight."*

The central subject of the discussion that day was simple yet very complex in finding a solution. How to defend France from that point on, and how to make sure the French Army followed suit. The French forces had been badly mauled by the heavy fighting of the fall, with casualties numbering in the hundreds of thousands. Territory losses were terrible, and it was obvious more ground would be lost to the north as they struggled to establish a coherent line of defense in the south.

The meeting was held only three days after the President of the Republic and the Prime Minister met with the British leaders at the

London War Office. With Great Britain and the British Empire's full support, the war would be continued. No one in England wanted to give in to the damned Germans.

General French, the British BEF (British Expeditionary Force) had already started to receive reinforcements and would get more as the recruiting offices in the UK filled up with new soldiers. But the subject of the day was more short-term. How to resist here and now, since without a firm stand and a solid defense, there would be no future.

"Gentlemen, if you will let me propose the plan," said Foch, handing out folders outlining the details of the deployment orders he was about to give them. The army commanders started to leaf through the paperwork, and then Foch continued.

They soon got to the thick of the subject when they found the proposed frontline Foch wanted to talk with them about. *"The red line you see here is the one we will entrench and defend to the last man and the last bullet."* He waited for any reaction from his generals, but these proud men had been ashamed enough to feel a little intimidated by the current situation, so they stayed silent. *"Everything north of that, we will defend the main harbors and cities, helped by our British friends. The goal is to get those siege battles (Le Havre, Calais, Cherbourg, and Brest) to last as long as possible to give us the time to consolidate our line of defense south and in the east."*

Foch saw a few of them straighten their shoulders and lift their chin up in expectation of a firm plan and a potential way for hope in the future. *"We will soon get more troops from the colonies and more from the British. General French will, of course, help hold the line near here."*

"Gentlemen," Foch said to conclude the first part of the meeting before they got to the details of where troops and generals would be ordered. *"We will prevail, and we will win over the Huns."*

25th Royal Field Artillery Brigade
Near Versailles, September 25th, 1914.

The big 18-pounder artillery gun exploded in fury as it fired its round, catapulting a cloud of billowing dust everywhere around. The gun servants around it, who had their hands to their ears to protect them, were temporarily obscured in the dirty grey cloud.

These proud men had their faces black with soot and were as dusty as a man could be. They had long, tired faces, but they seemed determined. They were the men of His Majesty's artillery, a part of the British Expeditionary Force in France.

Artillerymen Archibald Totenkam rubbed his eyes for a moment to remove the sting of the dusty, cordite-heavy smoke and turned around to fish another shell for his comrade, William Thorpe, another one of the gun team's handlers.

The two men and their other comrades were members of the 113th Battery RFA (Royal Field Artillery) within the 25th Brigade, a component of the 1st British Division. The 1st was one of the (rare) permanently established Regular Army divisions in Great Britain. Consequently, it was amongst the first to be sent to France at the outbreak of the First World War.

In this capacity, its men had fought a gallant war to date, first at Mons, and then at a multitude of battles that led to the Marne. There, the Entente forces were defeated by the Germans, and following the French infantry's retreat, they were forced to move south of Paris.

The battery was now installed in the sandy equestrian courtyard of the Versailles' Royal Stables, just opposite the Palace, across the street from Louis XIV's statue. The Great and Small Stables, commissioned by Louis XIV and built by Jules Hardouin-Mansart, constituted the greatest royal construction project for housing horses that was ever undertaken. Situated opposite the Palace, they mark the edge of the Place d'Armes and the start of three main avenues. It was a big place, and it was why the 113th's officers had decided to set up shop there.

Archibald was yet another poor orphan from London's slums and had not been lucky enough to get to know either his father or his mother. Raised in an orphanage where violence was prevalent, he joined the Army at 16, lying about his age to escape his dreadful life. And ever since then, he'd found his purpose in life. Military discipline was harsh, but at least it was just, unlike what he'd come to experience as a youngling. He was now twenty years old (officially 22 by the Division's books), and he was now a seasoned artilleryman.

"*Reload,*" said Lance-Bombardier Stimms to his men. The officer was in command of the gun within the battery. A four-guns Royal Field Artillery battery consisted of 115 men, of which 46 of these were drivers. Other batteries were scattered around the city of Versailles, and they relentlessly pounded the Germans lines, not eight miles away.

Archie, as the rest of the team called him, was by now a seasoned artilleryman. If he had been experienced when he arrived in France, he was now, like the rest of his comrades, bloodied. They were steady, solid, and stoic under fire. As of yet, no enemy shell had landed on their position or in their area in general, as the Germans were unusually quiet.

Some blokes in other batteries had told him that it was because the Huns were attacking northward. Whatever it was, it was fine with Archibald since Versailles, and the stables were quite a nice place to live in. Since his arrival in France, and especially since his first battle, Archie had become a heavy smoker and had a cigarette hanging by the corner of his mouth whenever possible. It helped him relieve the stress he felt. Once he was done handing out the shell to Thorpe, he stood straight and pinched his cigarette butt between two of his fingers to finish it with a long drag. He then exhaled the smoke and felt peace for a second.

The war was not going well, and it was difficult for every Allied soldier to keep his morale up, but they remained committed to the cause and kept a steadiness that surprised even their own officers. These men were defeated and beaten, but they continued to fight hard.

"Ready, sir," said one of the other gunners. He was some new guy from Dorsetshire who arrived a couple of days ago. His uniform was getting dirty, but it still had the look of newness coming with every new green recruit arriving, and starting to fight at the front. *"Well, by all means, Mr. Bitten, fire."*

And then the men put their hands on their ears, and the gun recoiled hard again as a blast of fireball burst through its muzzle. Smoke again drifted in a billowing cloud, and the entire affair started all over again. *"Reload,"* was said again by Lance-Bobardier Stimms. By that time, Archibald had already lit yet another cigarette.

Raiding the British Coast
The Raid on Yarmouth, September 27th, 1914

Three weeks after the British victory at Heligoland Bight, the German Kaiserliche Marine was finally sailing to get its revenge on the Royal Navy and those pesky British. The defeat at the Bight still stung, as the British had moved in very close to the German coast, and nothing had really been done to stop them. German Admiral von Hipper had devised a new plan to get back at the Brits for their insolence. The man was standing proud on the deck of his flagship, the battlecruiser Seydlitz. The ship had been bloodied in the last fight and had received some boiler damage. He turned toward the still-blackened hull where the enemy shell had hit. The workers at Wilhelmshaven had repaired most of the damage, but the look of the ship was not important at this stage since the vessel was needed for another mission. He walked casually as the ship slid out of the protected harbor, while his sailors went about their business of getting the ship underway.

He was proud of his men and had seen them in action at the recent battle. He was confident that they would again perform well. He then turned toward the western horizon, where his mission lay, and had a quick thought for the ships he'd lost at Heligoland Bight. The loss of the Moltke and the Deerflinger was a black mark on his honor, and he knew the Kaiser wasn't pleased. Yes, he'd sunk the Queen Mary, a British battlecruiser, but the entire affair was a tactical and strategic defeat for the Empire. He vowed to himself that he would have his revenge on the Royal Navy. *"Sir,"* said a tall and sharp-looking officer walking by him. He was holding his navy cap as it was windy, while Hipper didn't have anything on his head. *"Yes, Vice Admiral Raeder,"* he answered casually to his chief of staff. *"We are about to clear the Wilhelmshaven harbor and should be heading out to sea with the squadron within an hour at the most." "Thank you, Vice Admiral. Let's head back in"*, answered Hipper, gesturing to his officer to walk back toward the bridge.

With the imposing Royal Navy's numerical superiority in ships and firepower, the German Navy was seeking ways to attack the British fleet in the capacity it could. The German naval command felt it was inadvisable to enter into any direct fleet-to-fleet engagement, as was clearly shown by Admiral Hipper's defeated battle force. They had been outnumbered from the start and could not produce miracles when fighting with a five-against-one ratio. Instead, the Germans looked for opportunities to fight British ships individually or in small groups. The Kaiser had given orders that no major fleet action was to take place, but small groups of ships might still take part in raids.

The next big German fleet action was thought to happen when the German Army took over the French harbors the High Seas Fleet needed to rebase to better position itself. However, in the meantime, it had no intention of staying idle and doing nothing.

German 1st battlecruiser squadron, Admiral Franz von Hipper		
BC Seydlitz,	CL Strassburg	CL Stralsund
BC Von Der Tann	CL Graudenz	
CA SMS Blüche	CL Kolberg	

Thus, in retaliation for the British attack at Heligoland, a raid was decided. The operation had several objectives. One was to lay mines which might later sink any passing British ships. Another was to pick off any small isolated vessels or to provoke larger fleets to wander near Germany (as they gave chase) to come within range of the German High Seas Fleet. Another reason for the plan was that attacking a British coastal city would get the damned Brits to move their ships to protect those towns and affect the civilian's morale.

The Royal Navy's game plan was to keep most of its warships together, and near the North Sea in order to keep an overwhelming superiority over the German Fleet. Germany hoped to encourage Britain to send more ships from the main fleet for coastal defense, thus changing the ratio of force if the Kaiser's warships sortied to give battle.

For his mission, German Admiral Franz von Hipper had under his command the battlecruisers Von der Tann and Seydlitz, the armored cruiser Blücher, and the light cruisers Strassburg, Graudenz, Kolberg, and Stralsund. The plan was to lay mines off the coast of Yarmouth and Lowestoft, and the ships were also to shell Yarmouth proper. From there anything was good if they could fight a smaller number of ships or get chased by the Royal Navy's bigger squadrons back to the German coast where the High Seas Fleet would be waiting.

By early evening, Hipper's battlecruiser squadron left its home base on the Jade River near Wilhelmshaven. Two squadrons of German battleships followed them from the harbor slightly later to lay in wait for any ships that the battlecruisers might be able to entice to chase them back.

Hours later (the next morning), the German battlecruiser squadron neared the Yarmouth coast. The area was patrolled by the minesweeper HMS Halcyon and two old destroyers, the HMS Lively and Leopard. Halcyon spotted two cruisers, which she challenged.

The Germans didn't wait and sent an answer with the mouths of their guns. Destroyer Lively—some two miles behind—started to make smoke to hide the ships while Halcyon was straddled on every side by shells from Hipper's squadron. The Kaiserliche Marine gunnery was not as accurate due to the battlecruisers firing simultaneously, making individual aim a lot harder because none of the ships could discern where their own shells landed. Nonetheless, Von Der Tann slammed two of its 11-inch shells on the smaller ship, igniting one hell of a fireball in the morning light. The hits killed the small ship's momentum, and it was soon dead in the water with a wrecked engine and half of its crew dead. The other two British ships steamed away at full speed and managed to avoid getting hit by the German ships.

By that time, the squadron was in sight of Yarmouth, and Hipper ordered the Stralsund to lay the planned mines and for the other light cruisers to finish off the stricken minesweeper.

Hipper ceased firing at the fleeing destroyers and instead directed Seydlitz and von der Tann's guns toward the city to achieve his second objective. As if God himself had decided to strike the small British harbor and city, large columns of fire and smoke rose in the air as the two German battlecruisers rained fire and death on the area. The shelling went on for a few minutes, and Hipper decided that it was enough, seeing the fires blossoming all across the city. *"Vice Admiral Raeder,"* he said, lowering his binoculars. *"It's time to leave. Order the helm and the squadron to turn about and head back toward Germany, quickly now,"* he said with a gleeful smile. *"Let's hope the British take the bait and pursue."*

Once out of immediate danger, the two fleeing destroyers radioed a warning of the presence of German ships, and the city also blared to whomever could listen that they were under attack. The destroyer Success moved to join them, while three more destroyers in the Yarmouth harbor started to raise steam. The submarines E10, D5, and D3—also inside the harbor—moved out to join the chase, but D5 struck a just-laid mine and sank.

An hour later, the message finally got through to the Admiralty, and Admiral Beatty was directed southward with a British battlecruiser squadron, with more units of the Grand Fleet following from Ireland.

By then, Hipper was fifty miles away, heading home. As it happened, the British ships had no idea where Hipper's squadron had sailed and thus moved in a straight line down toward Yarmouth and the other British coastal towns in the area to ensure the Germans wouldn't raid another city. Yarmouth burned fiercely for the rest of the day, and many people died, with an ammunition factory severely damaged by fire and battlecruiser shells.

The fleets of the major powers in 1914 Part 1
The contenders and their warships

If one thing was certain in 1914, it was that every European power had a decent fleet to call upon at the start of the war, a result of the arms races of the last fifteen years between the rival nations. In short, Europe was not just armed to the teeth on the ground, it was ready for action on the naval side of things as well.

One of the dominating factors and events of the last ten years was the naval race between Germany, the ascending power, and the British Empire, the major naval power of the time. While the Kaiserliche Marine remained smaller than the Royal Navy, it was growing in size and power, and the British worried very much about it.

With a fleet, the Germans could threaten the British Isles and challenge the English on the sea. The implications were multiple for Great Britain as it could not keep its dominance on the sea if it lost to the German High Seas Fleet.

The dynamic of the conflict between the two was, however, dominated by Germany's land-locked position in the North Sea. As a result, all the British had to do was to make sure they contained the Germans there. The unfolding events in France threatened to change this dynamic to the advantage of the Germans, and that did not bode well for Great Britain.

The other powers, like France, Italy, Austria-Hungary, Russia, and the Ottoman Empire, all entertained healthy (and very costly) navies. The French were concentrated in the Western Mediterranean as they needed the link with their North African colonies, while the Italians kept control of the Central Med. The Austro-Hungarians were bottled up in the Adriatic but remained a force to reckoned with there.

The Eastern Med was a British affair, as the Royal Navy kept a very strong squadron in Alexandria, while the Black Sea was for now dominated by the Ottomans over the Russians because they had three dreadnoughts to none for the Russian Navy based in Sebastopol.

ROYAL NAVY

At the beginning of the war, the biggest, most numerous, and most powerful fleet was the Royal Navy. In fact, it was the undisputed naval superpower of the time. The idea of the British naval strategist was to have a fleet larger than the next two naval powers' combined strength.

By early 1914, the Royal Navy had eighteen modern dreadnoughts (six more under construction), ten battlecruisers, twenty cruisers, fifteen scout cruisers, ·two hundred destroyers, twenty-nine pre-dreadnought battleships, and a hundred and fifty armored-heavy cruisers built before the year that the battleship Dreadnought was launched and changed everything in naval warfare.

After the outbreak of the First World War, most of the Royal Navy's large ships were stationed at Scapa Flow in the Orkneys, ready to block, fight, and defeat any German breakout attempt by their ships. Britain's cruisers, destroyers, submarines, and light forces were clustered around the British coast to protect against enemy raids.

The Mediterranean fleet, consisting of two battlecruisers and eight cruisers, was based in Gibraltar. There were also naval forces across the Empire's colonies and former colonies, like Canada, Australia, and New Zealand.

The Grand Fleet was, by far, the largest battle fleet ever assembled in history. It contained a humongous amount of capital ships. In total, the fleet sported forty-nine battleships, of which twenty were dreadnoughts and twenty-nine of pre-dreadnought design.

The Grand Fleet - British Home Waters

1st Battle Squadron

BB Iron Duke	BB Colossus	5 DD
BB Malborough	BB Hercules	6 CA
BB St. Vincent	BB Neptune	
BB Collingwood	BB Superb	
BB Vanguard	CL Bellona	

2nd Battle Squadron

BB King Georve V	BB Monarch	Cl Boadicea
BB Ajax	BB Conqueror	5 DD
BB Centurion	BB Thunderer	7 CA
BB Audacious	BB Orion	

3rd Battle Squadron

Pre-dread BB King Edward VII	Pre-dread BB Commonwealth	CL Blanche
Pre-dread BB Hibernia	Pre-dread BB Dominion	5 DD
Pre-dread BB Africa	Pre-dread BB Hindustan	4 CA
Pre-dread BB Britannia	Pre-dread BB New Zealand	

4th Battle Squadron

BB Dreadnought	BB Bellopheron	BB Temeraire
CL Blonde	3 CA	2 CL

5th Battle Squadron

Pre-dread BB Agamemnon	Pre-dread BB Venerable	Pre-dread BB Implacable
Pre-dread BB Prince of Wales	Pre-dread BB Queen	CL Topaze
Pre-dread BB Bulkwark	Pre-dread BB Formidable	5 DD
Pre-dread BB London	Pre-dread BB Irresistable	8 CA

The Grand Fleet Part 1, September 1914

The Grand Fleet - British Home Waters

6th Battle Squadron

Pre-dread BB Russell	Pre-dread BB Duncan	5 DD
Pre-dread BB Cornwallis	Pre-dread BB Exmouth	7 CA
Pre-dread BB Almermale	CL Diamond	

7th Battle Squadron

Pre-dread BB Prince George	Pre-dread BB Jupiter	5 CA
Pre-dread BB Caesar	CL Sapphire	
Pre-dread BB Majestic		

8th Battle Squadron

Pre-dread BB Albion	Pre-dread BB Vengeance	CL Proserpine
Pre-dread BB Canopus	Pre-dread BB Goliath	5 DD
Pre-dread BB Glory	Pre-dread BB Ocean	3 CA

9th Battle Squadron

Pre-dread BB Hannibal	Pre-dread BB Mars	4 CA
Pre-dread BB Illustrious	Pre-dread BB Victorious	6 DD
Pre-dread BB Magnificent		

1st Battlecruiser Squadron

BC Lion	BC Princess Royal	8 CA
		5 DD

2nd Battlecruiser Squadron

BC New Zealand	BC Invincible	5 CA
		5 DD

Channel Fleet

Pre Dread BB Lord Nelson	4 CA	3 CL
		7 DD

The Grand Fleet Part 2, September 1914.

The Mediterranean Fleet was a lot smaller but had to contend with fewer potential enemies with the small Austro-Hungarian and Ottoman fleets. Combined with the French Navy, it was responsible for the overall defense of the theater, it was thought to be enough to cover the important convoys for the British, that is if the Italians stayed neutral or didn't join the Central powers.

BRITISH MEDITERRANEAN FLEET (Gibraltar, Malta, and Alexandria)

Vice-Admiral Sir Archibald Berkeley Milne

BC Indefatigable	4 CA	18 DD
BC Invincible	4 CL	

The British Mediterranean Fleet in 1914.

KAISERLICHE MARINE

At the outbreak of World War I, the Imperial German Navy was the second-largest navy in the world. It had twenty-two pre-Dreadnoughts, fourteen dreadnought battleships, four dreadnought battlecruisers, and around thirty cruisers, a hundred and forty destroyers, ninety torpedo boats, and forty-five submarines.

Following the Franco-Prussian War of 1870-1871, the German Empire was proclaimed at Versailles on 18 January 1871. It was a combination of the Prussia-dominated North German Confederation and a host of other smaller states like Bavaria, Wurttenberg, or Hanover. The Empire's navy was formed from the North German Confederation's navy, which had itself only been formed in 1867 from the Prussian Navy. The navy soon became an intricate part of Germany's armed forces and foreign policy upon the ascension of Wilhelm II to the throne.

Kaiser Wilhelm II greatly expanded the navy, making it his priority as he wanted to build a colonial Empire. The key leader who drove the show on the fleet's development was Admiral Alfred von Tirpitz. The all-powerful Minister of the Navy was responsible for expanding the Navy into the second-most powerful naval force in the World. While this was great for German prestige and enabled the Kaiser to obtain some overseas colonies in Africa and the Pacific, the net result was the souring of the relationship with Great Britain, and a naval arms race.

When the war began, the High Seas Fleet was not in an enviable position. The Kaiserliche Marine was the second most powerful navy in the world, but it was fighting the first. The discrepancy in forces made it impossible for its leader to think of any kind of direct main fleet against main fleet action. The British Grand Fleet consisted of twenty dreadnoughts and five battlecruisers, with another six battlecruisers scattered around the world, plus twenty-nine pre-dreadnought battleships. The Germans, on the other hand, could only match this with thirteen dreadnoughts, four battlecruisers, and twenty-two older pre-dreadnought battleships. Not a very good battle ratio.

In short, there was no way the fleet could sortie and hope to win one grand battle. But the future seizures of the French Atlantic and Channel ports opened a world of possibilities for the German Navy. Assuming it could rebase there eventually. With these harbors, it could rebase and directly threaten the Atlantic convoys and break the developing British blockade.

As war exploded all around them, the sailors of the German High Seas Fleet believed in themselves and knew they could have a major impact on the outcome of the conflict.

The High Sea Fleet		
1st Battle Squadron, 1st Division (Vice-Admiral Wilhelm von Lans)		
BB Ostfriesland (Flagship)	BB Oldenburg	4 CA
BB Helgoland	BB Thüringen	5 DD
1st Battle Squadron, 2nd Division (Rear-Admiral Friedrich Gädecke)		
BB Posen (Flagship)	BB Rheinland	4 CA
BB Nassau	BB Westfalen	5 DD
2nd Battle Squadron, 3rd Division (Vice-Admiral Reinhard Scheer)		
Pre-Dread BB Preussen (Flagship)	Pre-dread BB Hessen	3 CA
Pre-dread BB Deutschland	Pre-dread BB Lothringen	4 DD
2nd Battle Squadron, 4th Division (Kommodore Franz Mauve)		
Pre-dread Hannover (Flagship)	Pre-dread Schlesien	4 CA
Pre-dread Pommern	Pre-dread Schleswig-Holstein	4 DD
3rd Battle Squadron, 5th Division (Rear-Admiral Felix Funke)		
BB Grosser Kurfürst	BB König	4 CL
BB Markgraf	BB Kronprinz	4 DD
3rd Battle Squadron, 6th Division (Rear-Admiral Carl Schaumann)		
BB Prinzregent Luitpold (Flagship)	BB Kaiserin	4 CL
BB Kaiser	BB König Albert	4 DD

The High Seas Fleet was the most powerful component of the Imperial German Marine, with the most modern dreadnoughts and the best pre-dreadnought battleships. It was the component of the Kaiserliche Marine that was expected to sail and fight the Grand Fleet.

Battle squadron		
4th Battle Squadron, 7th Division (Vice-Admiral Ehrhard Schmidt)		
Pre-Dread BB Wittelsbach (Flagship)	Pre-Dread BB Schwaben	2 CL
Pre-Dread BB Mecklenburg	Pre-Dread BB Wettin	2 DD
5th Battle Squadron, 8th Division (Rear-Admiral Hermann Alberts)		
Pre-Dread BB Braunschweig (Flagship)	Pre-Dread BB Zähringen	1 CL
Pre-Dread BB Elsass	1 CA	
5th Battle Squadron, 9th Division (Vice-Admiral Max von Grapow)		
Pre-Dread BB Kaiser Wilhelm II (Flagship)	Pre-Dread BB Kaiser Wilhelm der Grosse	3 DD
Pre-Dread BB Kaiser Barbarossa	1 CA	
5th Battle Squadron, 10th Division ((Kommodore Alfred Begas)		
Pre-Dread BB Brandenburg	Pre-Dread BB Kaiser Karl der Grosse	3 CL
Pre-Dread BB Kaiser Friedrich III (Flagship)	Pre-Dread BB Wörth	3 DD

The Battle Squadron was still a powerful element of the German fleet, but was composed of older battleship designs, most of them built before 1900. They nonetheless had solid guns and were expected to join in in the case of a fight with the British Fleet. They were just slower but if the battle happened near the German coast, it was expected they would fight as well.

THE FRENCH MARINE

The French Navy, rather small compared to the large fleets that were the High Seas and the Grand Fleets, still had important responsibilities in case of war with the Central Powers. *According to the terms of the 1904 "Entente Cordiale,"* the French Navy was to police and master the Mediterranean against the Italians, Austro-Hungarians, and any other nation who joined the German alliance.

The French Mediterranean Fleet (1st Armée Navale) had twenty-one battleships (including four newly-commissioned dreadnoughts and six "*Danton*" class pre-dreadnoughts), fifteen cruisers, around forty-four destroyers, and fourteen submarines. It was a force capable of going head-to-head with the Italians and the Austrians in the unlikely scenario that both nations would join their ships in one grand fleet.

The 1st Armée Navale's first objective was to escort and protect the troop transports carrying North African divisions to France in case of war.

1st Armée Navale (Toulon and Malta)

Battleships

BB Courbet [Fleet Flagship]	BB France	1 CA
BB Jean-Bart	BB Paris	3 CL

1st Battle Squadron, 1st Division

Pre-Dread BB Diderot	Pre-Dread BB Vergniaud	2 DD
Pre-Dread BB Danton	2 CL	

1st Battle Squadron, 2nd Division

Pre-Dread BB Voltaire	Pre-Dread BB Mirabeau	1 DD
Pre-Dread BB Condorcet	1 CL	

2nd Battle Squadron, 1st Division

Pre-Dread BB Verite	Pre-Dread BB Republique	1 DD
Pre-Dread BB Patrie	1 CL	

2nd Battle Squadron, 2nd Division

Pre-Dread BB Justice [CA]	1 CL	2 DD
Pre-Dread BB Democratie		

AUSTRO-HUNGARIAN NAVY

Austrian Battle Fleet, Admiral Montecuccoli

BB Prinz Eugen,	BB Viribus Unitis	Pre-Dread BB Radetzky
BB Tegethoff	Pre-Dread BB Franz Ferdinand	Pre-Dread BB Babenberg
Pre-Dread BB Zryniy	Pre-Dread BB Arpad	Pre-Dread BB Habsburg
Pre-Dread BB Ferdinand Mac	Pre-Dread BB Friedrich	Pre-Dread BB Karl
3 CA	4 CL	12 DD

In the mid-nineteenth century, the Austro-Hungarian Navy, always a very small component of the imperial military capability, gained importance as world affairs turned toward the sea and colonialism.

While weak compared to Germany, the Austro-Hungarian fleet was strong enough to give pause to anyone. It fielded three dreadnought battleships, five pre-dreadnoughts battleships, three heavy cruisers, four light cruisers, and twelve destroyers.

Austria-Hungary had the industrial infrastructure for warship construction and could continue to expand it if needed or willed by the Emperor. The fleet that entered the war in 1914 was nothing more than a force in being, but it nonetheless would soon play a major role in the conflict.

French 14th Division
Versailles, September 28th, 1914

Private French soldier Armand Bonnier dropped his head to the ground with his head on his helmet as he got showered in a mountain of dirt lifted by a nearby exploding enemy shell. The German artillery was shelling their trench, and it wasn't good to be there at all. *"Merde!"* he said, almost buried in the catapulting dirt. He lost his balance and fell on his back. The enemy ordinance had slammed the sandbags just at the edge of the trench and almost blasted him out of existence. But he had been well-protected at the bottom of the hole, or so he'd thought.

His world swirled as he gasped for air (he even had dirty soil in his mouth), and he struggled out of his earth coffin. A steady hand picked him up. *"That was a hell of a lot closer than we have seen so far, Bonnier,"* said his broad-shouldered friend Philippe Cren. Armand gave him a tired smile. *"Thanks, buddy. This artillery shelling is bad,"* he answered. A dirty-faced Philippe (he was smeared with black dirt all over his face and uniform) just nodded and gestured him to keep low, as flying shrapnel could kill.

The French 14th Division, or at least what was left of it after the terrible losses at the Battle of the Marne, was just north of the small city of Versailles. The men had dug deep trenches to await the German arrival, and it was now time to defend it. The German 3rd Army was pushing hard on them.

Since the day before, they had been through three, two-hour-long artillery barrages, and three infantry attacks. So far, they had defeated every German attempt to reach their lines. Their overlaying fields of fire and the numerous machine guns they had killed and repulsed all the enemy soldiers who attempted to cross the by-now corpse covered no man's land.

"When do you think the bastards will stop firing," continued Philippe, as he tried to crouch as low as possible, holding his rifle close to his chest. Armand was about to answer when the German artillery shell explosions started to thin out noticeably. Within a minute, it was over, installing an eerie stillness in the air. Where a moment before, there had been a maelstrom of noise and death, silence had now replaced it. Then, the two friends, surrounded by other French soldiers, started to hear the wailing and the crying of the gravely injured amongst them. Some seemed to be near them, and an enemy shell had probably landed right into the trench. A rare occurrence but something possible nonetheless.

A sergeant came by, yelling the same message over and over again. *"Get ready; the Boches are coming. Get ready, the Boches are coming..."* he moved right by Armand and Philippe and stepped over the mound of dirt. *"Well, boys,"* he said, looking at the two black-sooted soldiers and the dirt all over, *"that was a close one. Everyone okay here?" "Yes, Sergeant,"* answered Armand mechanically. *"Good,"* he said, turning again toward his next part of the trench. *"Get ready, the Boches are coming. Get ready, the Boches are coming..."*

And both of them sat down crouching in the shallow, narrow trench, almost shoulder to shoulder with their comrades. They felt nervous, as with all the other enemy assaults before. Philippe, always a good lad to know when the enemy was attacking (Armand wondered how he could anticipate this), said: *"only five minutes to go..."*

(...)

On the other side of the field, the German whistles blew, and the soldiers prepared to attack and die. The poor lads were anxious to be over the top, and at Zero Hour, every one of them climbed out of the trenches. Not a man hesitated.

Once out of the relative safety of their trenches, the attacking troops were ordered to advance slowly toward the French in long lines. Most Germans – like many others – didn't think much of this order.

It was just as if they were at a training exercise, which was really, they supposed, absolutely mad when you came to think about it. They were just in extended order with everything on their backs, their rifles and bayonets, their entrenching tool, and everything else. They were just walking straight towards the French lines in extended order.

As a consequence, as with all the previous assaults, they were sitting ducks all the way. It was just walking straight into the death trap, hundreds of us. It seemed hopeless, but nevertheless, we obeyed. We were told that there was going to be this bombardment that would knock the hell out of the French, and all we had to do was get up and walk across – and we only had to walk, on no account had we to stop for anything – just walk straight through to the Versailles Palace. And there wasn't one of us in the German lines advancing that ever got to the enemy lines.

(...)

"Keep firing into the bastards," yelled their Lieutenant and their NCOs as they poured rounds after rounds into the thick mass of grey-clad shapes advancing in a long line toward them. Armand went through the rapid, rhythmic motions of loading and firing, then loading and firing again and again. Near him, two Hotchkiss machine gun positions clattered heavily and sent a stream of tracers into the German line. Philippe, just beside him, was doing the same. From the distance the enemy troops were, he could see them falling in droves. It was crazy, it was like a carnival shootout. The enemy troops made it to the barbed wire, and then they stopped and or dropped to their bellies since it was not possible to walk across. The artillery barrage had not destroyed it.

The assault looked like it would peter out just as the ones before had done. Armand smiled and just thanked God for yet another enemy attack repulsed.

The fleets of the major powers in 1914 Part 2
The contenders and their warships

THE ITALIAN NAVY

If there was one neutral country that could have a major impact on the war it was Italy. It possessed a large army but, most important, a large navy capable of going head-to-head with the French or the Austro-Hungarian Navy.

Reerina Marina		
BB Dante Alighieri	BB Conte di Cavour	BB Andrea Doria
BB Giulio Cesare	BB Leonardo da Vinci	BB Duilio
Pre-Dread BB Regina Elena	Pre-Dread BB Vittorio Emanuele	Pre-Dread BB Venice
Pre-Dread BB Napoli	Pre-Dread BB Benedetto Brin	Pre-Dread BB Saint Bon
Pre-Dread BB Roma	Pre-Dread BB Regina Margherita	Pre-Dread BB Emanuele Filiber

The combination of the Italian fleet with the Austrian one would certainly be difficult to manage for the allied forces. The Royal Navy had a handful of ships in the Mediterranean as it needed to concentrate in the North Sea to guard against the Germans.

The two combined fleets (Italy and Austria-Hungary) could have two-to-one superiority in dreadnoughts compared to the Anglo-French. In the case of "classical" battleships (including pre-dreadnoughts), the two fleets would have aligned twenty-two units against twenty-three for the French. As for cruisers finally, they would align thirty-five against thirty-six to France. The simple fact of the matter was that if Italy joined the Central Powers (and it looked like a real possibility after the fall of Paris), the British would have to send ships, especially if they wanted to execute the bold plan proposed by Winston Churchill.

RUSSIAN NAVY

The Russian Navy of 1914 was but a shadow of itself, its forces having suffered a severe blow at the Battle of Tsushima in 1905 against the

Japanese. It began to be painfully reconstituted after the disaster of 1905. It was not going to be a big factor and would contribute to Russia's isolation from the rest of the Entente powers.

In the Baltic, it could not sortie because of fear of the large German fleet, and in the Black Sea, it had just been completely shattered, with only a handful of ships left facing the three-dreadnought-strong German-Ottoman Navy.

Baltic Sea Fleet		
Pre-Dread BB Andrei Pervozvanny	Pre-Dread BB Slava	20 old DD
Pre-Dread BB Tsessarivich	5 CA (old)	5 CL

Black Sea Fleet		
Pre-Dreadnought BB Evstafi (flagship) in repair yards, Jan 15	3 CA	13 DD
BB Imperatritsa Maria (in construction)	BB Imperatritsa Ekaterina Velikaya (in construction)	BB Imperator Alexander III (in construction)

JAPANESE NAVY

The Imperial Navy was still somewhat modest in 1914, but the Japanese leaders felt it could take on what the Kaiserliche Marine had in the Pacific and help the Empire conquer the German colonies in the theater. It sported two dreadnought battleships, one dreadnought battlecruiser, five pre-dreadnought battlecruisers, and ten pre-dreadnought battleships, plus a plethora of support ships, including over twenty cruisers and fifty destroyers.

The Japanese Navy, now back under the command of legendary admiral Heihachiro Togo, had already fought an important battle against the Germans in Tsingtao.

Japanese Imperial Fleet Admiral Heiha		
fire	damage	Pre-dreadnought BB MIKASA
BB Kawachi armor belt damage reduced	Pre-dreadnought BB IKI light damage	CA X22
	Pre-dreadnought BB IWAMI	CL X 6
Pre-dreadnought BC Tsukuma damage	Pre-dreadnought BB SAGAMI	DD X47
	Pre-dreadnought BB SUWO	~~6 DD~~
Pre-Dreadnought BC Ibuki light damage	Pre-dreadnought BB TANGO	~~2 CA~~
Pre-Dreadnought BC Kurama	~~Pre-dreadnought BB FUJI crippled by Fort Bismarck mortar~~	
Pre-dreadnought BB KASHIMA,	Pre-dreadnought BB ASAHI	
Pre-dreadnought BB KATORI	Pre-dreadnought BB SHIKISHIMA	

OTTOMAN NAVY

Recently reinforced by two British-built dreadnoughts and the German battlecruiser Goeben, the Ottoman Navy was now a force to be reckoned with in the Black Sea and even in the Adriatic. With its three powerful ships, it could even rival and overpower the British Mediterranean Fleet, a lot weaker with only two battlecruisers.

Now led by the excellent German Admiral Wilhelm Souchon, it was poised to dominate and support the Turks in their war with the Entente. It had already won a substantial naval battle at Cape Sarych and almost eliminated the Russian Black Sea Fleet and its obsolete Pre-Dreadnoughts battleships.

Ottoman Navy- Admiral Souchon	
BB Sultân Osmân-ı Evvel	CA Hamidiye
BB Reşadiye	CA Mecidiye
BC Yavuz Sultan Selim (HMS Goeben)	8 DD
Pre Dreadnought BB Barbaros Hayreddin	
Pre Dreadnought BB Turgut Reis,	

The Battle of the Four Harbors Part 1
The fight for Calais September 25th to October 15th, 1914

If there was one critical area the Entente needed to resist as best they could, it was all along the French coastline, especially where major harbors and military facilities were present. The simple equation gave an easy-to-understand answer. With harbors, the German Navy could rebase there and create a world of problems for the Entente. With its powerful High Seas Fleet, it could first break the British blockade, send raiders into the open seas, and also attack Allied convoys critical for the British Home Island's war effort. Finally, submarines could also sail from there (for example, from Brest) to greatly extend their range far into the Atlantic Ocean and truly impact the convoy routes.

As a consequence, the French moved a lot of their garrisons into the four major ports the Entente did not want to lose, and the British Royal Navy vowed to help them. The plan was to send more troops directly from England and to make sure the troops were properly supplied with regular ship convoys.

The entire British 3rd Battle Squadron was thus sailed from Scapa Flow to Southampton, where it would base itself for the probable future.

3rd Battle Squadron		
Pre-dread BB King Edward VII	Pre-dread BB Commonwealth	CL Blanche
Pre-dread BB Hibernia	Pre-dread BB Dominion	5 DD
Pre-dread BB Africa	Pre-dread BB Hindustan	
Pre-dread BB Britannia	Pre-dread BB New Zealand	
Channel Fleet		
Pre Dread BB Lord Nelson	4 CA	3 CL
		7 DD

The squadron joined the Channel fleet, giving the British nine pre-dreadnought battleships to escort them and supply troopships. The old battlewagons would also be used in an infantry support role as offshore artillery platforms, a task that suited the warships very well.

The other intended objective of moving the 3rd Battle Squadron to the Channel was also in the case of a German breakout attempt. The majority of the Grand Fleet remained in the Orkneys (Scapa Flow) and in the vicinity of London.

The first clash between the Germans and the Anglo-French happened at Calais, where a full-blown fight blossomed into a maelstrom by September 26th, 1914. The Germans launched two major assaults at the Allied trench lines and harbor fortifications but were repulsed by the combination of artillery, infantry in prepared position, and the three battleships offshore (three more were in an escort role, and the last three were coasting just offshore the harbor of le Havre, where the Germans approached and where a battle would soon happen.)

(...) The Battle for Calais (...)

The defenses of the Harbor of Calais included three French divisions, an assortment of units hastily assembled together from nearby cities and other smaller harbor garrisons, and a newly raised British Division. The four units, totaling 42,000 soldiers, were supported by a half-battalion of Royal Field Artillery and some Moroccan troops from French North Africa. They were entrenched in well-prepared positions since they had advance notice of the enemy's arrival. From the moment the defeat at the Marne and the fall of Paris was announced, preparations were put in motion to get the town and the harbor fortified for a prolonged siege.

Facing them were the German Second Army's 4th Reserve Corps, including the 14th Division, the 58th Division, the 18th Reserve Division, the 30th Division, and the 44th Reserve Division. The 4th Reserve Corps was formed on the outbreak of the war in August 1914[1] as part of the mobilization of the Army. It was commanded by General der Artillerie Hans von Gronau, who was recalled from retirement. It was thus 65,000 strong.

By the time of the Battle for Calais, the German 4th Corps was a seasoned unit compared to the relatively green Allied troops facing them. They had laid siege to and took the Belgian fortresses around Liege and fought General Charles Lanrezac's French 5th Army at the Battle of Charleroi and Mons in August 1914 and again at St. Quentin a few days later. It was, finally, involved in the conquest of Paris and the Battle of the Marne that preceded it. It was one hell of a battle unit, and it was about to launch itself at Calais.

In order to reach a successful conclusion rapidly, the German High Command (OHL) also ordered the transfer of the heavy artillery pieces involved in the sieges around Liege: First, a battery of the state-of-the-art 420 mm guns (nicknamed "Big Bertha") and second the Austrians battery of 305 mm Skoda Mörser M. 11 mortars,

The road-transportable heavy artillery was first railed as far north from Paris as possible and then rolled to within range of Calais. Their travel was impeded by the French demolition of railway tunnels and repeated small, scattered Allied unit attacks.

The battle opened up with the expected fury by the evening of the 25th of September. The battery of the two monsters, Krupp 420 mm, and the 305mm Skoda guns, were unleashed to bombard first the trenches, and then shells were lobbed into the city as the Germans noticed the Entente had a unit of counter-battery fire.

The Central Powers guns rolled inside the town and it looked like they would succeed once more as they had in demolishing the Belgian forts, doing considerable damage in the process.

However, contrary to the Austro-German's beliefs, the situation would be completely different in the Battle for Calais. No longer were the guns the only big boys on the battlefield. Two pre-dreadnought battleships lurked some distance offshore but well within the range of the siege guns. After a couple of hours of range-finding and positioning, the two battleships opened fire on the enemy positions inland.

The first ship was the Hibernia, the 3rd Battle Squadron's flagship. The Hibernia was a King Edward VII-class pre-dreadnought battleship. The 17,000-ton warship was armed with four powerful 305 mm guns and a plethora of smaller caliber guns. The vessel firing in anger just beside it was the battleship Africa, with the exact same stats since it was also of the King George VII Class.

All of these guns were in the range of where the Austro-Germans had installed their siege artillery, and thus, the counter-battery fire had a devastating effect on the poor, unfortunate gunners. Shells first started to land near them, and they first thought they came from the town itself. But soon, they realized something was awfully wrong. The calibers of the shells were too big for British and French field artillery, and they thus found out too late they were under fire from battleships. When the Hibernia and the Africa found the range (they were helped by a couple of French biplanes spotting for them over the battlefield and having relayed to them the coordinates to fire at), they simply smashed the siege guns to smithereens. By the time the first three salvos were landed and had exploded amongst them, over half of the weapons were destroyed, the rest were unlimbered and rolled back into nearby woods for cover.

By the time the whistles blew in Oskar Dantz's area and sent the 14th Division to the assault, the guns were no longer able to support the unfolding German attack on the town.

The Dover Barrage and the mining of the Dover Strait
The Royal Navy prepares for the unavoidable, End of September 1914

War with Germany suddenly became a real possibility for the British as the Germans started their frantic naval building program and as they embarked on the acquisition of overseas imperial colonies. Both countries had been traditional Allies since the time of Frederic the Great, but this was now far in the past.

Now sporting a gigantic battle fleet, Germany posed a serious threat to Britain's continued existence as a maritime empire. The British had commerce ship convoys, and most of their industrial production relied on shipping these goods to the Home Islands.

The British strategy was thus concentrated on destroying the German Fleet. As the Kaiser continuously poured money and resources into building more and more battleships, so did the British. The Royal Navy had begun the naval race with a head-start and never lost the pace. IF Germany started to build a battleship, the British immediately countered, by building two to one every single time.

The result was the Grand Fleet, three times superior to the German battle fleet. As part of the war plan against the Kaiser's forces, the Royal Navy was to implement a total blockade of Germany. With this strategy in mind, the British deployed their warships accordingly at the start of the conflict in August 1914.

While the constant patrolling and overwhelming numbers of ships were key components of this strategy of blockading the Germans, naval mines were also produced by the thousands, and a deployment plan was put in place the moment the war began.

This entire state of affairs (British strategy and the imminent fall of the French coastal ports) meant that the Strait of Dover was now of critical importance since it was the obvious and shortest route the German High Seas Fleet would take to sail there. It was thus critical for the Royal Navy to be in a position to first interdict the German entry into the Channel and then execute its grand finale battle to smash the pesky Kaiserliche Marine once and for all.

The Strait of Dover, or Dover Strait, was the narrowest part of the Channel. It separated Great Britain from the rest of the European continent. The shortest distance across the strait was 20 miles. While that kind of distance was worrisome to the Brits because the Germans didn't have far to transport ships from one side of the continent to the other, it also represented an opportunity to block it with the number of mines the Royal Navy had in its inventory.

Following the grave defeat at the Marne River, the Royal Navy altered its plan again, this time banking on a heavy minelaying of the Strait. A naval mine was a floating (most often just below the surface) explosive device intended to explode on contact or in near proximity to a metal ship (or submarine, for that matter). Unlike depth charges, mines were a passive weapon. They were launched from ships, kept in place with anchors, and left to lie in wait for an unsuspecting ship.

By the end of September, as it became obvious the fight would now move on from Northern France to elsewhere (and probably the Channel or the Atlantic Ocean), the Royal Navy started to execute its minefield plan near Dover. Because of this proximity to the British town, the operation was called the Dover Barrage. The Royal Navy minelayers toiled for days on end and put up a wall of mines for the Germans to run into if they decided to be so bold as to attempt a breakout and sortie to move into the Channel.

By the end of September, and as the fight for the four harbors raged, the ships of the Royal Navy laid over 8,000 mines in the Strait, which was pretty much most of the British inventory at that time. When they were done, the Dover Barrage was one hell of a formidable naval obstacle, and the worst thing about it all for the Germans was that they didn't know about it.

2nd German Army – Fighting for Calais
14th Imperial Division, Infanterie-Regiment Graf Schwerin

The world around him was a maelstrom of artillery blasts and tracer fire. Private Oskar Dantz, a soldier in the Infanterie-Regiment Graf Schwerin (14th Division), ran as hard as he could toward the knot of small half-demolished buildings that had been designated as their objectives.

He had watched the big siege guns at work for the second time since Liege and had been awed once more at their power. Sergent Wilhelm had told them the guns would hit their little corner of the battlefield and that their job was to charge the buildings they could see at the edge of the town of Calais once they were done demolishing the defenses. They'd been told the guns would fire for well over an hour. However, they inexplicably stopped twenty-five minutes into their shelling for some unknown reason.

Regimental commander Colonel Theodor von Dücker had not cared much about why the guns had stopped, and decided to send the assault anyway half an hour later, as no countermanding orders came for him. Thus, the whistles had blown; Oskar, his friend Florian Storch, and the rest of the platoon had climbed the ladders from the bottom of their trenches and into the hail of fire he was now facing.

"Keep running!" he heard Sergeant Wilhelm yell over the cacophony of sounds. He was then rocked hard and thrown to the ground by a nearby artillery blast. For a moment, he thought he was dead or seriously hurt as he had blood splattered all over his uniform. The falling earth then hit him, and he was half-buried. A few seconds later, and as he regained his senses, he shrugged off the dirt and patted himself all over, rolling on his back. He found no injury and no pain; thus, he decided he was good.

He was about to get up when he noticed the stream of tracer bullets blazing about half a meter over him. Momentarily checked, he further regained his senses and realized he was still dazed. Looking to find his rifle, he was able to locate it right to his right. He pulled it toward him and held it with both hands on his chest. He was breathing heavily. Well, no, panting hard. He had not realized how winded he had been with the sprinting.

He saw soldiers running on each side of him and noticed none paid any attention. He tried to find the courage to get up but couldn't. It was very dangerous out there, and he decided to stay prone for a minute or two.

Fully recovered, he noticed the vortex of fire, earth, and death around him. He rolled on his stomach and watched the horrifying scene unfolding. His comrades were falling everywhere, hit by enemy bullets or shrapnel.

He decided to wait some more and play dead or unconscious. Eventually, soldiers stopped streaming by, and he noticed the enemy fire had significantly slackened. He got up and started running toward the knot of houses that was their objective, seeing his comrades were engaged in a hand-to-hand fight right over the French trench line.

Placing his rifle right in front of him, he yelled out of his lungs and lunged inside the trench, falling right on top of a French soldier but missing him with his bayonet. The fall was, however, enough to knock the Frenchmen to the ground, stunned. The man had been busy fighting with one of Oskar's German comrades. He was then killed by a couple of blows to the chest by his former adversary.

Oskar soon got up, rolling to the side to avoid an enemy blow, and fired his rifle right in the face of the offending man. The entire scene was a mad blood rush of death. Soldiers fought with rifles, hands, knives, and everything they could get their hands on.

Many wounded men from both sides lay in slowly accumulating pools of dirty blood, furthering the gory scene. Within another minute and two more kills, Oskar noticed that the fighting was suddenly over; there were no more enemies to despatch to hell.

"Get ready to repel the enemy and face the other way," yelled some NCO near him, and he followed suit with the rest of the German soldiers in putting their rifles on the opposite side of the Trench, facing inward toward Calais, where the French charge was coming from.

Royal Field Artillery 113th Battery
Versailles Royal Stables, September 28th, 1914

If the machine gun was the lord of battle in 1914, the artillery was the master of it. The explosive power, range, shrapnel, and other technological advances had made the weapon the real killer on the battlefield.

Artillery acted like a giant hammer to smash large areas, troop concentrations, fortresses, and trenches, or else anything standing in front of the advancing infantry, like knots of resistance of a simple barbed wire. The 1914 novelty was that artillery suddenly became the best way to stop an enemy attack, that is, destroy the infantry before it reached friendly lines.

The saying went like this: *"The artillery conquers, the infantry occupies."* In plain terms, the artillery was expected to destroy anything that stood in the way in order to clear the way for the grunts on the ground to occupy the ground

Gunner Archibald Tottenham was in the middle of an artillery and counter-battery duel with a bunch of nearby German artillery batteries. The entire area in and around the Royal Stable was under fire, and it seemed like their world would end. They had been firing non-stop on the Germans not so far north and about 100 yards north of the Anglo-French defensive lines and had been plastering the bastards for a couple of hours when the Kraut's counter-battery fire started to hit them as well. They were being hit by what was called, in artillery tactics terms, a box barrage.

There were many ways and tactics an artillery men could use in a battle and as it shelled the opposing side. A standing barrage was static and could be used for defensive reasons in order to slow down or stop the movement of enemy troops and break up attacks. A creeping barrage was for when you wanted to stand in any one place, like making a *"wall of blasting and explosions"* for some time, for example, to wait for the infantry to catch up or else to simply hammer an enemy trench line and stay there for a while to do more damage.

The standing barrage was based on where the artillerymen and their commanders knew the enemy positions were. The concept was to shell the area and then get the infantry to advance within, say, a rough distance of four hundred yards. Then, the standing barrage would move on the same distance (300-400 yards) and shell that area to protect the newly gained ground. This was what the 113th Battery and the ones near them had been doing, trying to blunt the German attack underway at the trench line.

They were sending shell after shell at the enemy, as the officer at the front had reported it was a heavy push by the damned Germans. And then the enemy counter-battery (a box barrage) fire had landed amongst them.

Artillerymen formed a rough *"box-like"* form and fired several barrages around one area or position to try and isolate it. These types of artillery tactics were more often than not used for defensive reasons, like for example, when the barrage was set on a pre-determined area, in case the enemy attacked that spot. But a box barrage could also be employed to fire at targets far in the rear where the artillerymen tried to locate an enemy gun position. This was what the Germans had decided to use on the British. They weren't exactly certain where the British were, but had decided to attack the area facing Versailles where the Royal Stable was located. It was a known set of buildings, and thus easy to get the coordinates to attack it. In addition, the large stable area inside the main building was a great position for artillery guns.

While Archie and his colleagues were worried about what the next seconds and the next minutes would bring, Lance-Bombardier Stimms was like marble and as cool as a cucumber. Tottenham liked that about his officer. The man was a steady hand. *"Keep at it, lads,"* he said.

The Germans were firing blind but had a rough idea where the British fire came from, and thus had decided to saturate the area with as much ordinance as possible. So far, none of the shells had landed in the Stable's sandy courtyard, and Archie nervously looked at the sky, wondering when the enemy shells would hit. Blasts and explosions could be heard everywhere, and it was obvious the small city of Versailles was getting hammered. Since they were firing high and above the Royal Stables, he couldn't see the Palace in front (there was a large wall blocking his view), but he figured that it must be hit as it was a hell of a lot larger than the stables. Probabilities dictated it would be.

Their own gun barked once more and recoiled in a cloud of dust and smoke. An eerie, dusty fog hung everywhere around the courtyard, only disturbed by the blasts and concussion waves of the cannons firing one after the other in an uncoordinated fashion. Archie wondered for a moment if he was going through the motions for no reason, as any moment could be his last. One well-placed shell and he would be dead.

A French Morane-Saulnier LA biplane fighter flew overhead the old Louis XIV palace and was thus privy to a hell of a sight. The entire city of Versailles was being peppered by blasts of fire, smoke columns, and catapulting pieces of stone from the being-blasted houses. The Versailles Gardens and the Grand Trianon's great pink marble hall were getting hammered hard, crumbling, and burning.

Archibald looked at the fighter droning up there and, for a moment, wished he was the pilot. Damn, these guys looked free. *"Hurry up, Totenkam, get that shell in,"* yelled Lance Bombardier Stimms. Archie wasn't too fussed about it since the ambient artillery noises and the rocking blasts made Stimm's voice quite faint. He just went through the motion and handed the shell to William Thorpe, one of the gun team handlers, who then shoved it into the breech. Moments later, the 75mm gun fired and recoiled backward in a cloud of billowing smoke. *"Reload,"* yelled Stimms over the ruckus of noise.

Archie's face, as well as the ones from all the gun handlers around him, harbored determined, busy looks, but were all dirty with black soot and gunpowder. Their ears rang because of the many loud blasts. He fished another shell, but just at that moment, a catastrophic explosion vaporized the gun beside his own, and everyone in the gun team was thrown to the ground. He turned around to see where the blast emanated from and saw that the area where the gun had been was now a flaming and fuming crater. He suddenly retched, seeing that several human body parts had been thrown about his feet. Looking at him from the chest to his feet, he realized he was covered in blood and what looked like flesh. He turned his head around in shock, seeing the other men from his gun team starting to stand up while some didn't. It was then that he noticed the sound of it all. Men yelling, some dearly, as they were injured. *"Go to cover,"* yelled the Lance-Bombardier. That meant going to hide from the enemy shelling. While the ground of the stable was mainly occupied by guns, in between them were located small round holes surrounded by sandbags for the gun team handlers to hide in in case of direct enemy attack, like the one happening now.

Archie saw that William Thorpe was stunned on the ground and picked him up, and they both ran to the relative safety of the hole they had for their gun team. Relative safety means that it would help them survive anything but a shell landing directly on top of them.

All around Archie and the bundled-up men, the stable was being smashed, the world was on fire, and buildings tumbled down to the ground in an oblivion of smashing and exploding. The Morane-Saulnier LA pilot, seeing the incredible destruction below him, took some notes for his reports. Trianon and the Versailles garden were being hit hard, while the stables and the city behind and around it were also being slammed to bits. He then put on the gas throttle to find where these enemy shells were coming from. After all, his mission wasn't to check up on the damage amongst Anglo-French lines; it was to find exactly where the Germans were firing from to get these coordinates to the artillery boys to shell it like the *"Boches"* were now doing to them.

The Battle for the Four Harbors Part 2
The fight for Le Havre, Cherbourg, and Brest, October 1st to October 11th, 1914

(...) Le Havre (...)

Since the 16th Century, when a French King had needed new harbors for his fleets and new money to come in via naval trade, the city of Le Havre has been a small, nondescript town on the coast of the Channel. He thus had the large harbor built in 1517, adding fortifications and gun defenses around it. Over the years, the town increased in size and importance. In 1914, it was a very important military and civilian port, with a sixty-four-meter-long quay capable of sheltering many ships.

A little over four centuries later, the harbor was the main base for the British Expeditionary force. Well, had been, before the German 51st Corps (2nd Army) approached it. Le Havre was the port of choice in military terms for anyone wanting to cross the channel to England or land in France from England.

Following the defeat at the Marne, the conquest of Paris, and most of the Entente forces retreating to a new line of defense south of Paris, La Havre became an immediate target for the Imperial Army and the British logistical apparatus that had followed the British Expeditionary force when it arrived moved to Bordeaux as it was designated the new harbor for British reinforcements.

The German 51st Corps, some 82,000 soldiers strong, included the 2nd Cyclist Brigade, the 243rd Division, the 121st Division, the 54th Division, the 1st Guards Reserve Division, and the 22nd Reserve Division. The corps was also involved in the Marne victory and the storming of many forts in Belgium. As the 4th Reserve Corps fighting in Calais, it was now a crack unit with many experienced, bloodied soldiers.

Facing them were 22,000 French soldiers and a Brigade of British troops with some good artillery units from the Royal Field Artillery and French leftovers from the Battle of the Marne. The troops were less experienced as a whole, but the entire area was well fortified.

The defenses of Le Havre were a roughly strait line of forts protecting its northern approaches (St Adresse, Tourneville, and Mont Joly) with a few artillery batteries set on a range of low hills near the city. They were about three miles from the town's outskirts and included nearly 100 heavy guns, both modern and ancient, and ranging from 3 inches to 6 inches in caliber. The Le Havre infantry lines were strewn about over an area of six miles in length, and all were either entrenched or sheltered in fortified positions. The Anglo-French defenses could only be approached by a set of two roads, both of which were well-swept by the aforementioned artillery batteries. The defensive preparations of Le Havre were thus pretty formidable since the troops had over two weeks to prepare their trenches and defenses.

Offshore, two more British battleships from the 3rd Battle Squadron roamed in artillery support. They were the pre-dreadnought battleships Britannia and Commonwealth, both again King Edward VII-class pre-dreadnought battleships with the same guns as the ones offshore Calais. They started to inflict heavy damage on the German troops the moment they were in range and would do so for the duration of the battle.

The road by which the German units approached led directly into Le Havre. At right angles with this road was a range of hills ringed with batteries. The fight for the hills took them four days to clear out, and then they arrived at the northern forts, where some heavy artillery had to be called to get them reduced.

The final fight for the city was initiated by one last German charge through the Fort of Tourneville, and by October 5th, the city center was reached, and the Allies surrendered. Several ships were scuttled in the harbor's entrance before they left, but the two British battleships refrained from bombing the Germans in the city itself to avoid killing civilians and angering the French. On the 6th of October, the German Imperial Flag was hoisted above Honfleur et Harfleur.

(...) Cherbourg (...)

Cherbourg was flanked by its harbor between La Hague and Val de Saire. The city itself and its neighboring port were one of the most important Channel ports. It housed important military facilities, a large landing area, and equipment. It was said the entirety of the French fleet could sail in and be protected by its defenses. It was consequently a prime target for the Germans, who eventually wanted to sail their fleet out of the German coast. Cherbourg was one of their prime targets.

Once called the "keys to the kingdom" by Vauban, the great Louis, the 14th fortress builder, it morphed, following herculean work, into a first-rate military port as Napoleon Bonaparte had prepared to invade England in 1804; it also had one of the largest French Navy naval arsenals. A stopping point for prestigious transatlantic liners before the beginning of the war, Cherbourg was now in the German target sight for its value as a prime military port.

The battle for the city started when the German 1st Army's 2nd Corps (3rd Infantry Division and 4th Infantry Division) and 3rd Corps (5th Infantry Division and 6th Infantry Division), supported by the Guard Corps (1st and 2d Guard Divisions), approached the city. In all, over 72,000 soldiers bore down on the small town of Cherbourg to assault it.

The Anglo-French troops numbered 18,000 men, supported by battleships from the Royal Navy's 3rd Battle Squadron, the Pre-dreadnought battleships Dominion and Hindustan. The Allied units entrenched themselves right into the city proper and into the old Vauban fortress in the northwest, where the military harbor was located.

While the defenders were ready and supported by two great warships, this time, the Germans had finally learned how to deal with them. Several large artillery units with longer range than the two King George Class VII class 305mm guns were brought to bear.

In the preceding years before the beginning of the world war, the Germans built several large artillery pieces for siege warfare, as it was becoming obvious very powerful shells would be needed to smash the plethora of modern forts springing up everywhere across Europe. The powerful guns were used to good effect in the Battle of the Frontier but also in Belgium. And now it was going to be used against British ships. The Germans moved in with mighty mortars ranging in caliber from 150mm to 250mm and a few 305mm Austro-Hungarian Skoda pieces for the coming fight.

The fight had thus opened with a heavy shelling from the sixty heavy guns far outranging the British battleships. The attack continued unrelenting for a full day, and the decision was taken to remove the two warships when Dominion was rocked by a series of 210mm shells, quickly followed by Hindustan with a boiler explosion that raked the ship with fire and secondary blasts. When the two battleships sailed out, they were burning and smoking hulks headed to the shipyards in England for lengthy repairs.

With their heavy support gone and not much artillery, the battle was thus a foregone conclusion. The heavy artillery pounded the town with abandon as the German infantry moved in and positioned themselves for the final assault, and on October 10th, the final series of bloody assaults was launched at the town.

The Anglo-French repulsed the first four attempts, but on their fourth one, the Kaiser's troops penetrated the northwest perimeter (the Vauban fortress), and then all hell broke loose.

The battle was over by the 12th of October, but not before the British set off the charges they had brought to destroy the military port facilities.

(...) Brest (...)

Brest was located to the north of a magnificent landlocked bay and occupied the slopes of two hills cut in two halves by the river Penfeld. It was one of the premier French ports in terms of military and commercial usage.

There was no battle proper when the German 1st Army's 7th, 8th, and 9th Corps arrived at the city since the Anglo-French had decided to evacuate it, but not before completely demolishing the harbor facilities to deny them to the enemy. By October 15th, the city, harbor, and all of the Britanny Peninsula were under German control.

The Storming of Battleship Hibernia Part 1 - Calais
14th Division, Regiment Graf Schwerin, October 15th, 1914

Private Soldier Oskar Dantz tried to keep his wits together as the motorboat he was in bobbed into the small waves. The engine worked at minimal power, as stealth was of paramount importance. As he watched left and right, he saw the outlines of numerous other boats all converging toward a pair of large, ominous-looking ships in the darkness off the coast of the city and harbor of Calais. The ships were also flashing in existence every now and then as they fired at the coast, briefly lighting the area around them.

He was nervous as hell, as it was his first time on a boat. Beside him sat his equally anxious and wary friend, Florian Storch. *"It's just like when we took the ferry to get over the Danube to Weltenburg Abbey,"* said Florian as he tried to convince himself and Oskar that all was well. Located near their hometown, the Weltenburg Abbey sat at the mouth of the Danube Gorge near their hometown. It was a place the two friends liked to go often, as the monks made the best beer in the area. To get to the place (there were no roads), you had to take a ferry. Oskar laughed softly. *"Storch, the Danube is like twenty feet deep where we cross, and we can even swim if the water is warm enough. This is something else entirely."* *"True enough, but stop being nervous; a boat is a boat,"* countered Florian. Oskar laughed nervously again. The memory of the Weltenburg Abbey did help to calm him down.

What they were trying to attempt was one hell of a risky and desperate move. The German 1st Army, Oskar's own 14th Division, and his Infanterie-Regiment Graf Schwerin had been fighting to try and conquer the city and the harbor for over three weeks. For his part, he'd been involved in heavy fighting and had taken some houses from the French, but as a whole, the city continued to resist stubbornly.

The Anglo-French had done a great job of entrenching themselves and had two powerful battleships just offshore supporting their defense, while the Germans, five times their numbers, struggled to advance inside the city. Oskar had heard they were called the Hibernia and the Africa.

Oskar and the Infanterie-Regiment Graf Schwerin had made some progress in the northeast corner of the city's defenses a week and a half ago, but the two British battleships had sailed right up the coast and shelled them to oblivion. He remembered the retreat and the maelstrom of fire that had slammed the unit. The casualties were horrendous.

The troops then settled in their trenches, dug in some more and the battle sort of stalemated. Every time an attack was attempted, the two British battleships, which the Germans could clearly see from the shore, intervened. It was then that some crazy First Lieutenant named Erwin Rommel proposed a plan to the Regimental commander Colonel Theodor von Dücker. The young officer's idea was to assault both British ships with infantry at night and try to board them. The enemy vessels were so close to the shore and Rommel's plan so well presented that it was accepted.

Theodor von Dücker was desperate for a solution since heavy pressure was being put by the OHL on the officers of the 14th Division and others to finish the siege. He thus gave Rommel 500 men and a week to prepare. Gathering boats and everything that could float with a reasonable degree of stealth. Both Oskar and Florian were chosen since they were known soldiers in the unit and were pretty good in a scrap.

Rommel was a peculiar officer, having come from the ranks. Well-educated, smart, and overflowing with energy and dynamism, he was one hell of a commander for the mission. As soon as he could, he obeyed his father's instruction and joined the 124th Infantry Regiment (based in Weingarten). Within a few months, it became obvious to his superior that he was a man of talent, and he was thus moved up to corporal with another promotion quickly following to sergeant. He was then recommended for officer school (the Kriegsschule) in Eastern Prussia (Danzig). He had finished his time there just in time for the beginning of World War One.

Oskar didn't know much about the man but knew he was already some sort of celebrity because of his heroic fighting. On August 2, 1914, he was sent to the Western Front, and he fought in the Ardennes area and then was part of the execution of the Schlieffen Plan to conquer Belgium and France. On August 22nd, in the town of Bleid, he and three men captured a whole platoon. During the conquest of Paris, he captured an enemy general and apparently covered himself with glory. He was wounded in the thigh when he went on the attack and defeated three French soldiers with an unloaded rifle. For this, he earned the Iron Cross Second Class.

Which brought the crazy daredevil here and then with Oskar, about to execute a crazy plan to board the battleship Hibernia. *"Don't worry, soldiers,"* said Rommel, sitting beside Florian and Oskar. He had chosen their boat for the assault, and it looked like the Lieutenant had no intention of avoiding the fight himself. *"The Brits are busy firing at the town and won't see us approach from the other side in the middle of the night."*

The plan was to circle around and attack while the battleships were half-blinded by their own guns firing since they were hosing the German position in the middle of the night. Oskar looked at the large flashes in the night and was awed at the power of the two ships. *"We'll soon be there; get ready and make sure you have everything."*

BEF, somewhere East of Paris
Fighting and the developing stalemate

Following the Battle of the Marne and the fall of Paris, the Allies switched to the defensive. They were entrenched and waited for the Germans to come at them. Opposed by machine gun fire and heavy howitzers, the Kaiser's troops were unable to penetrate the British and French positions on the heights and positions of choice chosen by the Anglo-French south of Paris and toward Verdun by the end of October. As a result, the war quickly descended into a stalemate, where neither side could advance. Weapons of modern industrialized warfare inflicted horrendous casualties on an unprecedented scale. A hail of machine gun bullets and a torrent of shells could stop any attack. Soon unable to make a breakthrough, the opposing sides began to consolidate their ground by digging trenches. They wouldn't stop trying to attack, but from then on, advances would not be counted by the miles, instead being measured in feet.

(...) Random fighting, Anglo-French lines (...)

Some elements of the 1st Royal Sussex Regiment were positioned in a nearby wood southeast of Paris and near Versailles (a platoon). They were busy trying to keep the damned Germans at bay, like many other units in the trench. The entire area was alive with bullets, fireballs, and men fighting hand-to-hand. Many casualties were inflicted by shells exploding when they hit the tree trunks around them, while others were good old slash wounds by bayonets. The soldier's world was a maelstrom of death, ground shaking, and streaming firearm ordinance. Earth catapulted in the air, tree splinters flew all over the place, and men died.

A blazing artillery shell zipped just over them. If it hadn't hit anything, it wouldn't have mattered, for those shells did not explode unless they hit did hit. However, the heavy round slammed a tree just behind them and exploded in a cataclysmic fury. That shell killed three men and wounded seven, as well as burrowing a deep crater, which in turn showered earth, rocks, and other debris around.

The 1st Royal Sussex Regiment and the 1st Loyal North Lancashire Regiment had been sent forward to support the beleaguered King's Royal Rifle Corps. The enemy was attacking in strength at one of the small villages they fortified as part of their defensive line supposed to stop the Krauts from further advances into France. They, too, suffered heavy casualties. An anonymous 2nd Lieutenant from the battalion recalled:

"I had only run fifty yards, trying to avoid the hailstorm of bullets streaming toward me and the rest of my comrades, when I heard a loud whistling sound on my right. Four enemy rounds exploded thirty yards to my right and blasted a few men from my platoon to the oblivion of a horrible, gory death. The sounds of the German shells were followed by an earth-shattering, ground-shaking moment, and I fell to the ground. The things were truly terrible instruments of war. After putting my helmet back on and re-shouldering my rifle, I aimed again in the direction of the incoming Germans. As right as rain, there they were, and I started shooting again in the withering grey-clad mass of men running toward our lines. I was joined by many of my comrades and a few machine gun teams, and so soon after that, the Germans (the surviving ones) ran back toward their lines in disarray. The fight in the woods north of Versailles was truly appalling."

Private Donny Loyd's letter to his mother was only a tiny account of the truly terrible fighting that day in France. Both sides had learned to hate each other and attacked with abandon. The Germans were under order to try and pierce the Allied line in what the OHL called *"the last push on the door before the whole barns comes down on its own."* The Anglo-French, in a similar fashion, viewed the fight as critical to the future conduct of the war. As Marshal Foch put it in an edict to the troops the day before, *"The line must be held at all cost and every French soldier must understand that, if need be, they are to give their life for the future of France."*

Both sides suffered heavily. Casualties amounted to nearly fifty percent in many of the German, French, and British units. The 1st Loyal North Lancashire Regiment was decimated to the point where it had to be taken out of the line for an indefinite period of time pertaining new reinforcements. In most units from both sides, three out of four officers were listed as casualties within a few days of the battle. The scale of such losses was almost bewildering to even the sanest military mind. It was hard to fathom why the commanders on both sides sent their men to such a massacre. But since one attacked (the Germans), the other side had to defend.

However, such casualty rates could not be sustained, especially on the German side, since they were the attackers. Regardless of how brave their soldiers were and how good their weapons or training were, the defender side always held the ground and thus was fighting from behind trenches, machine gun nests, and bunkers.

All across the front from the south of Paris to Verdun, the stalemate was slowly establishing itself while the dead and injured continued to mount because the generals would not accept to stay idle and find a better solution than sending their soldiers in futile charges at the enemy trenches.

French High Command (New French HQ, Versailles)
The situation on the 30th of October, 1914

The newly-minted Commander-in-Chief of the French forces, General Foch, tried to remove the dirt that had just fallen on the situational map they were looking at from the bottom of the cave in the city's mayor's building. The entire room was lit by flickering lights from the constant ground shaking due to the enemy artillery shelling.

Foch was at his field HQ not very far from the frontlines. In this, he was not the typical military commander of the time and was very near the frontline. He had decided that with his *"not giving one more inch of French soil"* order, leadership at the front was needed.

"So, Colonel Bronsard," you were saying, said the commander, as he put his fingers on his chin, looking closer to the map once the dirt that had fallen from the ceiling was removed. *"Please tell me of those reports of enemy attack slackening."* *"Yes, sir,"* answered Louis Bronsard, one of his staff officers attached to his HQ.

"The situation is stabilizing all across the frontline as the Germans seem to be removing a lot of troops for the East and have sent two of their armies northward to conquer the northern harbor and the territory north of us." *"Have we retreated anywhere?"* *"Well, sir, apart from a few enemy frontline penetrations in Belfort and Verdun that were quickly counterattacked and retaken, we have not given any significant ground at the frontline ranging from the Atlantic Ocean to Verdun to the Swiss border."*

A large blast rocked the entire building, just as if the Germans wanted to remind Foch and his men that while this was true and they had not gained anything in the last two weeks, they were still trying hard. *"That was close, sir,"* said one of the Lieutenants in charge of telegram communications, standing beside the stone stairway. He was soon clouded in dust billowing from above.

"It was," intervened Marshal French, the commander of the British Expeditionary force. The man was making no secret of his profound disagreement with Foch over the matter of being too far forward near the frontline. *"A commander's place is not near the fighting as we are now. What happens if a shell lands on top of the building and buries us in stone debris? Who will command and direct the troops?"* "John, stop being so pessimistic, will you," countered the French general. *"We need to show ourselves and act like we mean it. My predecessor was not of the same type, and look where it got us."* "General Foch," said French with an exasperated look. *"We both know that the all-out attacking French military doctrine was the problem there and that Joffre stuck to it for too long."*

The British BEF commander had been called to the French HQ to discuss the tactical position of the troops and where some of the reinforcements he'd just received from England (through Bordeaux) were to be placed. The entire Entente troop placement was now defensive-minded, as it was not capable of being able to do anything else.

The Allied armies had been decimated by first the Battle of the Frontier, then by the German breakout from Belgium and the subsequent battles. The defeat of the Marne then compounded the issue and made certain that no more attacks were possible for the time being. Reinforcements were coming from the colonies (French and British), but that took time. The English were madly recruiting and it was planned that the British Army would eventually reach in the millions like the French. The Canadians, Australians, French North Africans, and South Africans were all coming. This was why no offensive plans were being made against the Germans.

Present at the meeting with French and Foch were several of the British corps commanders, along with French Generals Gallieni and Lanzerac, both men who had proved their worth and strategic understanding of the new unfolding war. Foch had not gone through a crazy spree of replacing unit commanders but did reinstate what he considered the only cool mind during the fall before disaster befell on the Anglo-French, General Lanzerac. The man had been the only one advocating defense while Joffre continued on his offensive obsession, even in the face of overwhelming odds.

"General Lanzerac," continued Foch. "How are your troops doing?" "As well as can be expected in this very difficult situation, sir. They are suffering heavy casualty rates, and I am cycling the units from the frontline to the rear to give them a break, but the pace of enemy attacks, while relenting a little, is still frantic." Foch grunted. "Very well, but the real question I want answered is, can you hold and perhaps spare some troops?" Foch gave a quick look to French. Both men had received new orders pertaining to a future operation in the south.

Taken aback, Lanzerac answered carefully. "You need troops elsewhere, sir?" "Yes, General and I need to know if you can spare a division or two. I am also sending orders and instruction to the other army commanders in the West to send me five divisions while I will use three of the newly arrived Moroccan and Algerian units for the operation I have been ordered to prepare."

Lanzerac took some time to decide and conferred with Gallieni. Both men were working together in stemming the enemy tide south of Paris. "We both will have to confirm to you but we'll get you your two divisions, sir." "Very well, Generals. You are dismissed, but I will await your answer by tomorrow. Time is of the essence," answered Foch, satisfied. The two men gave their commander a stiff military salute and then turned away from the table where the operational map was to leave the basement of the mayor's building by going up the dusty stairs, leaving both French and Foch alone.

"That crazy Churchill," started French unhappily. "He will be the end of us. Too bold, too aggressive, not enough brains," he continued. "Well, Marshal, while I agree with you that this entire affair is a bit risky and might backfire on us, what have we got to lose? It isn't like we have a choice in the matter. The bastards have decided to join the Central Powers." French, always in a sort of perpetual bad mood since the terrible defeats at Mons and Charleroi (he had wanted to leave France, after all). Brooding over the map as he put both his palms on the table, French continued with his negative thoughts. *"I tell you, Foch, that bastard Churchill is an adventurer. No patience, no planning, no strength. All bluster."*

Foch crossed his arms behind his back, temporarily leaving the discussion as one of his staff people walked by him to show him a telegram from the commander in Belfort. *"We'll just have to see how it plays out, Marshal. In the meantime, we've got the two divisions, I asked of the Belfort Army commander."*

The French commander-in-chief moved to the table, shoulder to shoulder, with the British Marshal. *"Shall we plan this,"* he said, sitting down, looking intently at southern Europe and the area they needed to plan the operation for.

French 14th Division
Trench life and warfare, 1914

Private soldier Armand Bonnier and his friend Philippe Cren sat in a makeshift chair dug from the side of the trench wall and slowly smoked a shared pipe. That very morning, Philippe had been lucky enough to barter for some tobacco in exchange for a luger pistol he'd picked up a week before and that some asshole officer wanted. He was some sort of collector for the things. To the two very tired and worn soldiers, the why didn't matter very much. They were now enjoying a divine pause from the horror of war, enjoying the taste and the buzz the hard tobacco was giving them. Sitting both side by side on their earthen bench, they looked at empty air, surrounded by a grey cloud of billowing smoke.

Below their feet lay a dead German soldier from the hard fighting of the previous night. Several other bodies were strewn around, tossed to the sidewalls of the trench as other French soldiers walked by on the wooden planking at the bottom of the trench that made them avoid being always inches deep into dirty, stinky water. "Where do you think that bastard's from," asked Philippe as he exhaled a puff of smoke with great satisfaction. The two men were just making small talk as they lazied the day away following their harrowing night of battle. *"As far as I know, the German Empire is composed of twenty-five member states, so this could be any one of the fuckers."*

Another soldier passing by stopped to speak to the two smokers, having heard them talking about the dead German's parent unit. *"I'll tell you if you give me a puff of this excellent-smelling tobacco pipe."* The arriving soldier seemed to be from another unit but as bloody-fresh as they were, meaning he had also been involved in the fighting the night before. *"Well, be my guest,"* answered Armand with a smile. The man picked up the pipe and took a long drag, closing his eyes in satisfaction.

"From the black markings on his collar and the crest on his helmet, that bastard," finally said the soldier, pointing to the corpse on the ground with his hand holding the pipe, "is a Saxon engineer. I was told by my Captain that we got hit by a couple of Saxons and three Bavarian Divisions last night."

Night-time raids were becoming more and more frequent now that the front was stabilizing into trench warfare. Every night was one of fear of what the enemy would do. In the case of the night's previous fight, the Germans hadn't been subtle about it, shelling the Entente lines for a couple of hours after dark and then sending a full night assault by several divisions.

"Name is Max Killerman," added the passing soldier, giving the pipe back to Philippe since it seemed to be his turn. "Gotta go guys, have a nice day, and if I were you, I would toss that Boche over the trench before it starts to stink," and then he walked away toward the errand he'd been sent on.

Both Armand and Philippe just shrugged their shoulders, their curiosity finally satisfied. For a moment, they wondered if they should heed the man's advice and pick up the corpse, but they decided they didn't care for now. They had tobacco smoke to cover the smell, and anyway, some asshole officer or NCO would eventually come by and tell them to do it. If the German was gone, the ordering might concern something else, and they preferred not to know what it was. Leaving the dead man there was sort of their insurance that it would be their only instruction if it came to it.

The Storming of Battleship Hibernia Part 2 - Calais
14th Division, Regiment Graf Schwerin, October 15th, 1914

Private Soldier Oskar Dantz only heard muffled sounds as he had earplugs in. It was the first time he put any (he hadn't even thought about the idea), but he decided he would keep them as it made a hell of a difference in the middle of an artillery barrage. During the assault, he was just about to execute with his comrades; it would also come in very handy.

Rommel's entire plan rested on the fact that one didn't stand on the deck of a battleship when it fired its main gun. The concussion blast alone could kill, and it burst eardrums. This meant, in essence, that no British sailor would be crazy enough to stand and see or spot the approaching raiders. The boat was right on the battleship hull, and he was almost done climbing the grapple-tipped rope to the so-called gunwale or the rail that went along the edge of a vessel.

As he moved over and up on the deck, he was almost thrown back into the water as the concussion blast from the forward 305mm gun firing hit him. It slammed hard on his chest, and he almost lost his balance as he felt tremendous pressure on his entire body. He steadied himself and tried to see where the others already up on the deck were. He noticed, for the first time, that the deck was made of wood and wondered why that was since he'd always believed that battleships were made of steel.

What Oskar didn't know was that the wooden deck of a pre-dreadnought battleship was typically not directly attached to the armor plating beneath it. Battleships traditionally had an armored belt around the waterline to protect against incoming fire, and the deck was usually located above this armor belt. The wooden deck was typically laid over a steel structure that formed the actual deck of the ship.

The wooden deck served several purposes, such as providing a non-slip surface for the crew to move on, reducing noise levels, and helping to protect the underlying steel deck from corrosion. The wooden deck was usually attached to the steel deck structure using methods such as bolts, screws, or other mechanical fasteners. Additionally, the wooden deck was often coated with various sealants and paints to protect it from the elements and to improve its longevity.

Of course, all of these details didn't matter one bit to him as he gathered near the men huddled behind one of the main gun turret's hatch, where Rommel and a few more men were. A second later, Florian joined them, and yet another of the forward gun blasts reverberated across the deck. The ship had 2 turrets, one facing forward and the other one located near the stern. Both were raining gunfire on the helpless German trench lines facing Calais. Oskar was able to see the blazing tracer rounds as they arced in a quick path to slam earthside. For a moment, he was mesmerized by the sight, but quickly, his attention was reined in by Rommel.

The assault was planned to attack the rear one and also try to enter the ship to overtake it. He shook his head again, wondering how they would pull this off, as it had never been attempted. It was crazy! Battleship Hibernia was one hell of a big warship and had over 700 men. Oskar remembered their quick study of what was known about their layout and design with Rommel before they launched the mission. Hibernia was launched in January 1907, and it became the flagship of the British Atlantic Fleet. The eight battleships of the King Edward VII Class (of which Africa and Hibernia were part) were the top technological developments before the advent of the dreadnought class battleships.

In 1914, the outdated battleships were considered expendable items, and this explained the reason why the Royal Navy had accepted to sail them so close to the shore and put them at such risk. Keeping Calais out of dirty German hands was a higher priority than keeping an obsolete battleship out of harm's way.

Rommel pointed toward the hatch of the main gun, then toward the ship's citadel, central tower, and finally toward the stern, and the men fanned out in their assigned directions as per the plan the young maverick officer had given them prior to the attack.

Oskar was part of the group that was to assault the BL 12-inch Mk IX naval gun right beside them. One of the soldiers in the group tried the hatch, and it was unlocked. The twenty-man group almost all smiled at the same time, and Florian, also part of the attack on the gun, gave him a quick elbow in the ribs, showing his enthusiasm and anxiety for what they were about to do.

On the count of five with his left hand, he signaled to another soldier to open the hatch. Oskar clutched his rifle, and the hatch was opened, the men ahead of him entering the gun house. As he entered the small room, where the back of the gun barrel was and where the final ammo-loading procedure was located, Oskar was hit by a heavy smell of cordite, a clear indication that the gun was firing. The moment he was in, shots were already being fired as there were four British sailors in the small room.

The fight was quick, and the British were quickly dispatched. Four men were now dead, their blood pooling on the steel deck. As quickly as the blink of an eye, they neutralized the main bow gun. They fanned out in the rest of the turret, going down ladders to where the ammunition was stored. The enemies below were certain to have heard the gunfire above, and Oskar braced himself for a fight as he followed the men ahead of him down the ladder.

The shots started to ring and ricochet with sparks all along the corridors. Oskar was miraculously unscathed, while the two soldiers in front of him, still on the latter, were slammed with bullets, letting go and dropping down to the ammunition storage compartment, dead. They dropped like a sack of potatoes and made a sickening thud as they hit the deck twenty feet below.

Knowing he only had moments to live if he didn't do anything quickly, Oskar also let go of the ladder and dropped down the shaft, landing right on top of a crouching British sailor, who was peering into the ladder shaft to fire again. He slammed hard on the man and knocked him prone.

The landing hurt his leg and ankle, but adrenaline made him move like lightning, rolling to the side to avoid more enemy fire. Some shots rang again and hit the two German bodies who had fallen down the ladder as if they were sandbags.

He finally unslung his rifle (that had been strapped to his back) and rolled to his side again to face where the bullets came from. He emptied his Gewehr 98 rifle magazine in quick succession, firing the five bullets in the cartridge. The bullets ricocheted all over the place, luckily killing the two British sailors holed up in the ammunition magazine and injuring the third one he'd landed on moments earlier.

The next instant, more German soldiers dropped from the ladder, quickly taking control of the entire room. The forward gun turret of Battleship Hibernia was under German control. Oskar sat up and gave a cursory inspection of the dead comrades. They were gone alright.

The rest of the battle for the British warship lasted another half-hour. Over thirty German soldiers were killed, but it wasn't that bad considering the Hibernia's crew of over 700 sailors. Most were unarmed at the moment of the assault, and the Germans had taken them by surprise. Part of Rommel's plan had been to trap most of them in parts of the ship they sealed off.

While the assault on Hibernia had been a success, it had not gone as well on the battleship Africa. There the German assault was defeated by some quick-witted actions from brave British sailors and an armory lieutenant who armed enough of them to make a difference. Furthermore, and to Rommel's crew's predicament, some of the crew of Hibernia were able to signal that they had lost control of the ship.

Thirty minutes into the battle for the ship, Africa opened fire on the now German-controlled pre-dreadnought. And all hell broke loose for the raiders because the British captain, still under control of his vessel, decided that he could not leave the other ship in enemy hands.

305mm shells slammed into the hull of the ship in quick succession, and it didn't take long for the men to reach the conclusion that it was time to leave the Hibernia. After all, they were soldiers and had no training on warships. The first sign that there was trouble for Oskar and Florian was when the ship rocked, and a heavy clanging noise was heard. It didn't take long for smoke to be everywhere and a rolling fire to spread from section to section.

Oskar eventually climbed up the ladder as the ship rocked hard and was able to dive into the churning sea around the ship. The next morning, the Africa left the scene, leaving a half-sunken Hibernia, still smoking and burning.

With the British battleships gone, the defense of Calais didn't last one more day. The Germans, moving their heavy artillery back in position, made short work of the already beaten-down defenses.

Thus, the last of the four French harbors had fallen, while Oskar, his friend, and their newfound crazy officer Rommel waded to shore tired, wet but victorious, and with a potential medal ceremony.

CHAPTER 2
THE WAR IN THE EAST
"Now, we can no longer hold back. It will be a terrible war."
Quote by Austro-Hungarian Emperor Franz Joseph I about the start of World War I.

The Siege of Tsingtao Part 1
Von Spee vs Togo round 2 and the land battle, September 21st, 1914

The battle for the German Tsingtao Fortress had started over two weeks before, and it still stood proud against overwhelming numbers of Japanese troops and ships.

Following an intense naval battle, both the German fortifications and the ships on both sides were greatly damaged. Tsingtao naval forts (Hui-Tchien-Huk-damaged, Bismarck-damaged, Tsingtao battery-destroyed, and Hsisuniwa Battery-destroyed) were seriously damaged or taken out. In addition to these heavy losses, the Germans had lost a pre-dreadnought battleship, the Pommern, with damage ranging from light to heavy on the rest of its fleet. The city was damaged beyond repair and was now a mass of smoking rubble because of the constant Japanese bombardment from the Imperial Navy Fleet, and the artillery landed north of the fortress. In fact, the entire area was plastered with shell impact, reminiscent of the surface of the moon.

The Japanese were not unscathed to achieve this level of damage. They had to move in with their main fleet to confront Graf Spee in what history books would soon call the First Naval Battle of Tsingtao. In the critical, intense, and ship-sinking action that followed, the pre-dreadnought battleship Fuji was first crippled and then destroyed by Fort Bismarck's heavy naval mortars. Togo also left two sinking cruisers and six wrecked destroyers in the waters near Tsingtao, while the rest of his vessels were damaged.

And then the land battle had started, the Japanese thinking the deed done and the German forts-warships reduced. But it was not to be as the Germans had built and prepared well for this battle.

By the 8th of September, and seeing that there would be no easy walk-into-Tsingtao-scenario, Japanese forces installed their siege around the fortified area in a concentric ring and entrenched themselves for a long battle. With Tsingato's main fortress guns still active, the Japanese land commander-in-chief, General Kamio, ordered his troops to approach and entrench while the German Commander withdrew his forces closer to the town by his well-prepared defenses.

The Japanese started shelling the fort and the city three days after the naval battle (September 12th) and dug siege trenches, just like nine years earlier during the Russo-Japanese War and the Siege of Port Arthur. Their goal was to approach and avoid the enemy gunfire's very large 11-inch guns without incurring too many casualties. Every night, the Japanese dug further and further toward the German defensive lines, covered by their artillery shelling through the darkness. The bombardment was still going on by September 21st (employing around 100 siege guns with thousands of shells on the Japanese side) when a coordinated assault was ordered for Kamio and Togo by the higher-ups in Tokyo. The Navy and the Army would attack as one and try to overwhelm the stubborn German defenses.

Meanwhile, the Germans didn't stay idle waiting for the end. They used their heavy weapons to slam the Japanese trenches, even if difficult to hit. They still had some very strong defenses, and it looked like they would continue to resist for a while.

By September 1914, the Germans had been at Tsingtao for twelve long years, giving them plenty of time to prepare adequate defenses. The peninsula around the port was spanned by two ranges of low hills. On the nearest hills to Tsingtao, they had constructed three ferroconcrete forts (named Moltke, Iltis, and Bismarck) protected by a number of 4-inch, 6-inch, and 9.4-inch naval guns; in addition, Fort Bismarck, perched on the highest hill in the center of the peninsula had four 11-inch naval defense cannons. The Japanese troops approached them every night with their moving trenches, but it was still not enough, and they had to stay hunkered down during the day or else be obliterated from above.

Concrete redoubts had been built with 10-foot ditches running from sea to sea. A 6-foot wall had also been constructed with the immediate area strewn with land mines.

The third defensive line (the one the Germans planned on retreating to if the Japanese stormed the 2nd line) on the second range of hills northeast of Tsingtao and beyond the river was the 1,200-high Prinz Heinrich Hill on the eastern side of the peninsula, which was ten miles wide at this juncture.

Admiral Maximilian von Spee, the German commander of the Pacific Squadron, still had a powerful fleet following the naval battle with Togo and the Imperial Japanese Navy. With the added protection and cannons of the harbor defenses, it remained a formidable opponent for the yet-still-small Japanese Imperial Navy.

German Pacific Squadron	
Admiral von Graf Spee	
damage	CA Sharnhorst
BB Kaiserin rudder damage, deck damage	CA Gneisenau
~~Pre dreadnought BB Pommern heavily damaged~~	CL Emden
Pre Dreadnought Schleswig-Holstein	CL Nurnberg
	CL Leipzing

The fight for Tsingtao was taking too much time, and the more it remained in German hands, the more the Japanese leadership perceived its prestige was affected. It was why, even against Admiral Togo's quite prudent and logical objections, the combined assault was ordered.

Russian Second Army
The Siege of Koenigsberg, September 21st, 1914

A Russian general of German extraction, Paul von Rennenkampf commanded the Russian Second Army, the northernmost of the imperial forces, in 1914. Rennenkampf and his army moved slowly into East Prussia in August, were bloodied in a skirmish in Stallupönen, but emerged victorious from the Battle of Gumbinnen, again in August. The man was of German descent, like many other officers in the Russian Imperial Army, following a long tradition of military officers starting from the time of Catherine the Great in the 18th Century.

Baltic Germans were perfectly integrated with the Russian society. Indeed, they were over-perfectly integrated and over-German in their attitude. As Tsar Nicholas the first once put it, *"Russians serve Russia, Baltic Germans serve the Romanovs."* Having sworn their loyalty, how could they break their oath? Anyway, the concept of nationalism was not prevalent at the start of the 20th Century; thus, it was perfectly normal for people of other states to serve a sovereign in another country.

By the time the war broke out, General Rennenkampf had forty years of experience in the Russian Army, having fought in the Crimea, also in the Chinese Boxer Rebellion at the turn of the 20th Century, and finally in the Russo-Japanese War in 1904-1905.

The man at the head of the 2nd Russian Army was a very cautious man but had nevertheless been able to clinch a victory at Gumbinnen and was now besieging Koenigsberg. Perhaps some could criticize his way of making war, but not his results. Tsar Nicolas II himself had sent him congratulatory letters, and he was quite proud of the Tsar's praise.

If he had to be honest with himself, however, it wasn't like he had yet faced a major German force since the start of the war. The new enemy commander-in-chief in the East, General Paul von Hindenburg, had retreated before him and General Samsonov's 1st Army as they greatly outnumbered him by a three-to-one ratio. Now that the Germans had gained a major victory in the West, Rennenkampf dreaded the fact that the OHL could send troops toward Prussia.

The General was walking toward the ridge where he would be able to get a good view of the city fortress of Konigsberg that his forces had been assaulting for the last ten days.

In September 1914, German field defenses surrounding the fortress were attacked by 40 infantry battalions of the Russian 2nd Army; the attackers enjoyed significant numerical superiority, but the defenders were well-entrenched and behind some solid fixed defenses. By the 19th of September, the Russian advance brought the fortress proper within range of Tsarist artillery, further reinforced with sixty additional guns of calibers up to 203mm, but these could only be brought into action in the next few days. The day before, a Russian frontal assault that Rennenkampf had ordered was repelled by German artillery and its entrenched troops. The day afterward, two Russian flanking counter-attacks forced German artillery to relocate deeper into the city.

For centuries Konigsberg had been one of Germany's iconic cities. Kings had been made there, and philosopher Kant had come from the city. Conquering it would, therefore, not only be a strategic victory for Russia but also a significant setback for German morale. Rennenkampf tried to think of all the honors he would get if he stormed the critical fortress.

He finished his walk as he walked over the hill to a scene of mayhem and destruction. The entire area was on fire, dotted with smoke columns and blazing tracer rounds landing into the fortress and firing from it, trying to smash the Russian artillery guns pounding the German defenses.

General Rennenkampf, recognizing the strength of the defenses, had moved his troops to entrench in a ring around the no less than nine powerful forts protecting Koenigsberg. A large tract of land was also protected by interlaying trench positions and minefields, filled with grey-clad German soldiers milling about like mice in tunnels. Rennenkampf could see the dots moving to and from the trench, and the flashes of their guns. These flashes were killing Russian soldiers, and he didn't like it one bit. Not all of the forts were modern or could necessarily withstand a true artillery bombardment and it had shown in the first few assaults since the beginning of September. Some were now in Russian hands.

But enough still stood that the battle for the fortress was far from over. The fortifications of the city included numerous defensive walls, forts, bastions, and other structures. They made up the so-called First and the Second Defensive Belts, built in a first phase (1626—1634) and a second (1843—1859). The fifteen-meter-thick First Belt was erected due to Koenigsberg's vulnerability during the Polish–Swedish wars. It was, however, never tested in battle. *"Well, until now,"* said Rennenkampf as he chuckled to himself. *"Sir, do you need anything,"* said his chief of staff as he heard him laugh softly. The entire top of the hill was ringed with trenches, guns, and bunkers, and the General was observing the scene below from the safety of a log and earth bunker. It was the forward Russian HQ, and Rennenkampf was paying it a visit to see the progress of the battle. He was starting to get worried at the time it took to storm Konigsberg because there were persistent rumors and reports of trainloads of troops arriving west of the Vistula River. He was certain a German counteroffensive was in the works.

"Here, sir," continued his chief of staff, giving him a pair of binoculars. *"This is where our troops are fighting. The so-called Second Belt includes twelve bastions, three ravelins, seven spoil banks, and two fortresses surrounded by a water moat."* He paused to the left: *"Red brick gates seem to serve as entrances and passages through defensive lines and were equipped with moveable bridges. All of them*

are bristling with machine guns and artillery. Our soldiers are having quite a hard time."

Between the 1890s and 1914, the Germans committed a lot of resources to building new fortifications and reinforcing old ones to meet the latest artillery developments. Königsberg, the key position in East Prussia, had twelve Biehler-era forts from the 1870s, one newer fort from the 1890s, three interval works, and forty-one I, A, and M Raume. They were built amongst the older constructions or else replaced decrepit ones from the 17th Century.

"Looks good so far, but the troops aren't advancing fast enough," answered Rennenkampf. The chief of staff dropped his binoculars to await his commander's further comments or orders. Instead, the General countered with a question. *"Do we have any news of General Souvorov's army on the Vistula?"* The question took the Colonel by surprise, since he didn't understand what was the point of speaking about an army so far away? "Well, sir, the last report puts it being about to cross the river to attack the Germans there."

Rennenkampf seemed thoughtful for a moment. If Souvorov was on the attack, then he felt he still had more time. *"Very well, Colonel. Tell the troops to keep at it."* Yes, sir."

Friedrich Wilhelm I Fort
1st Grenadier Regiment "Crown Prince" (1st East Prussian)

Astronomic Bastion	
Bronsart Fort	
Dohna Tower	Reinforced with concrete and steel, with several machine guns and field guns.
Friedrich Wilhelm I Fort	The largest fort of Konigsberg, equipped with the most modern defenses and guns.
Gneisenau Fort:	
Grolman Bastion:	Strengthened with casemates and caponiers inside its wall and also included the lesser Oberteich and Kupferteich Bastions.
Pillau Citadel	
Stein Fort	
Barnekow Fort	

List of the forts around Konigsberg

Captain Mikael Lundbeck, an officer in the 1st Grenadier Regiment (part of the German First Division, 1st Corps, based in Konigsberg), looked with attention at his men firing in the embrasures in the walls of the fort.

Well, not with that much attention as he had people for this, but nevertheless, he tried to keep his attention to the men fighting it as the moment was critical. After all, he was in charge of a company of men, or of 240 soldiers. His job is to direct the fight, not participate. But sometimes the enemy doesn't cooperate, like in this instance, as once they entered the fort well, then he would fight. Since he thought about fighting, he felt his P08 Luger pistol holstered to his hip.

Mikael was trying his best to lead his men as the 1st Grenadier Regiment was stuck in the main German fort defending the city of Konigsberg, Friedrich Wilhelm I (in honor of the former Kaiser). The building was the biggest and strongest in Konigsberg, and it couldn't fall.

They were in the middle of an attack, and he tried to keep his composure while his men fought the latest Russian assaults. The bastards did not let go and kept coming. Their artillery pounded the fort every day and night, their only reprieve from the shelling being when an enemy infantry attack was underway.

The soldiers manned the holes and fired one shot after the other, with more of them behind busy reloading Gewehr 98 Rifles to help with the firing rate. Left and right, two Maxim Machine guns chattered away at the attacking Russians. Billowing smoke and a cordite smell prevailed in the large room he was in with his men,

"Captain," his Lieutenant yelled as he ran right beside him. They were in one of the main towers of the fort, facing the river that was crawling with Russians. *"Yes, Lieutenant."* *"I think we will need more reinforcements, sir,"* continued the young officer. *"The enemy has breached the lower levels."* A wave of fear washed over Mikael, and for a moment, he almost ordered everyone to retreat deeper into the fort. But then, his training and sense of duty surged back to the surface. *"Take two squads and kill the bastards. I'll get more men from other parts of the forts, Lieutenant."* *"Thank you, sir,"* said the man as he turned to go and pick up his men for the counterattack below.

The overall situation for the fight for Konigsberg wasn't doing so bad to date. The siege was a little over ten days old, but German forces were holding, supplied by sea. There were also rumors that some battleships would soon come to support them with their big guns, just like the British were doing in the Battle of the Four Harbors in the West. While the enemy having infiltrated the fort's lower levels was unsettling, he wasn't overly worried since he knew they had enough men in the fort to defend it and repulse the attackers. Other captains would also send troops to the beleaguered area and all would be fine.

The world around him seemed to shake as if the Hammer of God had slammed against it. The wall in front of Mikael exploded in a fury and a large cloud of dust, the men firing from it obliterated by the blast.

Mikael fell on his back, coughing hard. He noticed his ears were ringing, and his eyes stung because of the dust. *"Captain, are you alright,"* said one of the soldiers, walking by him to give some assistance. *"Yes, Private,"* he said with some hesitation, *"I am good. Get me Lieutenant Strolker and any sergeant or Corporal. I need an assessment of the situation." "Yes, Captain,"* answered the soldier.

This was going to be a close fight.

The Siege of Tsingtao Part 2
Von Spee vs Togo round 2 and the land battle, September 21st, 1914

(...) Fort Bismarck, the assault commences (...)

The German Governor commanding the defense of Tsingtao, Captain Meyer-Waldeck, watched with apprehension at the stream of Japanese yellowish uniforms streaming in the open and trying to overwhelm the land defenses. The enemy assault started with a mad soldier rushing and yelling at soldiers. *"What are they yelling, Colonel Lettow,"* asked the German Governor. *"Something like Banzai, sir,"*

He grunted, not liking what he was seeing. He didn't fancy the Japanese and didn't hold any love for the Chinese either. In fact, he hated Asia as a whole and wondered why he'd been stuck with this godforsaken job of defending an untenable position. But by God, he'd been given a job, and if it entailed him killing as many of the wretches as possible, he was fine with that,

His fortifications were formidable, but that was a lot of soldiers charging the fortified area. *"How many do you think there are, Colonel,"* he continued the discussion with another question. *"I would estimate at least ten thousand, sir."* He gave a long glance at the entire scene and the battlefield. The approach along the peninsula and thus to Tsingtao was dominated by Prince Heinrich Hill and by three concrete and steel hilltop forts on Moltke Berg, Bismarck Berg, and Iltis Berg. The three positions were his trump card and how he hoped to repulse this first attack. He'd lost half his cannon defenses with the Imperial Navy's attack, but most of what he'd lost had faced the sea and were intended to defend against warships anyway. He took a deep breath. It was time. He turned toward Colonel Lettow, giving him a grave face.

"Order all forts to commence firing," he said to his chief of staff, who nodded and then rapidly moved to the background to relay the order. Meyer-Waldeck stood high, almost on top of Fort Bismarck, and

watched from one of the main guns' embrasure. *"Sir, if you may,"* said one of the soldiers walking beside him and gesturing that he should move in the background. The main 282 mm gun he was standing beside was about to fire, and it would not be good for him to be too close. *"Indeed,"* he answered.

The Japanese attack began at dawn on the 21st of September. Two of the defending forts were heavily damaged by the naval attack a couple of weeks before (destroyed even), but the Germans kept at it and fought hard. Some of the damaged positions and the guns were repaired by the time the land attack started, giving Meyer-Waldeck more firepower.

The guns up in Fort Bismarck and Fort Hui-tchien-huk exploded in their fury, slamming the attacking Japanese with a storm of fire and shrapnel. Then, the German Maxim Machine guns started to clatter their blazing bullets from up high in their trenches in the hills. Perched higher up over them all (Meyer-Waldeck and Lettow had moved to the concrete-fortified rook of the bunker housing one of Fort Bismarck's 283mm guns), the two men also saw the lines of tracers crossing the field from both sides. The Nipponese soldiers died in droves and left a long trail of blood as they tried to advance up the hill toward the forts and the trenches. But advance they did, and that was not good for the Germans.

The battle for the hills and for Tsingtao beyond them was on.

Fort Hui-tchien-huk
4 x 24cm/40 naval rifles. 3 destroyed, 1 remaining
8 x 8.8cm/35 naval rifles 5 destroyed, 3 remaining
Searchlights in armored cupolas. Destroyed
A generous ammunition stockpile.

Fort Bismarck
4 x 28.3cm coast defense mortars. 2 destroyed, 2 remaining
8 x 8.8cm/35 naval rifles 4 destroyed, 4 remaining
Searchlights in armored cupolas.
A generous ammunition stockpile.

~~Old Tsingtao Battery.~~
~~4 x 21cm/40 naval rifles.~~
~~8 x 8.8cm/35 naval rifles~~
~~Searchlights in armored cupolas.~~
~~A generous ammunition stockpile.~~

~~Hsiauniwa Battery.~~
~~4 x 21cm/40 naval rifles.~~
~~8 x 8.8cm/35 naval rifles~~
~~Searchlights in armored cupolas.~~
~~A generous ammunition stockpile.~~

The German forts following the First Naval Battle of Tsingtao and their fight with Togo's Imperial Navy

After five hours straight of fighting, artillery shelling, and death, the Japanese assault seemed to falter. Not helping was the weather. In short, it was atrocious; rain transformed the field into a quagmire, and the roads or rather tracks used by the Japanese to reach the assaulting area were in bad condition, narrow, and heavily congested by the movements of the large forces and their equipment using the same road. From up high, it seemed like a swirling mass chugging away in the mud and in a sea of blood. The attack was about to fail, but it was at that moment that Admiral Togo Heihachiro joined in.

(…) German Dreadnought battleship Westfalen (…)

"Admiral," said the lookout officers, relaying a radio communication from up in Fort Bismarck. "*Yes, Lieutenant,*" he said, turning around. Admiral von Spee was on the bridge of his dreadnought battleship, Kaiserin. "*Governor Meyer-Waldeck reports that the enemy fleet is within sight.*" Von Spee tried to keep a straight face. "*Very well. Commence firing as soon as the forts relay a firing position.*" "*Yes, sir,*" answered the man. The reason he mentioned this was that while his ships were protected within the confines of the harbor and the surrounding hills, they couldn't see the approaching Japanese ships very well. They thus relied on the lookouts in the forts and in the coastal watch stations scattered across the coastline.

German Pacific Squadron	
Admiral von Graf Spee	
damage	CA Sharnhorst
BB Kaiserin rudder damage, deck damage	CA Gneisenau
~~Pre dreadnought BB Pommern heavily damaged~~	CL Emden
Pre Dreadnought Schleswig-Holstein	CL Nurnberg
	CL Leipzing

Half a minute later, the guns of the great battleship boomed in anger, filling the Admiral's view with fireballs and billowing smoke. A couple of minutes later, it was quickly followed by heavy cruisers Sharnhorst, Gneisenau and then by the light cruisers. Von Spee did not harbor any illusion about this renewed action. The forts had protected his fleet during the last fight, but now that most of their guns were gone, it would not go as well for his ships. He decided to prepare for the contingency plan he'd talked about with Meyer-Waldeck, the Tsingtao Governor and military commander.

(...) Dreadnought Battleship Setsu (...)

Legendary Japanese Admiral Togo Heihachiro stood, both arms crossed behind his back, looking at his powerful fleet firing at the distant outline that was Tsingtao and the enemy fleet. It was far, but he was certain he could see the fires of the burning city and fortress.

Japanese Imperial Fleet Admiral Heiha

BB Setsu serious deck damage, internal fire	Pre-dreadnought BB HIZEN light damage	Pre-dreadnought BB MIKASA
BB Kawachi armor belt damage BC Kongo funnel damage speed reduced	Pre-dreadnought BB IKI light damage	CA X22
	Pre-dreadnought BB IWAMI	CL X 6
Pre-dreadnought BC Tsukuma	Pre-dreadnought BB SAGAMI	DD X47
Pre-Dreadnought BC Ikoma light damage	Pre-dreadnought BB SUWO	~~6 DD~~
Pre-Dreadnought BC Ibuki light damage	Pre-dreadnought BB TANGO	~~2 CA~~
Pre-Dreadnought BC Kurama	~~Pre-dreadnought BB FUJI crippled by Fort Bismarck mortar~~	
Pre-dreadnought BB KASHIMA,	Pre-dreadnought BB ASAHI	
Pre-dreadnought BB KATORI	Pre-dreadnought BB SHIKISHIMA	

The Imperial ships involved in the developing action were the very same ones that fought in the first battle, and there had not been enough time to repair them properly. Several would have needed some time in shipyards, but it had not been possible. The ships had sailed to Chosen (Korea), and some summary repairs were done; new sailors embarked to replace the dead and injured, but overall, it was the same fleet that had not succeeded in destroying the German one the last time.

The sound of the guns reverberating through Setsu's hull gave him some comfort that this time, he would succeed in silencing the powerful forts towering over the town and, if he was lucky, to also sink the German fleet in the harbor.

(...) The naval brawl (...)

As one would expect, a battleship vs battleship fight was sure to produce severe casualties on one of the two fighters or on both sides. The German forts (the ones that still had guns and that were not fighting against the infantry assault) produced the first strike, with the pre-dreadnought battlecruisers Tsukuma and Ikoma being hit. Tsukuma was punched in the funnel, and two more shells splashed on the stern portion of the deck, destroying the forecastle and igniting a big fire, also killing eighty-three sailors. While Tsukuma could not be considered lucky, his lot was a hell of a lot better than Ikoma. The Japanese warship was not only slammed by ten hits from the 8.8 cm naval guns of both Fort Bismark and Hui-tchien-huk but also by four torpedoes fired from SMS S90, a torpedo-boat of the Imperial German Navy based in Tsingtao. The underwater weapons opened the older battleship's hull to water, and the vessel started to sink almost right away.

The brave German ship was rapidly destroyed by one of the main guns from the Kongo, exploding in a spectacular ball of fire.

The Japanese ships were not just there to get destroyed, however. Their own guns produced a lot more damage on the Germans by almost silencing Hui-tchien-huk, destroying its last remaining main guns, and leaving only one 8.8 cannon operational. Fort Bismarck suffered a similar fate, with only two 8.8 cannons remaining.

The German fleet inside the harbor remained relatively unscathed up to that point because Togo had ordered his ships to concentrate on the forts. Now that the fixed naval defenses were destroyed, he signaled his entire fleet to go for the killing stroke and ordered all ships to sail to the harbor and attack von Spee's fleet directly.

(...) The land battle (...)

With their high forts gone, the German defenders, numbered 10,000 infantry soldiers and marines, now relied on the defenses in the hills to stop the 50,000-strong Japanese assault.

The first Nipponese objective, Fort Moltke, was built on a promontory to the southeast and housed revolving 9.4-inch and 6-inch guns. The valley of the Hai-Po River four miles northeast of the port was over a mile wide, with bare sloping sides making it a formidable obstacle and an excellent defense line.

In between lay the killing fields in which the Germans manning the forts killed or injured thousands of Japanese soldiers. Then, Nipponese General Kamio's men reached the fort itself, and yet another bloody fight erupted.

Concrete redoubts had been built with 10-foot ditches running from sea to sea. A 6-foot wall had also been constructed with the immediate area strewn with land mines. More Japanese died, but Fort Moltke was overwhelmed by sheer numbers, and the Kaiser's troops retreated backward.

The third defense line on the second range of hills northeast of Tsingtao and beyond the river was the 1,200 ft-high Prinz Heinrich Hill on the eastern side of the peninsula, which was ten miles wide at this juncture. The entirety of the German forces tried to resist there but had to fall back in the last forts around the city. The last hour was approaching for the German land forces in Tsingtao.

(...) German dreadnought battleship Westfalen (...)
(Six hours into the battle)

"Sir," said his Second-in-command to Admiral Maximilian von Spee. "Yes, Vice-Admiral Krenk?" "*All ships that can get their steam up report ready for action and to sail out, sir.*" Very well," answered a deep-in-thoughts von Spee. The man was executing his last-resort plan by executing a full sortie with all his ships. He knew he would lose some and that casualties would be heavy, but there was no helping it; Tsingtao would soon fall, and if his fleet was still in the harbor when it did, he would have to either surrender or scuttle his ships.

Thus, he had given the fatal orders condemning many of his sailors and ships to die in an all-or-nothing breakout attempt to sail free into the Pacific and try to rejoin the scattered German bases and colonies there. The Japanese fleet was a lot larger and was near, so it would not be easy.

The plan was simple. The pre-dreadnought Schleswig-Holstein, too slow to outpace the enemy, along with armored cruisers Sharnhorst and Gneisenau, would fork right into the teeth of the enemy fleet while his two precious dreadnought battleships would sail in the opposite direction and try to gain the deep Pacific, flanked by light cruisers Emden, Nurnberg, and Leipzig.

German Pacific Squadron	
Admiral von Graf Spee	
BB Westfalen stern damage, secondary gun damage	CA Sharnhorst
BB Kaiserin rudder damage, deck damage	CA Gneisenau
~~Pre dreadnought BB Pommern heavily damaged~~	CL Emden
Pre Dreadnought Schleswig-Holstein	CL Nurnberg
	CL Leipzing

He stayed on the bridge the entire time the Westfalen picked up steam and increased its speed. His two dreadnoughts were Nassau Class battleships, capable of making 22 knots, while he knew a ship like the Setsu could do 21. The only heavy ship capable of running down his vessels was the Kongo-Class battlecruiser, but he believed that if he could distance himself from the rest of the fleet, he would be able to smash the fast Japanese ship with his two dreadnoughts.

(...) Dreadnought Battleship Setsu (...)

Admiral Togo smiled broadly. He felt like a shark at dinner time. "Admiral," said the lookout officer. "*I can see, Lieutenant,*" he answered, lifting his hand to shut the other man up. "*Signal all ships to go to full speed and stop giving any attention to Tsingtao. We need to sink this German fleet before it escapes into the Pacific.*"

The Imperial Navy ships had already been cruising at near top speed since in a running battle with the forts and approaching the harbor; thus, it wasn't difficult to get them to full speed.

"Sir," continued the lookout officer, braving his superior's wrath since he had another message to relay. *"Some of the enemy vessels are turning toward us. Three heavy ships are presenting us their broadsides while the two main units continue to sail southward."*

He cursed inwardly, trying to keep a straight face with his men on the bridge. This complicated things and made him mad, but it was what he would have done if he'd been in the German admiral's shoes. To escape, he had to sacrifice something to keep his enemy busy. He made a snap decision. *"Signal the battlecruiser Kongo and cruisers Chikuma, Yahagi, and Hirado to launch themselves at the enemy. They should be fast enough to catch up with them. Also, signal our other dreadnought Kawachi and ten armored cruisers to follow suit."* "Yes, sir," said the signal officer. "What of the other ships, Admiral," asked his chief-of-staff. *"We go in for the kill on these bastards,"* he answered, pointing toward the gun flashes of the Schleswig-Holstein and the two armored cruisers.

The siege of Przemysl
4th Russian Army, September 18th to 30th

"The battle, which began on October 1st between our troops and the Austrians on the Galician front in front of a city called Przemysl, continued with great tenacity on October 4th, 5th, and 6th. The Austrians conducted a particularly intense attack along the front line of Sanok/Stare Miasto-Stryi, south of Przemyśl. Bayonets were used often. On the night of October 4th to October 5th, in the vicinity of Stare Miasto, the Austrians took the offensive five times, getting closer to our troops. At 7:00 a.m. on October 5, our troops, allowing the Austrians to approach as close as approximately 200 steps, suddenly loosed heavy fire from rifles, machine guns, and howitzers. The Austrians faltered. They tried to hide in trenches, but our troops launched a counterattack. Shouting 'Hurrahs,' we overthrew the enemy with our bayonets. The Austrians suffered heavy losses. We took an entire battalion prisoner, including 15 officers and six machine guns."
Luka Karadnoszl, Private in the Austro-Hungarian defense force of Przemysl, 1914.

The city of Przemysl was Austria-Hungary's best hope to stop the Russian juggernaut from rolling down with unstoppable ease in Galicia. Prior to the conflict, Austro-Hungary had extensively worked around the city to build a ring of formidable fortresses designed to stop and defeat a major Russian assault. When war was declared, Przemysl was designated as the HQ for all K.u.k. forces in Galicia. As the situation moved from offensive to defensive, troops were sent to the fortress in advance to build a trench and install barbed wire to increase the fortress' defensive strength and to house more soldiers than the space had been planned for. It had been thought that 85,000 soldiers could shelter in Przemysl, but with the retreating Austro-Hungarian forces, it looked like a lot more than that would have to use the fortress for defense.

Desperately needing German help that wouldn't come because the Kaiser had his own set of bad troubles with Russians in East Prussia (Tsarist General Samsonov was at the Vistula with the Russian 1st Army), the fortress was what could stop the enemy from completely conquering Galicia and spilling over the Carpathians and into Hungary proper.

The Russians encircled the city by the end of September and trapped 131,000 Austro-Hungarian soldiers inside the Galician city. On 24 September, General Radko Dimitriev (commander of the Russian 3rd Army) began the siege with his forces, and he was soon joined by more and more Russian units. After only a brief artillery bombardment (most of the artillery train had not yet caught up with his frontline forces), he ordered a full-scale assault on the fortress. The fortress was defended by 120,000 soldiers under the command of Hermann Kusmanek von Burgneustädten. For three days, the Russians attacked and accomplished nothing at the cost of 40,000 casualties, only inflicting 21,000 casualties on the defenders.

Soon, the Russian 11th Army (General Andrei Nikolaevich Selivanov) caught up with the front and arrived in front of the fortress. Senior to Dimitriev, he took command and the leadership of the siege. Selivanov did not order any frontal assaults as Dimitriev had and instead settled in to starve the garrison into submission.

By the middle of October 1914, the entire city was ringed with Russian siege trenches. It's numerous (and arriving more and more daily) artillery bombarded daily and kept at it, only stopping when they ran out of ammunition because of the bad Russian supply system.

The battle was only just starting and the Siege of Przemysl would end up being one of the longest of the entire war.

16th Moscow Regiment, 4th Army
Fighting in and around Przemysl, October 6th, 1914

Every time an Austro-Hungarian shell burst very close, Private soldier Dmitri Fedorov shriveled in his hole. The world shook, and the prevalent dust thickened. When the blast was close, he was even showered with dirt. Once, the day before, he'd received part of an arm as the explosion rocketed some poor bastard's body everywhere around.

At intervals, there would be the rat-tat-tat of an enemy machine gun, and bullets would whizz and split over his head as they swept the top of the trench. Dmitri took a moment to look himself up and down, just to make sure he was unscathed. The only thing he saw was dried blood from the terrible assault they'd had to execute a few days before. He also saw that he was beyond dirty. His crusted uniform stank and he was riddled with lice all over his body. His uniform, which had originally been a bright, nice brown, was now a dull gray.

Fedorov, a factory worker from Moscow, had been mobilized like many of his fellow countrymen for the war. He'd gone to battle with enthusiasm, but he now laughed at the person he once was. It was beyond stupid to be excited to go fight in this godforsaken war. He looked to his right, where Sergeant Radetzky lay, his face as unreadable as before.

He wondered if this would one day end. It was hard to believe the war was only two months old. From his perspective, and the one of most of his comrades, they had already had enough fighting to last several lifetimes of memories. Enough dead friends, terrible, gory scenes, stupid officers and their orders... He had gone through it all and couldn't believe it was going to continue for the foreseeable future.

Yes, the Russian Army was advancing across the frontline from the Baltic to Galicia, but Austria-Hungary was a large empire, and they had only made a dent (even if sizeable) into it by occupying two-thirds of

Galicia. He hoped that they could win a decisive battle in Przemysl, as there were, apparently, over 120,000 enemy soldiers trapped in the fortress. This meant that if they took the city, they would eliminate a full Austro-Hungarian Army and potentially have them sue for peace.

A Captain ran down the line, giving orders to the lieutenants in charge of the platoon, and Dmitri pretended not to hear or understand what that meant. Well, he knew what that meant, but his mind could not process it.

Soon, the hammer dropped. *"Listen up, lads,"* grunted Sergeant Radetzky out loud. The men around him reluctantly stood up and walked to their NCO. Fedorov also got up, and it seemed to him that every muscle in his body ached from the last time they'd gone over the trench.

The entire Russian position encircled the city from one end to the other with a network of intricate trenches designed to get the troops as close as possible to the frontline before attacking. He remembered the enemy fort's strength and did not look forward to facing that might once more.

"Orders came down from division HQ," started their Sergeant (Dimitri's unit was the 16th Moscow Regiment). *"The artillery will be shelling just in front of us with a rolling barrage, and then we will assault the bastards and take the fort facing us. Other units from the 11th and 3rd Armies will be assaulting all across the perimeter."* Radetzki paused, keeping a straight face, an obvious sign he did not believe one word of what he was about to say. *"The higher-ups say this attack should break the Austro-Hungarian's will to resist."*

Everyone grumbled their dissatisfaction but refrained from saying anything out loud. Discipline was harsh in the Russian Army, and no one wanted to give any ideas to the Sergeant about their enthusiasm or willingness to fight.

Half an hour later, the loud whistling sound of Russian artillery shells rolled from far away to the rear to above them, blazing fast toward the fortress they were about to assault once again. Then, the blast started to make themselves heard, and the ground was shaken by small tremors.

Twenty minutes later, the whistles blew all across the Russian forces encircling Przemysl, and the assault was launched. Dmitri scared out of himself once more, stepped on the ladder and climbed to the top, where he was greeted by a hailstorm of bullet tracers, blinding explosions, and overbearing sounds of death and war.

He picked up his rifle and started walking toward the front, like the rest of his comrades, and hoped to dear god that he wouldn't die that day.

Von Spee's escape and the fall of Tsingtao
Von Spee sails through the Maelstrom, Yello Sea, September 21st to 24th, 1914

(...) Battleship Westfalen, Yellow Sea, eighty miles from Tsingtao (...)

"Admiral," said the lookout officer. *"The enemy ships are firing,"* he continued. German Admiral von Spee didn't answer anything, as he could see the towering columns of water sprouting around his small forces of five ships (BB Kaiserin, BB Westfalen, and three light cruisers, Emden, Leipzig, and Nurnberg). *"Have we figured out what's pursuing us?"*

The man paused to look at his notes. *"Sir, two groups are closing in. The closest is composed of what looks like a dreadnought battlecruiser."* von Spee took a mental note that if this was the case, it was the sole modern battlecruiser in the Imperial Fleet, the Kongo), *"And three cruisers, Admiral. They are faster than our battleships and have caught up with us. A little further behind are what looks like a strong task force of a battleship (probably modern) and ten cruisers.*
The German Pacific Squadron commander was thoughtful for a moment, and his people on the bridge tried to keep busy at their post but eagerly awaited what the man would say. *"If we turn and give battle, then this second task force will catch up to us, and if we continue to sail out of the Yellow Sea, that battlecruiser will continue to fire at us,"* said von Spee out loud. While this wasn't good by any means, it wasn't that bad a state of affairs. Yes, the Kongo was a faster ship, but it would probably not sail too close to his two battleships for fear of being destroyed. And, while the Japanese battlecruiser could fire with its two twins Vickers 14-inch 45-caliber gun forward main gun, his own ships, Westfalen and Kaiserin, could counter with three turrets each, as the innovative Nassau-Class design had a peculiar but numerous turret arrangement. *"Thoughts, Captain,"* he asked to the ship's captain. Von Spee was the admiral in charge, but the Westfalen, his flagship, still had a captain. He normally asked advice from Vice-Admiral Krenk, second in and chief of staff, but the man was in his

cabin plotting a course and trying to find the best way to find the coal his ships would need to execute what he had in mind. Germany had some coaling stations across its Pacific Empire, but some were already in Allied hands or would be soon.

With each six twin 11-inch SK L/45 guns, it meant that the firing ratio was on the German side, albeit the Japanese had the bigger caliber and could do more damage if they landed a shot.

The Westfalen's captain, Johannes Redlich, eagerly answered. *"Sir, my ship can outgun and outfight the Japanese battlecruiser, and we have enough guns for a running battle without turning to present our broadside."* Von Speed put his fingers on his chin. *"Indeed, Captain. However much I would love to cross the T on these Japanese bastards, I believe the prudent course of action is to keep going straight ahead to avoid having to fight the second task force that isn't far behind."* He paused. *"OK, let's keep on our current heading. I have Vice-Admiral Krenk plotting the best course to the next coaling station."* *"Very well, sir,"* answered Redlich.

(...) Meanwhile, on land (...)

As the fleet was leaving and concentrating its guns on the approaching Japanese Imperial Navy and with the destruction of the high forts' main batteries, the fight on the ground quickly turned in the Japanese Army's favor. After all, the Nipponese land commander, General Kamio, attacked with a five-to-one ratio, so there wasn't very much the overwhelmed German defenders could do about it. By the end of the afternoon, and following thousands of casualties, the Japanese troops penetrated Fort Molkte on Prince Heinrich Hill. This success signaled the end for the German line of defense on the hill, and they retreated to the inner forts for the last fight.

The battle lost in intensity as the Japanese ships got busy fighting the German ones, and General Kamio's artillery did not want to hit its own troops as they assaulted the city. By the end of the 21st of September, most of the first, second, and third lines of defense were in Nipponese hands, and the commercial harbor (north of the city) was also occupied.

After a terrible night of fighting where the Japanese soldiers launched assault after assault, the Governor of Tsingtao, Alfred Meyer-Waldeck, called for a cease-fire. Meeting up with General Kamio in the afternoon, the surrender of the German fortress was formalized.

The battle for the German Chinese outpost was over, but its ships remained loose in the Pacific.

(...) Meanwhile, facing Tsingtao Harbor (...)

At roughly the same time as the fight for Tsingtao unfolded on land, Japanese Imperial Navy commander Admiral Togo Heihachiro fought the slower elements of Admiral von Spee's fleet, the pre-dreadnought battleship Schleswing-Holstein and its two flanking cruisers, the Sharnhorst and the Gneisenau. The fight that happened then was not an equal one. The Japanese had sixteen pre-dreadnought battleships and a dreadnought (Settu), plus ten cruisers, ranging from old to modern, with light cruisers and destroyers.

While Schleswing-Holstein was a powerful ship, it stood no chance against the storm of steel and might that rain down its fire. It was the same for the two cruisers. And anyway, their mission was to cover the rest of the fleet's escape. It only took half an hour, and most of the work on the German pre-dreadnought was done from long-rage by the Setsu, Togo's own ship.

Its gunners landed five hits on their fourth salvo, smashing the German ship. The bridge was hit, and its captain was killed on impact, and the resulting fire incapacitated most of the gunnery stations. The proud Imperial German Navy vessel was then riddled with multiple hits (over fifty) by numerous Japanese ships, and it finally exploded in catastrophic fury.

The same fate was reserved for Sharnhorst and Gneisenau, and after forty-two minutes, the battle was over. Admiral Togo had his victory and soon ordered his ships to turn about to the open sea and join in on the pursuit of Admiral Graf Spee.

(...) Westfalen-Kaiserin VS Kongo (...)

A splash of fire blossomed on the forward deck of the Japanese battlecruiser Kongo as yet another volley of 11-inch guns was fired from both German dreadnoughts. The entire bow section of the ship was now smoking and burning, its metal badly mangled. The ship's captain now had a decision to take.

While Kongo had powerful 14-inch guns, its armor was not on par with its two opponents. It had only 8 inches of belt armor and 2.5 inches on the deck. This lack of armor was in common with British battlecruiser philosophy at the time: firepower and speed over armor protection. And at a speed of 27.5knots, the Kongos were definitely fast. After all the Kongo was built in England, based upon the Royal Navy's own Lion class Battlecruisers. The ship faced the Nassau-Class with 11.8 inches of armor around the Belt, 11 inches on the turret, and 6.3 inches on the battery.

Its 14-inch main gun had succeeded in hitting the Kaiserin on the stern, badly mauling its rear and destroying one of its main 11-inch guns, but staying in range of the German avalanche of fire would eventually kill his ship. The cruisers flanking him in the chase had not yet been hit, but they would not react well to enemy fire as they were protected by even lighter armor.

From above and afar, it seemed like a gigantic fire was burning on the water, with towering columns of black smoke. Columns of water also populated the area as the ships from both sides maneuvered madly in order to dodge the incoming shells. Sprinkled by tracer shells and blast of fire when a shell hit, it was a hell of a sight.

The situation was a little different on the German ships. Von Spee's dreadnoughts were slower; thus, he couldn't choose whether to disengage or not. This was the Japanese commander's prerogative, although von Spee was fine with that for the moment, as he was mangling his opponent.

"The Japanese battlecruiser is still on course, admiral," said the lookout officer. Every one of his men was at his battle station, and the moment was tense. Admiral von Spee looked toward the large smoke cloud that was now Kongo, watching gleefully as yet another set of 11-inch shells slammed the billowing darkness and then, with the resulting blossoming of fire. He tried to will the enemy vessel to turn away or reduce its speed so his own could slip away. "Admiral," said the gunnery officer. *"We estimate that the three enemy cruisers will soon be in range with their own guns. Do you still want us to belay firing on them or now give them some attention?"* The German commander thought for a moment. Perhaps it was time to spread the love a little. "Order one gun turret per dreadnoughts to target one cruiser each. Let's see if the Japanese like this."

The fight continued for another few minutes, and then the Kaiserin was hit again by the Kongo. Von Spee watched in horror as a big ball of fire blossomed on the ship's stern and central boiler. *"That looks serious, sir,"* said his second-in-command (now back on the bridge), Vice-Admiral Krenk.

Almost immediately, the Kaiserin's forward speed slowed down, the ship losing momentum. *"Damn!"* said von Spee. *"I have no intention of losing our sister ship to that enemy bastard. All ships, including the three light cruisers, turn-about and cross the T on the Kongo and these three cruisers."* "Yes, sir," answered the helm and signaling officer, who relayed the order to his men so they could also give the same instructions to the other vessels.

Von Spee was taking an extreme risk with his maneuver since the second task force, not far behind, might be able to catch them. But the German admiral was an old, experienced hand and knew how to maneuver. *"Once the broadside maneuver is completed and we have fired three salvos each, we turn back toward our original heading."*

The signaling officer spoke up. *"Sir, we have just received a message from Kaiserin. They had a boiler explosion but should be able to resume their speed within a few minutes, just the time to restart the boilers."* *"Good,"* answered von Spee, now happy that he had decided to order the turnabout maneuver.

A minute later, with a torrent of tracer shells exchanged on both sides, the blazing ordinance crisscrossing each other in bright flashes reminiscent of lightning bolts. Kaiserin was hit again, as well as Nuremberg (by the Japanese cruiser), destroying most of its main guns and boilers, making it almost dead in the water. But the Germans, now able to bring more guns to bear, inundated the Imperial Navy ships. Kongo's raging fires increased by a noticeable few notches, and the last few 11-inch hits finally silenced both its forward guns. Kaiserin's gunners also smashed one of the Japanese cruisers with a hit while Emden lodged a pair of torpedoes on another.

"Resume heading," said von Spee, now nervous that he had given enough time to the other Japanese task force pursuing them to catch up.

The flurry of hits convinced the Japanese commander on Kongo, now injured and with a heavily damaged ship, to abort the pursuit. As it happened, the group behind, with dreadnought battleship Kawachi and ten cruisers, did not catch up in time allowing the Germans to make their escape.

And thus, the German Asiatic Squadron melted away into the Pacific horizon.

The Third Austrian Offensive on Serbia
The fall of Belgrade and the push south to Kosovo, October 7th to October 15th, 1914

Quickly following the declaration of war by Austria to Serbia, the Austro-Hungarian invasion of Serbia crossed the border in early August, only to be badly defeated by Radomir Putnik's 1st and 2nd armies at the Battles of Cer Mountain and Sabac.

A second offensive, a few weeks later, was again attempted by the Austrian commander in the theater, General Potiorek. This time, the k.u.k attack was launched over the Drina River. But again, the Habsburgs were stopped and then pushed back across the border in abject defeat. Stalemate resulted from the offensive and the Austro-Hungarians were frustrated again in their intention of stomping Serbia into the ground.

Franz Conrad von Hotzendorff, chief of staff of the Austro-Hungarian army, was, however, not a man to get discouraged by such trivial matters as two (very) convincing defeats by a technologically and numerically inferior foe. He seemed to want a third one. He thus ordered the theater commander, General Oskar Potiorek, to launch a third attack to capture Belgrade.

While Hotzendorff was not the ideal realist and certainly not the best strategist in all manner of military subjects, he was encouraged by the fact that the Bulgarians were about to launch their offensive on the Serbs. Initially pretty cold on joining in the war, the German victory at the Marne had convinced the Bulgarian King that it might be a good idea to join in, while there was still time, in order to get the spoils of the victors. Furthermore, there was no love lost between Bulgaria and Serbia, having been recent enemies in the Second Balkan War in 1913. The Serbs had gained territories from the Bulgarians in that war, and King Ferdinand I wanted them back.

Thus, with a new army attacking the Serbs in the south, the Austrian commander was relatively confident that this would produce an overall victory.

After its startling second victory at the Battle of Drina, the Serbian army moved back inside its border to await further developments. The Russian offensive was going very well, and there were good chances that it could knock Austria-Hungary out of the war altogether. If this happened and the Serbian field armies were still operational, the country would be in an excellent position.

There was thus no good reason to risk it all in an attack on the Habsburg Empire, even if it was very tempting. General Radno Putnik, the Serbian Army's overall commander, had 250,000 battle-seasoned veterans (albeit poorly equipped), while the Austro-Hungarians had a well-equipped force of 450,000 men but with abysmal morale following its two defeats. As always, things seemed to favor the Austrians, and this time, it looked like it would be like the saying *"third time's the charm."*

On October 7th, the Austro-Hungarian Army group (5th and 6th Armies) was ordered to attack by General Oskar Potiorek. The Habsburg attack was, for once, overwhelming, as it crossed the rivers just north of Belgrade (the Danube and the Sava) and also the Drina.

The 5th Army crossed the Drina once again and attacked several border towns, capturing them with surprising quickness. In the south, the Austro-Hungarian 6th Army slammed into the 1st Serbian Army, pushing it out of the border towns and also from Mount Maljen on the 9th of October. By then, the entirety of Putnik's left wing was in a dire situation. A day later, the Bulgarian offensive crashed on Serbia's southeastern border, creating one hell of a sense of urgency for the Serbs as they only had token force on the border with Bulgaria. Putnik, knowing this would compound the problem with the Austrian offensive and probably help it succeed, sent the 2nd Army south to face the new invaders. While this reduced his chances to fight off the third k.u.k. invasion, it would not do to lose the rear of the country to the damned Bulgarians. Putnik could win all he wanted against the Habsburgs and still lose his country to the southern enemy.

The Serbian 1st Army fought well but was so overwhelmed by the enemy numbers that it was forced to abandon its current position in the defense of Belgrade. It retreated to new defensive positions further southward. Radomir Putnik did not fancy the retreat but had to reluctantly accept it because of the transfer of the 2nd Army south to face the Bulgarians; he could not send any reinforcement to the beleaguered forces defending the capital because he had none. They were all gone to fight south.

Austrian General Potiorek thus moved his two armies into Serbia and followed suit, occupying Belgrade in one fell swoop and continuing on to pursue the beleaguered Serbian 1st Army. Marshal Putnik had thus no choice but to order his troops to entrench where they were and await the results of the battle in the south. Perhaps, he hoped, that the situation could yet be saved if the 2nd Army defeated the damned Bulgars.

Potiorek decided to do the same, as his forces were tired and worn down. The front fixed itself in trench warfare on the 20th of October, but this time with Belgrade finally in Austrian hands.

21st Landwehr Division, 6th Army
The assault on Belgrade, October 15th, 1914

"Soldiers, exactly at three o'clock, the enemy is to be crushed by your fierce charge, destroyed by your grenades and bayonets. The honor of Belgrade, our capital, must not be stained. Soldiers! Heroes! The supreme command has erased our regiment from its records. Our regiment has been sacrificed for the honor of Belgrade and the Fatherland. Therefore, you no longer need to worry about your lives: they no longer exist. So, forward to glory! For the King and the Fatherland! Long live the King! Long live Belgrade!"
General Dragutin Gavrilovic, commander of the Belgrade defense force, left behind.

On October 15th, the Central Powers artillery opened fire, bombarding the Serbian lines. It was time to finish the work and take Belgrade. The Austro-Hungarian third offensive was finally making good headway, and the enemy capital was only defended by token forces, following General Putnik's (commander-in-chief) orders to send the 2nd Serbian Army south to fight the Bulgarians. Parts of the 5th and 6th Army continued to push the Serbs southward (the rest was attacking Belgrade), while the Bulgarians, now allies, did the same from the southeast. The offensive was in full swing, and it appeared the Central Powers would finally master the Serbs.

Private soldier Helmut Gottenburg and his weird non-German speaking comrade (and now friend), Radno Karacivs, a Slovene, looked at the arcing artillery shells. Helmut smiled as Radno mumbled something unintelligible. He still couldn't understand a word of what the damned man said, but he liked him nonetheless, so he smiled back. *"Yeah, Radno, impressive,"* he also answered, his Slovene friend not getting a word either. The shells whistled loudly above their heads, and they watched the concussion waves hit the buildings on the other side of the Danube, igniting balls of fire and catapulting black columns of smoke high in the air. They'd fought together, each saved each other's lives a couple of times, and took care of each other. And saying they did not understand each other wasn't true. They had developed a way to communicate, and each understood a couple of words from their respective languages. His friend handed him his secret schnapps canteen, and then he understood what the guy meant. He figured that the next time, he might understand when the guy offered him some good alcohol.

Very large guns, were the key aspect in Austro-Hungarian plans for Belgrade and the rest of Serbia. This was a lesson the Austro-Hungarians had learned in France and also in Galicia, either by being the one shelling or on the receiving end of the heavy guns. To attack and defend, one had to have an overwhelming artillery force, smash the enemy lines either if they advanced or hunkered down in trenches and fortifications, and then send your own infantry when the enemy was severely weakened.

It didn't take long for the enemy capital to burst into flames while the Austro-Hungarian forces crossed the Danube. Many K.u.k. units were already in Serbia, but the 21st was still on the other side of the Danube, and it was now finally their time to join in the fight.

Helmut, and Radno amongst them on ferry boats and some of their powerful river monitors. Radno said something again, and Helmut thought he understood. There were a couple of words he always said before battle. Perhaps it was a swear word or something of the sort. The ferry boat was a simple platform without any protective walls, so the Austro-Hungarian soldiers had ringed them with sandbags, and that was where the two friends were sheltering behind as enemy bullets slammed into them. The enemy soldiers were on the Danube's other bank, taking potshots at the multitude of boats and ferries crossing to the attack.

A loud noise was heard on their right, and Helmut could not resist but peer over the sandbags to look. *"Wow, Radno, have you seen, it's one of the river monitors firing. That's impressive!"* The moment he said it, several other soldiers peered over their makeshift protection to see the ship in action. The Slovene also peered and answered his usual gibberish, followed by a nervous laugh. *"Yeah, I know, it's good to have them on our side,"* answered Gottenburg.

The ship they were watching fired one round after the other, its shells blazing from river to shore and blasting away the heavy enemy troops' concentrations and or the machine gun nest scattered at different points on the shore.

The Sava was a magnificent ship. It was very low on the water and sort of looked like a submarine, with its main 120mm gun mounted on a central conning tower. The ships also fired a hailstorm of bullets with its six machine guns mounted at different spots on the hull. River monitors were an important part of the Austro-Hungarian strategy, as the Danube and its tributaries were large enough to take them. Belgrade was surrounded by water, and so the K.u.k. called upon its friend, the Austrian Navy, for help.

The Habsburg's employed a healthy flotilla of ten river monitors in 1914 and would continue to use them for the duration of the war. These vessels weren't made to go on the open sea, with very low freeboard. European rivers didn't have a lot of waves, and the boats didn't need a ton of stability. They were also squat and low on the water, like submarines, to reduce the target they presented. River monitors were designed to come in support of the infantry and to patrol the river in enemy territory.

To ensure the landings were successful, General Potiorek's plan was to storm the plethora of islands on the river facing Belgrade. Two in particular were targeted for their proximity to the shore and their size, which would enable the Austrian forces to get some artillery and machine guns to support further landings on the river's other bank.

The first targeted island was called *"Zigeuner Inseln"* (Gypsy Islands), and the second one *"Great War Island."* The two places had Serbian names but the Austro-Hungarians couldn't care less how they called them. Both were strategically placed where the Sava and Danube rivers met. The Serbs had also seen their strategic importance and fortified them heavily. They had machine gun nests covering all angles and approach, and a few guns were well placed to shell the crossing Austro-Hungarian barges.

The Sava River Monitor thus got busy exchanging fire with them and blasting most of the visible Serbian position to oblivion.

The 21st Landwehr Division had been given the task of storming the two islands, and in the case of Helmut's platoon, they were headed to Great War Island, facing the large and ancient citadel, only 200 meters on the other bank of the Danube, in Belgrade proper, the Kalemegdan fortress, another spot the Austro-Hungarian's needed to reduce and storm if they wanted to conquer Belgrade.

"Get ready," yelled one of the NCOs at the head of the barge. *"We're approaching our targeted landing zone,"* he continued. Helmut put his rifle right on his chest, tightening his grip on it as his nervousness and anticipation of the battle to come increased. He turned to look at Rado, who had seemingly lost all the colors on his face. His Slovene friend nervously gulped another sip of his Schnapps canteen and smiled back with a weary smile. Helmut hated that moment before battle, where anticipating what would happen (like the fact he could die) was almost worse than the fighting itself. When the battle began, all thoughts and nervousness were dispelled away as the need for survival, adrenaline rush, and simple combat took over.

The barge suddenly crashed on the swampy shore of Great War Island, and the soldiers were rocked forward, with many losing their balance to land on the wooden planking of the makeshift landing craft. "Go! Go! Go!" was the only thing the NCOs and officers had in their mouths, and both Radno and Helmut stood up. They were greeted by hell itself as enemy bullets zipped right beside them, smoke billowing everywhere, and the sound of battle. A few large explosions blossomed ahead, catapulting a machine gun position high in the air. They both stepped over the sandbags, rifles in hand, and yelled like their comrades. It was time for the assault, and they ran, ran hard toward the shore where the enemy bullets were coming from.

This was a desperate moment for the two friends and the 21st Landwehr Division, but they made it to the first line of enemy defenses. By the time they got there, other Austro-Hungarian soldiers had already cleared the position. As they thought they would dodge that fight, a powerful Serbian counterattack was launched at their newly-gained position, and soon, the 21st Landwehr and the two friends were involved in most of the heavy fighting, with knives, bayonets and very short-range firing. They survived and thrived, battling through and being involved in the conquest of Gipsy Island.

Following a couple of hours of that, most of the Serbian defensive position, their guns, and machine gun nest were silenced. By the end of the day, Great War Island was declared secure, and the Sava River Monitor, along with four of its brothers, moved on to duel with the Kalemegdan fortress, the ancient Ottoman stronghold. It was, of course, bristling with guns. The Serbs weren't stupid, and thus, the Austro-Hungarian ships and artillery on the northern shore of the Danube shelled it for most of the night. The fortress was not two hundred meters from Great War Island, and it was where the k.u.k. army engineers would build the pontoon bridge to enable the forces to cross into Belgrade itself. Only then (with a bridge and the Serbian shore defenses reduced to smithereens) could the crossings be made in relative safety. During the night, as Helmut and Radno slept the sleep of the warrior as they were dead-tired but alive, the same barges that brought them to the island ferried the artillery for the attack the next day. In the wee hours of the morning, Helmut and Radno (amongst others) were requisitioned to help with the hauling of the heavy pieces under fire from the enemy. By noon, the guns were ready to fire, and the engineers were already at work on building the pontoon bridge to cross into Belgrade proper.

The fighting reached the Kalemegdan Fortress by the end of the afternoon, and both friends were part of the assault on the old historical fortress. Fortunately for the Austro-Hungarian soldiers, it fell rapidly, thanks to the river monitor shelling and the fact that the

Serbian defenders had mostly evacuated the position a couple of hours before sunrise.

The city could not hold out much longer, not without help from the Entente, and none was coming because the Anglo-French couldn't reach a land-locked position so far from the sea.

"Step to the side, and I'll throw," said Helmut, gesturing to Radno with his hands, hoping he would understand. They were in some nondescript small street near the old medieval fortress, trying to assault one of the last knots of resistance in the area.

He showed the Rohr grenade he had in his hand. The Rohr hand grenade was a cast-iron cylinder concussion weapon filled with explosives and attached to a cardboard handle. Soldiers needed to ignite and throw to destroy hard-to-reach areas or create a lot of damage by throwing above the trench or inside concealed positions.

Radno got the concept and moved to the side, which Helmut followed by throwing the grenade through the already-broken window of the small store or café they were trying to assault.

The grenade flew to its destination and landed in the middle of the small room beyond Helmut's view. For a moment, he thought he heard some Serbian yelling, and then a muffled thumping noise was heard, followed by smoke and debris.

The next moment, Radno was running, rifle blazing, with Helmut following right behind. They got into the room but only found gravely wounded enemy soldiers. Radno smiled at Helmut and slid his wicked-looking knife out from his leather waist belt to kill the four Serbs by slitting their throats. Gottenburg turned toward the window (to watch if more enemies were in sight) as he heard the weird gurgling sounds the bastards made.

"We're almost done, Radno," he said out loud, knowing his friend would not understand him. Anyway, the Slovene was busy killing off the Serbs and emptying their pockets.

German Army East Prussian HQ in Elbing
(Battle of Marienburg Part 1)
Near the Bay of Danzig September 23rd, 1914

Paul von Hindenburg, the commander-in-chief of all German forces in Eastern Prussia, sat with his chief of staff, Eric Ludendorff, General Max Hoffman, the General staff's expert on the eastern sector and since a week ago, acting commander of the German 8th Army in the field. There was also a newcomer to the group, namely the Crown of Bavaria, Rupprecht von Bayern, commander of the German 6th Army, who had been railed from the Western Front to the west bank of the Vistula in order to prepare for the counteroffensive and the defense of the sacred lands of East Prussia.

Something would finally be done about the rampaging Russians. While Hindenburg had no intention of abandoning East Prussia to the Russians, there was a world of difference between that and launching the offensive toward Samsonov's Russian 1st Army prematurely. At the time (before the Kronzprinz's troops' arrival), he'd only had 200,000 men, not even half of what his opponent fielded.

The plan had thus been to leave Konigsberg to fend for itself. The city was a powerful fortress, and Hindenburg left 40,000 men to fight and man its defenses. The goal was for the great city to occupy half of the Russian force (Rennenkampf's 2nd Army) until such time that he either dealt a decisive blow on Samsonov's 1st Army or else received enough reinforcements to attack across the entire front.

They'd fought a major battle at Tannenberg but were unable to encircle or blunt General Samsonov's 1st Russian Army's advance. The Battle of Tannenberg had started well for the German army, but the number of Russians started to tell after a few days. The Tsarist armies' frontal attacks floundered on the strong German defenses, but General Samsonov, the commander of the Russian 1st Army, simply used his superior numbers and spilled around the enemy forces without the German commanders being able to do anything about it.

Hindenburg, Hoffman, and Ludendorff reacted well to the outflanking moves and defeated several of the attacks, but in the end, Samsonov just kept pouring more and more troops into the maelstrom.

By September 4th, Hindenburg had no choice but to call for a withdrawal. His armies were not defeated, and he was able to keep casualties to a minimum, but he was forced to move back because the situation called for it.

He might have been able to hold at Tannenberg if he'd poured everything he had within the 8th Germany Army into the battle, but that would have meant leaving Konigsberg defenseless. In addition, some of Samsonov's forces (a couple of light divisions) were attacking further west, and there was a danger of the entire German force being cut off from the country.

In the end, there was no simple answer to the overwhelming numbers of Russians pouring into Eastern Prussia (and the no-sending of reinforcement to the East policy from the OHL), and thus, Hindenburg did the best he could by preserving his forces and getting them to fight another day.

By the 5th of September, Tannenberg was in Russian hands. For the second time in history, the Slavs had defeated Germanic forces in the famed city (1410, 1914). The next day in the North, General Rennenkampf's 1st Russian Army arrived within sight of the powerful Konigsberg fortress and ordered his troops to lay siege to the city.

The entire German position in the East had threatened to unravel if nothing serious was done. Hindenburg called again for reinforcements, which fell on deaf ears once more. By that time, the Battle of the Marne was in full swing, and all hands were required on deck for the battle in the West. There was no choice; the future outcome of the war depended on it.

The Vistula River Line, initially envisioned by von Prittwitz, the former commander of the 8th Army, had then been (after all) a very good option for Hindenburg and the rest of the German Eastern commanders.

The fighting withdrawal behind the Vistula River was completed by the 13th of September, and it was at that moment that the OHL announced they would rail a full army to the East in order to beef up the defenses and perhaps turn the tide of the war there. Once he'd received his new troops, Hindenburg's operational orders were to try and hold as best he could, but the old, willy general had something else in mind: attack.

The newly-arrived Rupprecht Kronzprinz von Bayern's 6th Army had 220,000 soldiers, and these numbers were beefed up by a few more divisions, bringing the total number of troop reinforcements to roughly 300,000 men. Germany's rail system was the best and most efficient in the world, and in record time, the entire force was positioned East on the west bank of the River Vistula, bringing the German troops levels to about 460,000. This meant that Hindenburg had more men than Samsonov's force, which numbered around 400,000 men.

The Germans, believing in their tactical and technological superiority over the *"eastern barbarians,"* would have attacked with half that force, but now that they had the troops, there was nothing but offense in their minds.

"Your Majesty," said Hindenburg, bowing respectfully to the Crown Price *"Thank you for being here at the meeting, and I hope your travel was easy and safe?" "It was, General, thank you,"* answered Rupprecht von Bayern, or the Kronzprinz. The man had not traveled with his army, instead going back to Munich to see his father and his family. It had been a well-deserved rest following the great victory in the West.

"Kronzprinz, if you do not mind, we will start the presentation on the plan of attack right away, as we are all busy men," interjected Ludendorff, always the serious and dedicated one. "Please do, General," countered von Bayern.

"The plan is, in essence, what General Max Hoffmann here," continued the Chief of Staff as he pointed toward the General Staff tactician, "proposed a while back before the defeat at Tannenberg." The original idea was to get the 8th Army to disengage from Rennenkampf's Russian Second and concentrate everything on Samsonov's 1st Army. The only defense left in the North was Konigsberg, thought to be able to withstand a long siege, or at least long enough for the Germans to defeat Samsonov and come to the rescue.

Hoffmann's plan was to try and turn the tables on the Russians. And then he spoke following his commander's words. "Now that Rennenkampf's 2nd Army is stuck fighting in Konigsberg, we don't even have to watch for our left flank while we try and envelop Souvovov's 1st Army as originally planned. The enemy forces there are not advancing any more, concentrating on taking the fortress."

"Both the German 1st Corps and the 3rd Reserve Corps from 8th Army will be shipped here," continued Ludendorff, as he pointed at the map laid at the center of the table where the four men sat. *We'll also beef up the left flank as well with some of your troops, Your Majesty. The key will be to make the Russians think we are still in front of them, and this is where your army gets in on the festivities, Kronzprinz."* "Very well," answered von Bayern. "What do you need me to do?"

Hoffman spoke up as Ludendorff signaled for him to do so. "Well, Your Excellency, in essence, it will be to fill the gap the four other corps have left, but at the same time, we want you to pretend to retreat backward. If Souvorov can take the bait, we've got him."

The Battle of Marienburg Part 1
Near the Bay of Danzig September 23rd-27th, 1914

Since Rennenkampf stayed where he was, the Russian 2nd Army's fate would be sealed if the troops made good time to the flanks and crossed the Vistula fast enough.

The Russian commander was marching toward the city of Marienburg on the way toward Danzig, the main German town in the area. If that town fell, the entire East Prussian German position would unravel. The plan was to push the troops around by way of the excellent German rail network in places where the Russians had not yet reached: The southern would cross and position itself at Goudenz, and the second one would roll over the Vistula and go to the northern town of Elbing, where it would deploy for an advance south.

Oblivious to his enemy's plans, Samsonov was still pressing forward toward the glowing jewel of a prize, Danzig. He was urged to hurry by Northwest Front commander General Zhilinsky, located in Vilnius. The Tsar was getting impatient, and Zhilinsky had transferred the heat on his subordinates. The 1st Army commander tried to explain to his superior he was advancing as fast as caution permitted him, without halting, covering marches of more than 12 miles per day amidst supply problems. *"I cannot go quicker,"* was his constant answer to his superior.

Zhilinsky nonetheless insisted, and thus Samsonov resolved to increase the tempo of operation significantly, regardless of the risk involved. The man was not the best general in the world, but he understood the concept of advancing too far, too fast, and the potential for getting outflanked. In short, because of the Tsar's pressure (it was his uncle, the Grand Duke, in reality) and the high command making stupid decisions hundreds upon hundreds of miles behind the front, the Russians were blindly walking toward the German trap because they thought they had their enemies on the backfoot or were forced to advance too boldly by their masters.

1st Army's supply situation was not very good, with breakdowns in logistics obvious with several units having to husband ammunition and the men going hungry. Because of this, several German towns were sacked to the bone by desperate soldiers only looking for food. The fall season was rainy, and the constant water pouring down from the sky morphed the dusty trails into unmanageable mud quagmires. Samsonov, in one last attempt to soothe his superior's impatience, told Zhilinsky that *"the countryside is destroyed, the towns burnt down. The horses are thin and not well-fed when they are. The men are also getting restless since hunger is gnawing at their stomachs."*

But the overall theater commander in Vilnius didn't care one bit about supposed discomfort. He didn't mind the men suffering and couldn't care less about Samsonov's issues. He had a Tsar and a Grand Duke to please; these men were a lot more important on the pecking order.

And thus, the Russians kept on grinding forward, and it would have dire consequences for the Empire. By September 25th, just as the new German troops (von Bayern's forces) were being railed into position, Samsonov's army started pushing hard on the entrenched German 20th Corps, and the fighting began in earnest.

The Germans forces withdrew as planned; hence, the Russians pushed enthusiastically ahead and stormed Marienburg's outskirts, ten miles from the Vistula. The Tsarist soldiers were particularly motivated in their attack because they were eager to sack the town and snatch the civilian food stores. The Germans, however, didn't retreat and fought back hard. The city was put aflame, and the fight started in earnest.

The Battle of Sarikamish continued
October-November 1914

By October 15th, 1914, with the Ottoman assault on Sarikamish had stalled, out of steam. The weather, casualties, difficult terrain, and general lack of supplies stopped the Turks cold in front of the small mountain town. The Russians then sensed an opportunity to deliver a devastating counterattack was at hand and consequently acted.

Enver Pacha's (the Ottoman commander) 9th and 10th Corps at Sarikamish (left flank of the Turkish Army) relied on a very tenuous supply road going back into Anatolia proper. It ran through Bardiz and snaked its way to the frontlines across the difficult ground, rough mountain passes, and bad weather. The Russians concluded that if the bulk of their 1st Russian Caucasian and 2nd Russian Turkestan Corps held firm against the Ottoman 11th Corps pushing hard in Sarikamish itself, the rest of the enemy force could be outflanked, encircled, and destroyed.

A few Russian regiments were sent across the mountains in order to surprise the Turks in Bardiz and install a few artillery batteries on the heights around the Turkish-occupied town. They soon took the critical Ottoman supply town under heavy fire, creating a world of problems for Enver Pacha's forces.

The battle for Sarikamish continued to rage while the Russians tried their outflanking moves. The Ottoman 10th Corps continued to move south towards Sarikamish, regardless of the threats to its left flank and supply line. It was as if its commanders and officers were blind to the threat, even if they did receive several recon reports of large enemy movements on their flanks. They thus slugged mindlessly forward by marching across mountain peaks and through waist-deep snow, and the men suffered heavily. But they continued to press hard on the Russians, as they were ordered by Enver Pacha.

In general terms, the campaign was already over, Enver Pacha's plan having floundered because of bad planning, weather and unrealistic goals. The cream of the Ottoman Army was thus being quickly whittled down to nothing. While a 90,000-strong Army had entered Russian territory weeks before, only half now remained and it wasn't in the best of shapes.

It was in this setting that Private Soldier Mohamed, one of the still-alive men in the 10th Corps, was stuck in. The cold had seeped through his bone, and he shivered almost permanently now. His original unit was gone, and he had now been attached to a machine gun team. Well, the team itself was a hodgepodge of survivors from other units, and their machine guns were the same. They came from different areas of the battle. As he closed his eyes, trying to find comfort for a moment with memories of his home near Bursa in Western Turkey, while a couple of his comrades struggled and cursed as they tried to remove the ice in the machine gun barrel.

Bursa was a nice little town, a former capital of the Empire, near the Sea of Marmara. The weather there was always nice, and it was even rare one needed to wear anything more than a long-sleeve shirt or something similar. He certainly didn't need the thick, heavy fur coat he now had and needed to survive. He'd stolen from a dead Russian corpse, even if it was riddled with lice and had a terrible smell. In fact, here in the damned Caucasus Mountains, he wore two of them, and even that didn't dispel the damned cold.

"*Incoming,*" said the bastard of a Lieutenant who had assembled them a few days ago. The unit was positioned on a snow-covered mountainside and out in the open. There was nowhere to dig as the ground was rock solid and frozen beneath them. At least, the Russians had the same predicament. The enemy soldiers were trying to run as much as they could because of the sloping of the ground and the knee-deep white snow. Some were falling, others were awkwardly holding and or firing their rifles, but most bullets whizzed over the

Turk's head, which was fine with Mohamed. He wasn't looking to get killed anytime soon.

Their own machine guns started chattering away, mowing down the frontline Russians by the dozens. The enemy soldiers started falling backward and to the side, while the bullets themselves also lifted snow all around the perimeter.

Mohamed picked up his rifle and started firing in the moving mass of brown uniforms as well. He was comforted by the loud staccato noise of the German Maxim machine gun. The magnificent weapon was in short supply in the poorly-equipped Ottoman forces. They'd picked up the one they had from a dead crew as they got assembled by the bastard officer. Mohamed's small unit didn't seem to have any problems and had both weapons and ammunition aplenty. Mohamed had been pressed into the unit just for that reason in order to have an additional *"human pack mule"* to carry more of the drums. What he didn't know (and wouldn't have cared anyway) was that the reason they had so much ammo now, was because the previous, now-dead machine gun handlers had husbanded ammo from seven different (dead) machine gun teams as they'd retreated.

The battle continued for some time as Mohamed went through the motions of cycling from handing out 50-round ammo drums to the Maxim gun operator beside him to firing his own weapon (the Turkish Mauser Model 1887 rifle, an import from Germany).

The dead Russians started to pile up and accumulate into a mound. So much, in fact, that the following enemies had to jump or climb over the dead human *"wall."* From there, Mohamed took heart and knew they were going to win.

Then, all hell broke loose, with the head machine gunner beside him exploding like a ripe melon, spilling brain matter everywhere and, unfortunately, on Mohamed. In shock because of the gory moment, he tried to find which enemy soldier had shot his comrade but couldn't find any enemies right in front. Then a second comrades, this time to his right, got slammed, falling forward. His brain finally registered that the Russian fire was coming from behind. He turned to see, spotting a flood of brown uniforms running as awkwardly as the other group. The Russians were climbing the steep slope. He turned again to what used to be his only frontline and saw the enemy soldiers gathering again over the bunch of dead, with bullets starting to blaze by, now from both sides. There was nowhere to go, nowhere to run; they were encircled.

Bolstered by fresh reinforcements, the Russians launched a counterattack against the left wing (9th and 10th Ottoman Corps) and suddenly encircled the Turkish units, trying to do the same to them in Sarikamich. Over the next few days, the 9th Ottoman Corps fought a brave rearguard action but was completely destroyed, while the 10th Corps barely managed to escape, also suffering heavy casualties as ragtag bands of starving, demoralized troops fled through heavy snow back to Ottoman territory.

By November 5th, Enver Pacha's dreams of glory had ended in a complete debacle. The human cost was staggering. Ottoman losses came to nearly 90,000 dead, including 53,000 who froze to death and thousands more who perished from disease—especially typhus, the great nonhuman killer of the First World War.

With its best field army destroyed, the Ottoman Empire would never really recover and only trudge onward from that point to the war's conclusion. The Turks weren't done by any means, but most of their land offensive capabilities were gone.

The Battle of Marienburg Part 2
Near the Bay of Danzig September 23rd-27th, 1914

From the start of the battle to the 25th of September, the Russian 1st Army under Samsonov pushed westwards, driving into the Marienburg German defenses commanded by the Kronzprinz Ruprecht von Bayern, also commander of the newly-arrived German 6th Army.

The Russian forces succeeded in forcing the Germans back into several areas of the embattled city. Von Bayern let himself back up, reeling the Russians in like fish. Then, later that day, both Ludendorff and Hindenburg came by on a frontline tour, arriving at von Bayern's positions; they then insisted that the Germans attack to continue to pin down the enemy forces in Marienburg while the other troops on the flanks executed their outflanking moves.

In total, the battle would encompass 460,000 men of the German 8th and 6th Army plus other units against the 400,000-man strong Russian 1st Army.

The Russian commander's perspective was skewed by the fact that he had not sent enough recon troops around to watch for his flanks and to figure out what the enemy was planning. This move was because Samsonov was overconfident, even if he didn't have well-supplied troops. He was still under the belief that he had superior numbers, and that he would again spill his troops around the German position (just like Tannenberg) and force the enemy to retreat by fear of being encircled.

He never imagined it possible for the Germans to be able to redeploy so many troops in so short a time from the Western Front. Meanwhile, he was completely unaware of the enemy's heavy buildup on both his flanks in Elbing (north) and Goudenz (south). The Russians wanted to finish this by encircling what they thought were numerically inferior forces, but instead, they were getting encircled themselves.

On September 26th, the Germans center (6th Army under Kronzprinz von Bayern) followed Ludendorff's orders and began a powerful counterattack on the enemy, now halfway through the town of Marienburg. The attacks were slow and measured, but the fight in the demolished streets and burning houses was nonetheless very frantic and destructive. Heavy casualties mounted on both sides, but the Russians got the worse of the exchange as they continued to attack as well, while the German forces had better supply, more machine guns, and more reliable artillery because they always had shells compared to Samsonov's problematic supply. Von Bayern sensed that there was an opportunity to push harder and break the Russian lines, but he was the bait and couldn't overdo it for fear that Samsonov would order a retreat, hereby saving his army from envelopment.

On September 27th, both German northern and southern pincers launched their attacks. The artillery barrage was overwhelming, and Samsonov's left flank suffered considerable casualties and was pushed back. The right flank was also subject to a powerful German attack, and it, too, was pushed back. Meanwhile, the Russians continued the attack on the German center, with Samsonov being completely unaware of what was happening on his flanks.

By the capture of several towns south and north of Marienburg on the 28th of September, the Germans had broken right into the flanks of the Russian position.

Max Hoffman, the commander of the northern pincer (the one coming from Elbing and with the most successfully gained ground during the entire battle), gave orders for his cavalry to march on Marienburg and at 4:30 p.m., seeing that the Russian resistance was collapsing in front of him, he ordered the main bodies of his divisions to press forward through and around the town as he fixated the 1st Russian Army's right flank.

At the same time, the Russian's left flank was totally enveloped, while their center and right were engaged successively and driven back. Finally, Kronzprinz von Bayern didn't need to pretend to falter anymore. Starved and exhausted, the Russian soldiers perceived the hopelessness of their position as the Germans surged forward in a staccato of machine guns, bullets, and artillery shells. The attack was overwhelming, and they were starting to believe the rumors of enemy troops around the town and behind their lines. Their formations broke, and they surrendered in the thousands on the flanks, giving a taste of what was about to happen the next day.

The following day (September 29th), the Russian 1st Army was completely encircled. Retreating Russian troops ran into German defensive lines and were met with withering gunfire. Casualties were enormous on the Russian side as elements of the army attempted to break through the German lines to escape. But it was to no avail.

General Samsonov and a handful of staff officers, when they found themselves surrounded, dismounted from their horses. News of disaster had come in from every quarter. They set off into the forests on foot, heading south. Night fell. They had a compass but no maps. Samsonov could go no farther. He was heard to say: *"The Emperor trusted me,"* as he turned aside alone amongst the trees. A single shot was heard.

The Battle of Marienburg was a complete success for the Germans. A victory that would reverberate in the diplomatic world was much as in the military field. The Russian 1st Army was completely annihilated. 88,000 men were either killed or injured. 290,000 were captured. Less than 40,000 soldiers managed to escape back to Poland. Three hundred and twenty artillery pieces were also captured. Seventy trains were required to transport all the captured Russian equipment back to Germany, as nothing was wasted in war.

In one bold stroke, General Paul von Hindenburg had salvaged the situation from disastrous to hopeful. The Russians still had numerous troops inside Eastern Prussia, and the siege of Konigsberg was in full swing, but there was no more danger for central Germany, and the Army could now go on the offensive for a change.

Friedrich Wilhelm I Fort
1st Grenadier Regiment "*Crown Prince*" (1st East Prussian), October 29th, 1914

Astronomic Bastion	
Bronsart Fort	
Dohna Tower	Reinforced with concrete and steel, with several machine guns and field guns.
Friedrich Wilhelm I Fort	The largest fort of Konigsberg, equipped with the most modern defenses and guns.
Gneisenau Fort:	
Grolman Bastion:	Strengthened with casemates and caponiers inside its wall and also included the lesser Oberteich and Kupferteich Bastions.
Pillau Citadel	
Stein Fort	
Barnekow Fort	

List of the forts around Konigsberg

Captain Mikael Lundbeck, an officer in the 1st Grenadier Regiment (part of the German First Division, 1st Corps, based in Konigsberg), took a deep breath, trying to keep his cool. The Colonel was in a bad mood today, and he had taken the brunt of the bastard's foul mood. Colonel Thomas von Kracken was not what you could call a nice (or even competent) officer. The bastard was the commander of the 1st Grenadier Regiment, but it was more because of his imperial connection than his competency at his job. And since Mikael wasn't a noble, von Kracken hated him or at least found him beneath his stature.

"Lundbeck, are the repairs on bastion number seven complete, yes or no," continued the Colonel. *"Sir, as I have told you, no, they are not done; we do not have enough mortar. We need more."* Von Kracken made a face, the look he harbored when displeased. *"I do not care what you lack, Captain. Go get it somewhere, and I want it to be done by the end of the day."* Mikael knew it was futile to continue to argue with the man and thus gave him the military salute before he took his leave from the commander's office. The colonel was sheltering below

in the fort's fourth basement, where he was safe from anything the Russians could throw at him. *"Fucking bastard,"* he said as he stormed out of the basement and back to his unit on Bastion number 8.

Friedrich Wilhelm I Fort was a very large fort thus it took him several minutes to get back to his position. The exterior shell of the walls was built with red bricks and very thick; the center was made of ferroconcrete sand and reinforced with steel bars, made to withstand modern artillery fire. The exterior of the fort looked as if it was now a ruin, having been hammered for weeks on end by Russian artillery. Mikael didn't know why the enemy only shelled the fort in a scattered fashion, but that helped him and his comrades hold it. The reason, unknown to the Germans at this point of the war, was because Rennenkampf's forces, like most Russian frontline armies, did not have the necessary shells because of supply issues.

The fort was not just a gun position like some of the forts elsewhere (like the Liege forts of Fort Douaumont in Verdun), but rather built like large, towering buildings with several bastions ringing it. The fort's interior was a maze by design in order to confuse any breaching enemies. This had been a great thing during the enemy's penetrations inside the fort. They'd been repulsed every time, thanks in no small measure to the fact that they got lost or scattered inside.

He rounded the corner, saluted back a couple of soldiers giving him the military salute, and went up the curving steel stairs up to his bastion on the second floor. He stepped onto the rubble-strewn floor, again saluted by several of his men. *"Captain,"* said Lieutenant Werner Lotar, one of his best officers, *"How was the meeting with the Colonel,"* he continued with a smile, knowing what the answer would be. *"Charming, Lieutenant, charming." "Ah, well, that's good, sir. And what did he say about the still-ongoing repairs to the wall?"* continued Lotar, glancing toward a large hole in the wall that his men were busy filling up with bricks and mortar. *"He said it should be done already,"* answered Lundbeck with a dark face. *"So, he wasn't happy, as* always," he continued, moving to the hole to look at the Russian trenches ringing the Konigsberg fortress.

The entire ground was laced with large trenches, and the soil blackened. Mikael could hear the sounds of gunfire and some distant explosions, probably an attack on some other part of the German defenses. *"The Yvan has been quiet for the last two days,"* he said, putting his feet on the brick and leaning on his knee with his arm to be in a relaxed position. He was taking a chance since it was possible a Russian sharpshooter could fire on him. *"They have, sir."*

The last month of siege had been harrowing for the Germans, but Konigsberg held against all odds. The 40,000-something defenders were delaying the advance of a 300,000-man enemy army deeper into Eastern Prussia. And there now was hope while they fought like demons to hold the line in the fortress. The new general in charge of the German forces in Eastern Prussia, General Paul von Hindenburg, had won a great victory two days ago at a small town near the Vistula called Marienburg. Rumor now had it that he was on the move and launching a counteroffensive in Poland and toward Konigsberg to relieve the siege.

Turning back toward his Lieutenant, he took a deep breath. *"We have to finish the repairs by tonight, or else there will be hell to pay on my next visit to the Colonel. We need to find more mortar." "I'll see what I can come up with, Sir."*

The Bulgarian Invasion of Serbia and the Serbian retreat
King Ferdinand backstabs Serbia October 11th to October 29th, 1914

There was no love lost between Serbia and Bulgaria. The two countries had gone to war (1913) with each other in the Second Balkan War because of Bulgaria's dissatisfaction over the spoils of the First Balkan conflict a year earlier (1912). Serbian and Greek armies repulsed the Bulgarian offensive and counterattacked, entering Bulgaria.

Romania, also not very much in love with the Bulgarians, decided to snatch the opportunity to settle old border disputes with its southern neighbor. The Ottoman Empire also took advantage of the situation to regain some lost territories from the previous war. When Romanian troops approached Sofia, Bulgaria asked for an armistice, resulting in the Treaty of Bucharest, in which Bulgaria had to cede portions of its First Balkan War gains to Serbia, Greece, and Romania. In the Treaty of Constantinople, it lost Adrianople to the Ottomans. With its attack, King Ferdinand hoped to take his revenge on the Serbs and take back what he felt was rightfully his country's territory. The rest of the countries who had taken advantage of him would eventually be dealt with, starting with the dastardly Romanians, looking more and more like they would join the Entente Powers.

In July 1914, Germany and Austria-Hungary signed a secret treaty and alliance with Bulgaria to enter the war on their side in exchange for big chunks of Serbian Macedonia. While the King had not yet been ready to commit in order to see where the winds of victory were blowing in August, he decided by the end of September the time was ripe for entering the conflict on the side of the Central Powers because of the German victory at the Marne and the subsequent conquest of the French northern ports. The war appeared to be won already, even if the Russians were pushing hard in the East.

Thus, the Central Powers went from being three partners to four, and it looked like more would join soon. His Foreign Minister then met with the German ambassador in Sofia, and quick exchanges were processed by telegrams between the two sides, including Austria-Hungary and Germany. By the 4th of October, a secret alliance was signed, and an agreement for the Bulgarians to launch the offensive the moment the Austrians would do so in the north.

The Bulgarian 1st Army under General Kliment Boyadzhiev launched an offensive toward Nis, one of the top three cities in Serbia and a critical rail hub. In addition, the Bulgarian 2nd Army, commanded by General Georgi Todorov, launched an attack on Macedonia. Its objective was to conquer Skopje, the southernmost city and capital of the province Bulgaria sought to add to its own country.

The Bulgarian forces pushed hard and aggressively like the experienced troops they were (after all, all of the Balkan Armies were recently bloodied in the wars preceding the First World War). But initially (in the first two weeks), the Serbian Army put up a remarkable resistance before weakening. The reason for this was the rapid redeployment of the Serb's 2nd Army to the south to face the Bulgarians.

But it wasn't like Serbia had enough troops to cope with the four invading armies slashing across its land from the south and the north. Faced with war on several fronts (Belgrade had already fallen by then), the Serbian High Command decided that it was best for the army to try to hold its opponents for as long as possible and retreat slowly to the south.

The following week, The Bulgars took Nis and Skopje (October 27th and 28th). The Belgrade–Sofia–Constantinople railway could now be reopened (after some repairs) for the Central Powers, and a permanent land connection could thus be established from Berlin to the Middle East, opening a world of possibilities for Germany and its allies.

21st Landwehr Division, 6th Army
8th Austro-Hungarian Regiment, October 29th, 1914

Morale was high in the 8th Austro-Hungarian Regiment, and for once, Private soldier Helmut Gotternburg was not annoyed at his non-German speaking Slovene comrade, Radno Karacivs, as he chanted in his native tongue. The annoying sound of his voice and his language didn't bother Helmut anymore, for they were winning, at last.

The road was wet and muddy, as the autumn rains had started falling a while ago, and the tens of thousands of men ferrying from the north, south, and everywhere in between had soon done wonders to transform the landscape into a hard-to-describe grey quagmire of mud, water and greyness boredom. And then, that was one more thing that didn't bother Helmut anymore because they were winning. The Empire had finally been able to vanquish the damned Serbians.

After months of fighting, scores of dead, discouragements, and everything in between, the third offensive had done the trick. The Prague Regiment had been one of the first in Belgrade, as the enemy capital was abandoned by the enemy forces because they would have been encircled if they'd stayed. It had been a great moment, and the parade in the city center the next day had been one hell of an accomplishment for him, the Regiment, and the Empire as a whole.

Even Radno seemed happy. Helmut didn't know what the damned Slav wanted, meant, or said, but he could tell when the man was happy since he flashed his decaying, dark tooth smile more often than not, making him look a little like a dimwit.

Granted, they had been helped by their new Bulgarian allies, and without them, they probably would still be fighting for Belgrade instead of marching south of Nis on their way to push the enemy into the Montenegrin Mountains. But things were going so bad for Austria Hungary as a whole that every good news was stellar news.

The Siege of Przemysl would soon enter its third month, and the Russian enemies were pushing the last of the Empire's defense forces into the Carpathian Mountains. All of Galicia was now occupied, and losses were well over a million men dead, injured, and prisoners. News from home (from the letters the soldiers received) spoke of hardships, hunger, and restriction. No, things were not going well. Not well at all.

The last month and a half had been one of walking, fighting, then more walking, then more fighting. But now Helmut felt that there was light at the end of the tunnel. There were even talks of sending some of the troops away to help against the Russians in the East. God knew that the forces there needed good soldiers. *"Well!"* he thought proudly to himself. *"Not just soldiers, but victorious soldiers!"*

Coaling and naval pursuit in the Pacific
The German Pacific Squadron sails into Yap, October 12th, 1914

The Island of Yap, located in the western part of Caroline Islands, was a beautiful Pacific Island surrounded by a coral reef lagoon. It was part of the German Empire, and it was a very important place for the Germans. Purchased from Spain by the Kaiser along with several other outlying and neighboring territories in the area, it now housed a very important telegraph station.

Following their acquisition of their many far-reaching territories in the Pacific, the Germans began laying down undersea cables to connect to Shanghai, the Dutch East Indies, and Guam. The place was thus a very important communication center for the world, and consequently, it was protected by troops and some ships.

However, Admiral Maximilian von Spee, the commander of the German Pacific squadron and the recent escapee from the Battle at Tsingtao, couldn't care less about sending more messages to Germany. Of course, it was nice to be able to send a few cables to the Kaiser to tell him that all was well, but the real reason he was in Yap was to get coal.

The new technology (not that new, as in 1914, the British were switching to a better solution, oil) enabled the European Powers and anyone able to build coal-fired ships to have more powerful war vessels, but strategically, it reduced their range greatly. This meant that a fleet wanting to cross the Pacific line von Spee wanted to execute had to find ways to get coal to replenish its stores. The substance was good and performed well, but large battleships like the ones the Pacific Squadron tended to use a lot of it.

Thus, the first order of business for the German Admiral when he was able to escape the Tsingtao deathtrap was to sail to the closest spot with coal. While the Kaiserliche Marine needed to use Colliers (large transport ships carrying oil and able to get coal to the warships during operation), there weren't that many available in the Pacific at that moment in time, so Yap came in handy for von Spee.

The man's rough plan was to sail eastward toward South America to eventually go around Cape Horn at the tip of Argentina and sneak into the Atlantic. The ultimate idea was to rejoin the fatherland.

"Admiral," said the helm officer. *"The Kaiserin reports that she is in the lagoon. No problems, no issues. The rest of the fleet, including Westfalen, should be in shortly."* Maximilian von Spee nodded with a curt nod of the head and turned back with crossed arms toward the battleship bridge's viewport. *"Do we have an exact count of how much coal is available here?"* he instead asked, still looking at the distant island and the beautiful blue ring of water around it. The signalman officer has just reported..." continued another officer (the communication one). *"Ah yes, Sir. The quantities in Yap are quite satisfactory, as we expected. We will be able to fill our ship's hold to the gills." "Excellent,"* answered von Spee, happy about the little bit of positive news.

The Admiral had been thinking a lot about how he would get his ships and his sailors out of their predicament. The Pacific was large, and Germany still had many bases in the Carolines, the Bismarck Archipelago, and New Britain, but the Allies were certain to attack and occupy them. Furthermore, the Japanese fleet pursuing them since Tsingtao would not let any of these bases survive if it had anything to say about it. The trick for him was thus to find a way to sail out of the Pacific and get enough coal to do it. His first stop was a success, and his next one needed to be plotted accordingly. He believed that with one or two coaling's (depending if he got into a battle or not), he would be able to make it into the Atlantic.

"Signal the telegraph station; I would like to know if they have news or the whereabouts of enemy fleets, especially that pesky Japanese one on our tail?" "Yes, Admiral," said the communication officer. The signalmen on the side of the ships then went to work with lights and

flags to signal the admiral's demand. Twenty minutes later, the reply came in, also by signal flags. *"Sir, they say at the last news, the Japanese fleet was in Formosa a week ago for coaling,"* he finally told von Spee. The German commander readjusted his white cap (he was wearing, like most naval officers of his time, an all-white uniform) and spoke in a low rumble that only he could hear. *"Where are you, Admiral Togo; will you catch me, or will I escape?..."*

Saipan, Northern Mariana Islands

"Send the Marines," said Admiral Togo, looking at the tiny island of Saipan in the distance. The Northern Mariana Islands were a German colony, but not much had been attempted to settle it beyond what its previous owners, the Spanish, had done and built. The reason the Japanese fleet was in front of Saipan was because it was where the Germans had established an administrative office to officially take control of the Marianas.

Togo had thus decided to take possession of it for Imperial Japan. After all, the Empire had a secret treaty with Great Britain, giving it ownership of many of the German colonies in the Pacific, including the Marianas (except for Guam, which was American) once the war was over and the Central Powers defeated. In any case, it wouldn't be difficult as the island was mostly without any Germans; soldiers, or civilians.

The legendary Japanese admiral was frustrated by the German Pacific Squadron's elusiveness, and he'd lost the scent, although he had a pretty good idea the Germans had gone south into the Caroline Islands.

The stain on his honor was dire as he'd let the enemy ships escape from Tsingtao, and he had decided he wouldn't relent until he'd found Admiral Maximilian von Spee and his Pacific-roaming warships.

He had been pretty close to the enemy fleet and on its tail for days, but after another day, the Germans had continued onward while his own coal reserves got low to the point where he had to call off the pursuit to sail to nearby Formosa (Japanese controlled) to get refueled.

At that point, he guessed the enemy commander had more coal; he knew that von Spee would have to stop either in the Marianas or else the Carolines. The first option was unlikely unless he rendezvoused with Colliers which were not in abundance for Germany in the Pacific. The second option, now confirmed by the absence of anything German in Saipan but a few offices and administrators, was that the man and his vessels were now either approaching, or into the Yap Lagoon.

"Orders, Admiral," said his chief of staff. *"Leave a few destroyers here, but the rest of the fleet sails within the hour. Ah, also leave a couple of colliers here in case we lose the ones we have with the fleet as we make our way deeper into the Pacific." "Yes, sir."*

And just like that, the Imperial Japanese Fleet moved to the southern horizon. The noose was tightening on von Spee and his brave sailors, for at the same time, several British ships were also looking for him.

CHAPTER 3
Politics, diplomacy, and planning

"All treaties between great states cease to be binding when they come in conflict with the struggle for existence."

Otto von Bismarck, German statesman

Rome, Italy, Palazzo Montecitorio
A renewed friendship, October 15th, 1914

"Well, Mr. Prime Minister," said the German Ambassador to Italy, Hans von Flotow. *"Indeed, Mr. Ambassador. These talks have been most fruitful,"* answered Antonio Salandram as he sipped another big gulp of his glass of wine. The man definitely loved his alcohol, especially during diplomatic discussions.

Flotow was ecstatic. He had finally been able to do it and sway the Italians onto Germany's side. The man was the Reich's representative to Italy since February 1913 and, as such, had presided over the ebb and flow of Germano-Italian relations in the last year and a half. To say that it had been interesting for him was an understatement.

He had been berated by the Kaiser for not convincing the Roman leadership to uphold its treaty obligations when the war started. But he had never given up and had gone through the motions and waited for the military results on the field of battle. And then the German Army had delivered in a big way, smashing the Anglo-French and occupying Paris. His gamble had been sort of risky. By not insisting or doing anything else than his normal function as ambassador, he had played right into the hands of the Entente diplomats as he'd faded away in the background. But at the same time, he had been quite careful not to antagonize the Prime Minister and his people, and now it was paying off in a big way.

Following the fall of Paris, he'd been recalled to Salandra's office and new discussions were started. The Italians had first started to tell him how they valued the Triple Alliance principles and how they wanted to make sure the Germans understood that they had never wanted to do anything bad or leave the alliance. They had gone out of their way to charm him and please him, and he'd played along.

He knew the bastards had been really close to an agreement with the Anglo-French to join them in the war in exchange for promises of

Austro-Hungarian territories and other considerations. He didn't like Salandra; he thought the man was a slimy asshole and not worth a damn in terms of trust. His words didn't mean a thing, like most Italians; they were just opportunists.

But at the same time, they could be useful for the German cause. With Italy joining the war on the side of the Central Powers, Flotow was pretty certain that it was won. The Romans had a million and a half soldiers in arms and could mobilize a little over double that number within months. They had a fleet that fielded seven modern dreadnoughts, enough to tilt the balance of naval power in the Mediterranean in the Central Powers' favor.

Yes, they were bastards that couldn't be trusted. But he played along, since in exchange for promises of land from the French and the British once the war was won, Salandra had agreed to join the Central Powers. The date remained to be fixed and decided, but Italy WOULD join Germany and Austria-Hungary in their struggle.

"Mr. Prime Minister, I cannot begin to tell you how happy I am with the result of our talks. Rest assured that the Kaiser conveys to you his best intentions and looks forward to Italy expanding westward at the expanse of the enemies of the Central Powers."

"Indeed," said Salandra, gesturing for one of the dinner servants to refill the German's cup. *"As discussed, my dear Ambassador Flotow,"* he started, putting down his cup for one rare moment during the last ten minutes, *"I shall get back to you soon on the matter of when our armed forces will be ready for action."* Flotow smiled. *"Thank you very much, Mr. Prime Minister."*

The secret agreement between the Germans, the Austro-Hungarians, and the Italians was as follows: Italy joins the Central Powers thus it would attack France in the south, Malta in the Central Mediterranean, and the fleet would join up with the Austro-Hungarian Navy to sail with the objective of taking control of both the Eastern and the western Mediterranean.

In exchange, Italy would get the following concessions and territories once the war was over: Nice, Menton, Monaco, Corsica, the colony of Tunisia, and the entirety of the French Mediterranean Fleet (what would be left of it at the end of the conflict anyway). From Great Britain, it would get Malta and Gibraltar, plus concessions in Egypt so Italy could expand there.

Flotow inwardly smiled. The Italian Prime Minister thought himself so smart. But in truth, Germany had promised nothing. Only territories that weren't theirs, and the Italians played along.

The two men continued their excellent and pleasant evening, moving on to dessert and a cigar with grappa when things were said and done. They did not notice one of the servants in the room, for he had been in the employ of the Government for a while. But that man was also working for the British Foreign Office. The very next day, a message was relayed to a British ship in Taranto that relayed itself to Malta and then up the chain all the way to London.

By October 16th, the news of the Italian decision reached the halls of power in London, and a copy of this information landed on Winston Churchill's desk. The man had been expecting the news, and so had worked feverishly on a plan to make sure the Italians would not be too much of a nuisance.

OHL
Berlin, October 27th, 1914

"*So, basically, we are in control right now,*" said Kaiser Wilhelm, the German Emperor. "*Well, Your Excellency, I wouldn't put it that way as the Entente Powers are still very much alive, but yes, we have taken the initiative both on the military and diplomatic fronts,*" answered Erich von Falkeyhayn, the German Minister of War. The two men were discussing prior to the meeting of the OHL in Berlin on the overall strategic situation and the conduct of the war. The Kaiser was well-apprised of the military situation, but his natural tendency to boast and liked to be reminded that the war was going well.

As Falkeyhayn was done speaking, the Chief of the German General Staff, General Helmut von Moltke, entered the room. "*Your Excellency,*" he said, giving the Kaiser the military salute. "*Ah, my dear General,*" answered Wilhelm. The German Emperor was quite happy with his commander-in-chief as he had delivered a stellar victory in France and, with the latest success at the Battle of Marienburg, had been proven right in his choice of naming Paul von Hindenburg in command of the imperial forces in the East. "*How are things at the General headquarters,*" continued the ruler. "*All is well, my Emperor. It is not easy to manage the Army in war, but my staff is excellent, and General Falkenhayn here,*" answered von Moltke with a graceful gesture of the hand, "*provides the necessary tools for war.*" The Kaiser was a bit surprised by the praise from Falkenhayn's rival (the two men didn't like each other very much), and it was a well-known fact that the Minister of War wanted the job of the Chief of the General Staff. Falkenhayn smiled in return but didn't say anything, wary of praise from his rival.

The rest of the exchange was interrupted by the arrival of a few more people for the meeting about to take place at the OHL HQ in Berlin. First entered the German Chancellor, Theobald von Bethmann Hollweg. Right behind him was both the chief of the operation divisions, Gerhard von Tappen, the Information Division, Lieutenant

Colonel Richard Hentch, and finally, Hugo von Pohl, the Chief of the Admiralty Staff, who lorded over the Kaiserliche Marine. They all sat down and did some small talk together before von Moltke, with a signal from the Kaiser, put everyone to order. *"Please, everyone, settle down; we have a long meeting ahead of us and with many subjects."*

The room they were in was as austere as German minds could make it. Oak table with white walls, without any decoration of any kind except a portrait of the Kaiser above the door giving way to the hall. Chairs rubbed the floor and made some noise and after a few moments, everyone was still.

"General von Tappen, would you please give us an appraisal of the situation in the West, will you," continued von Moltke. *"Yes, sir. The frontline in France, now located on a roughly horizontal line from the south of Paris to Verdun and then down to Belfort on the Swiss border, is somewhat stalemated. Our best efforts to break through have been met with heavy casualties. It appears the Anglo-French have put themselves on the defensive. The four main French harbors in the north that we have just conquered are still being repaired and are not yet ready for naval operation."* Von Tappen stopped because he saw that Hugo von Pohl, the Navy commander, had a question with his raised hand. *"Yes, Admiral?" "When will the harbors be ready to receive my ships, and what is the state of each,"* Pohl said with unbridled enthusiasm. It was well-known within German leadership circles that the Kaiserliche Marine was chomping at the bit to sail into the new harbors since it would open a world of possibilities for its warships. While the sailing part from Wilhelmshaven to Calais or else Brest wasn't a done deal because the British would try to intervene and had heavily mined the Channel, it was nonetheless an enticing prospect for everyone. With the fleet in Atlantic ports, the damned Allies would not be able to have as tight a blockade as they were executing now. And until they were ready, the German High Seas Fleet was stuck in port with nowhere to go but the immediate vicinity of the North Sea.

"Calais should be operational within the week, as our naval engineers have almost finished clearing out the two large freighters the enemy had scuttled right at its entrance. Brest is still far from being done. The French and English were quite extensive in destroying its facilities. Furthermore, they have scuttled three ships in the harbor, and the naval people are encountering a lot of issues removing them. The port of Le Havre is operational, and Cherbourg remains closed to naval traffic for the same reasons as Brest."

"Ah," intervened the Kaiser with enthusiasm. *"This reminds me, von Moltke. Have you recalled the magnificent officer responsible for the assault on the British battleship Hibernia? I believe his name is Erwin Rommel, and I want to congratulate him personally."* Von Tappen made a sour face at being interrupted while Moltke seemed unruffled. *"Yes, my Emperor. I have sent two of my trusted people to hand out medals to his men, and Rommel himself has been recalled to Berlin for a personal meeting with you as you requested."* *"Thank you,"* answered Wilhelm with a smile. *"Von Tappen, please continue."*

"Thank you, Your Majesty, I was almost done. Admiral Pohl, the Harbors will be ready to receive your ships at some time in November or December; I will have to confirm to you on the exact timetable." *"Very well,"* answered the navy commander.

Von Moltke then retook control of the discussion. *"As matters stand in the West, we propose to stop offensive operations for the time being as our strategic objectives have been reached, and we need the offensive power in the East. I don't think anyone will object."* No one answered, apart from most nodding positively. Matters were pretty bad in the East, and yes, it was time to take care of the Russians. The Kaiser didn't say anything, and so, the subject was closed. What remained to be decided (in the discussion that day) was how many soldiers and to where they would send them.

Wilhelm was more interested in other matters that could fix the problem by adding more troops on the side of the Central Powers.

"Chancellor, can you give us a rundown of the diplomatic situation?" "Indeed, my Emperor. First and foremost, and as most of you already know, the Italians have agreed to join the conflict on our side, although they have not yet confirmed when. As the matter of our deal remains secret, we must thus await them to be ready to make a move. Hans von Flotow, the German ambassador to Rome, has confirmed that the Italian Army is getting quite busy moving troops to the French border. An attack should be imminent." "What of my dear brother-in-law, Constantine," interrupted the Kaiser, eager to learn the latest developments. "The country remains neutral, although my ambassador in Athens tells me that when Italy joins, this may give enough go-ahead to the King to get the country and his parliament to join us.

As you know, the Prime Minister and King Constantine are at odds, and Venizelos wants the country to join the Entente." The Kaiser didn't answer anything, his disappointment obvious. With this, Bettman-Hollweg continued. "The same is true with the Romanians, the King wants to abide by his obligations with the Triple Alliance treaty, but the parliament are not in agreement. There, the problem lies more with the fact that Russia seems powerful at the moment. If we can defeat the Russians and remove them from Galicia altogether," he let his words hand in the air as there was no guarantee that would happen anytime soon with the string of disasters befalling the Austro-Hungarian Army in that sector, "then maybe we have a chance to sway them to our side. After all, we can promise them much in the way of territory in Russia, like Bessarabia."

"Thank you, Chancellor Hollweg," answered von Moltke. "Lieutenant Colonel Hentch, what is the situation in the Balkans and the East in general?" "Sir, the Serbs are buckling, and it appears that the Austro-Hungarians, with the timely help of our new Bulgarian allies, are finally pressing hard. Belgrade is in their hands, and the Bulgarian Army has pushed the Serbs out of Nis and Skopje. The enemy is in disarray and is now retreating into Kosovo, where there is no way out." "That's great news," said von Falkenhayn. "This means we can reopen land communications with our Ottoman ally and send him some help, as events are not looking good in the Caucasus." The Minister of War was referring to the fact that the rail lines that went through Serbia and Bulgaria could now be repaired and repurposed to send supplies to the Turks and keep them in the war. It was no secret the Turks didn't have the necessary war industry to sustain a modern conflict for long and would thus need German coal, weapons and ammunition to keep going.

"Speaking of the Ottomans, what is the situation at the Battle of Sarikamish," said the Kaiser. The man seemed bored with the too-serious discussions. "Your Excellency, it appears that the Turkish Army is defeated. According to our information received from the head of the German military mission to Istanbul, General Liman von Sanders, Enver Pacha, the Minister of War and commander in chief of the Eastern offensive, has returned to the capital. The Ottoman Army is in full retreat, and tens of thousands of men are dead. One of their corps (the 9th) has been completely destroyed as it tried to cover the retreat of the rest of the men." The Kaiser grumbled. "That's not what I call great news."

"No, my Emperor, it is not," interjected von Moltke. "And there is more. While the reinforced German 8th Army under Hindenburg is advancing in Poland and reclaiming the lost territory in East Prussia following its grand victory at Marienburg, there are still a lot of dark clouds over the horizon. And that, despite the destruction of their 1st Army. Konigsberg is entering its fifth week of siege, and there appears to be more and more Russian reinforcements coming to the fore. We hope that General Hindenburg will be able to arrive in time to save the fortress. Von Moltke looked to Hentch for confirmation. "Indeed, Your Excellency, the Information Division concurs with the Commander-In-Chief. The Russian strength in the sector is now around 500,000 men, despite the complete destruction of their 1st Army. My recommendation to you and General von Moltke is to send at least another 500,000 men from the West to the East, bringing our forces to about a million soldiers when all is said and done." "I agree; let's make this happen," answered the Commander-in-chief without waiting for the Kaiser's confirmation, something that seemed to happen more and more since the war started. Von Moltke continued as Wilhelm didn't object or say anything. *"We also need to send a lot of help to the Austro-Hungarians in the Carpathian Mountains as the Russians are pushing them out of Galicia entirely."* The Siege of Przemysl was about to end with the fall of the last stronghold in the province, and with it, the Austrian outlook for the rest of the war looked bleak. *"Next is Hungary and the complete disintegration of our ally if we don't do anything. I have already taken steps to send 300,000 soldiers from the Western Front to Galicia. This, as you know, goes right in hand with my decision to stop all offensive operations in France. We will restart them once the Italians join."*

The Kaiser was more interested in less relevant stuff. *"Admiral Pohl,"* he started, completely oblivious to what had just transpired. *"I need to have news from Admiral von Spee and his brave Pacific Squadron."* It was no secret that the Kaiser was still sore about the loss of Tsingtao but was taking a keen interest in the romantic story that was von Spee's survival. *"My Emperor, I am happy that you mention it. I have just received word that the surviving German ships have arrived at our Yap telegraph and coaling station. The ships are well, and the Admiral sends his best wishes. He says he will continue to plunge deeper into the Pacific and that he will try to rally the Reich via Cape Horn and the Atlantic."* *"Well, well!"* answered the Kaiser with a broad smile, tapping on the table, even startling his Chancellor, who had been keeping quiet. *"Finally, some news about the heroes of the Pacific! Admiral, we need to find ways to help them rejoin the fatherland. What have you in the works?"* *"Well, we have no current capabilities to send warships, although an Austro-Hungarian heavy cruiser has joined Admiral von Spee in Yap. We are dispatching coaling ships in various spots south of Argentina and into the Pacific, as the squadron will need much to cross the expanse and face several potential naval battles."* *"Excellent, Admiral!"*

"Hum..." von Moltke made a noise to try and retake control of the situation. Von Spee's adventures were interesting but irrelevant in the grand scheme of things for now. *"So, now to the next order of business..."*

A bold plan – Operation Ares
Gibraltar, near Oharra's battery, October 29th, 1914

Sir Winston Churchill looked at the details of the plan of attack that was about to unfold and smiled at the Admiral in charge of the operation that would gamble a lot for the British Empire. On it rested the continued success of the Entente, the future of France, and the outcome of the war. The First Lord of the Admiralty wore his typical white uniform and harbored a white hat. A cigar was burning slowly between his lips.

Churchill walked to the edge of the rail surrounding the largest of the two guns on Oharra's battery, a 10-inch monster towering above Gibraltar's highest rock. The weapon was Britain's guarantee that it controlled the straits. Capable of destroying any ships trying to cross the area between Morocco and Spain, it was built squarely and well-armored to protect its gunners. Gibraltar bristled with guns on all of its sides, but the majority of them faced the water to interdict it to the enemy of Great Britain. And Oharra's battery lorded over them all.

Gibraltar was British since the War of Spanish Succession when an expedition landed on the rock and took control of it in 1704. The place was as strategic as it could get. The entire British position was built on a mighty rock that climbed to the sky and a natural harbor right beside it. It was reputed to be impregnable and had withstood several sieges during its two-hundred-year-old British episode.

"Isn't that a grand view, Admiral?" The blue water of the Mediterranean Sea shone brightly as the magnificent sun reflected on it. Many ships transited the strait at that moment, and all were flying either French or British colors. No neutral nation was permitted to sail through since the war had started, unless Britain said so.

Below, in the Gibraltar harbor, rested a great fleet. It was about to set sail for the landing that would change the face of the war. *"Indeed, my Lord,"* answered Admiral Beatty. The man had sailed from the

Home Fleet with the reinforcements Churchill had ordered him to bring. In fact, he had sailed with his boss the First Lord himself, because fighting Winston wanted to see to it that the operation was a success. After learning through the extensive British spy network that Italy was about to join the Central Powers, the British, upon the urging of the dynamic Churchill, had decided to act before Rome did any damage. The French, reeling from disaster to disaster with the fall of Paris and the entire north of France, were also eager to do something about the backstabbing Italians. It was about making certain the bastards didn't choose when and where to attack but that the Entente would.

Operation Ares, as it was grandly named, was soon to be the most ambitious amphibious operation of the war, and of history to date. In one fell swoop, the goal was to destroy the entire Italian Fleet, land in force, and force the Italians to surrender. At the same time, ten French divisions would launch at the northern Italian border from Monaco, Nice, and small towns like La Turbie and try to pry the frontline open.

"The fleet we have assembled here is incredible, my Lord," continued Admiral Beatty. Over twenty-seven dreadnoughts and pre-dreadnoughts battleships, flanked by over a hundred support vessels ranging from cruisers to destroyers, would escort four French and three Imperial British Divisions (two Australian and 1 New Zealander) in the most daring operation that could be willed by the aggressive British.

The strategic situation was completely desperate for the Entente. France was half occupied, and Paris was in German hands. Everything could unravel with one more defeat or with the Italians attacking in force. And thus, it had been agreed to go ahead with Churchill's bold plan.

With the loss of the northern ports, the French Navy had been forced to move its assets as far south as Bordeaux, and in the end, it was decided to move all of it to Gibraltar to join the large fleet the British were assembling. The decision wasn't a total and crazy gamble. The Entente could spare the troops. The front had stabilized south of Paris, Verdun, and Belfort as the Germans sent a lot of troops East to meet the Russian onslaught, threatening to drive to Berlin and also to knock the Austro-Hungarians out of the war. It was thus deemed a calculated risk to move troops south and attack Italy while they had the opportunity. The real danger lay in the stripping of the British Grand Fleet, supposed to keep the German High Seas Fleet bottled up in Northern Germany and keep up the blockade of the Central Powers. Perhaps the reduction in naval strength would trigger the Germans to take action and sail out of their den, but in the end, action was chosen over passivity.

"The fleet will leave tomorrow as planned, my Lord, and we should be within sight of Taranto in two days." "Good," answered Churchill as he tapped in the rail, straightened up, and took his cigar between two of his fingers. The smoke billowed all around him. *"The French Combined Fleet commander, Admiral Augustin Boue de Lapeyrere, should also be here shortly. He is in the harbor below. We are set to meet with him at the Wellington Redoubt, my Lord." "Just grand, Admiral Beatty. Just grand,"* answered the First Lord, looking down once more at the incredibly powerful fleet assembled below.

BRITISH MEDITERRANEAN FLEET (Gibraltar)		
Admiral		
BB Malborough	Pre-dread BB Russell (6th battle squ.)	18 DD
BB Ajax	Pre-dread BB Cornwallis (6th battle squ.)	4 CA
BB Conqueror	Pre-dread BB Almermale (6th battle squ.)	4 CL
BB Superb	Pre-dread BB Duncan (6th battle squ.)	
BB Dreadnought	Pre-dread BB Exmouth (6th battle squ.)	
BC Indefatigable	CL Diamond (6th battle squ.)	
BC Invincible	5 DD (6th battle squ.)	

British dreadnoughts Marlborough, Ajax, Conqueror, Superb, Dreadnought, Indefatigable, and Invincible would make up part of the fleet. Their older brothers (pre-dreadnoughts) would sail beside them and add their firepower to the invasion force. They were the Russel, Cornwallis, Almermale, Duncan, and Exmouth.

The French had brought everything they had for the battle since, at this point, they didn't have anything to lose, and no real military harbors in the Atlantic left. Dreadnoughts Courbet, Jean-Bart, France, and Paris would be flanked by pre-dreadnoughts Diderot, Danton, Verginaud, Voltaire, Condorcet, Mirabeau, Verité, Patrie, Republique, Justice and Democratie.

FRANCE
French Combined Fleet

	Battleships	
BB Courbet [Fleet Flagship]	BB France	1 CA
BB Jean-Bart	BB Paris	3 CL
	1st Battle Squadron, 1st Division	
Pre-Dread BB Diderot	Pre-Dread BB Verginiaud	2 DD
Pre-Dread BB Danton	2 CL	
	1st Battle Squadron, 2nd Division	
Pre-Dread BB Voltaire	Pre-Dread BB Mirabeau	1 DD
Pre-Dread BB Condorcet	1 CL	
	2nd Battle Squadron, 1st Division	
Pre-Dread BB Verite	Pre-Dread BB Republique	1 DD
Pre-Dread BB Patrie	1 CL	
	2nd Battle Squadron, 2nd Division	
Pre-Dread BB Justice [CA]	1 CL	2 DD
Pre-Dread BB Democratie		

The staff car arrived at the white gate at the base of the Oharra battery and honked twice, indicating to the Admiral and the First Lord that their ride had arrived. *"Let's go to that meeting, Admiral, shall we."* The battle about to take place would indeed decide much and would be one hell of a fight.

Stay neutral
Greece, Romania

Tatoi Summer Palace
Near Athens, October 17th, 1914

King Constantine I of Greece laid back in his chair, looking at the magnificent clock at the end of the room. It had been a gift from Kaiser Wilhelm II during his visit five years before. He smiled, remembering the visit. It had been a simpler time when the two men could just be friends and not worry too much about politics and war. Wilhelm had loved the Tatoi estate and both men walked the grounds a few times for several hours. He liked his cousin, the German Emperor, and would have liked nothing more than to join the Central Powers. Greece could have done what the Bulgarians were doing and joined in the fight against the Serbs and grab some territory. Constantine took a deep breath and again looked at the report from his royal counselor, Andralos Kostapukis, in front of him.

Rumors had it that the Italians were about to join the Central Powers. If that happened, he believed he had a good chance of toppling Prime Minister Venizelos from power and placing a more pliable man in his place. Venizelos was the leader of the faction that wanted to join the Entente, but the King could not accept it, would not accept it.

He stood up and walked to the large window of his study in the main Tatoi Palace building. The leaves outside were taking the beautiful red and yellow colors of the fall before they fell. The entire scene was taking the shape of a breathtaking painting. The scenery in front of him was magnificent, as the Tatoi Summer Palace was a sprawling 10,000 acres of buildings, gardens, and magnificent groomed forest.

For now, there wasn't much more to do than enjoy Tatoi while it lasted, as he would soon move back to Athens for the winter months. His attention was snatched back to more mundane matters as a few knocks on the door were heard. "Yes, please enter," he said in response. One of the royal majordomo, Mr. Itzakis, entered the room.

"Your Majesty," he started, bowing slightly in respect. *"Tea is ready to be served in the east gardens. Would you like to go now?"* Constantine smiled at the man and turned toward the door. *"Yes, Mr. Itzakis, why not."*

Peles Palace
The King is dead. Hail the new King.

King Carol went to bed on the evening of the 18th of October, 1914, with a bit of discomfort. He didn't feel good and had not been feeling well for the last week or so. It had first started with a pain in his left arm, and now it had spread to the chest. His doctors had told him it was his heart. At 75 years old, the First King of Romania, the very same man who was crowned King in 1881 following the country's independence from the hated Turks, had lived a long life.

He closed his eyes on that evening never to open them again. The next morning, the royal servants went to his room for his usual morning routine, but the King did not wake. Within a few hours of sunrise, King Carol was pronounced dead of natural causes.

From there, things moved quickly. The new king as sworn in the very same day. King Ferdinand, Carol's nephew, rose to power and moved to Peles Palace to take Carol's place as Romania's leader.

Meanwhile, the royal corpse was exposed in Bucharest (Curtea De Arge Monastery), and a National Day of Mourning was proclaimed by the new Prime Minister, Ion Bratianu.

Both men favored ties with the Entente and met on that very matter the day following Ferdinand's accession to power. Bratianu convinced the King to wait for an opportune moment to join the Entente, but that time wasn't now; the Romanian Army was not ready.

The British and French ambassadors were received regardless, and some discussions were had, but nothing went beyond pleasant discussions. The German ambassador was also received, as Kaiser Wilhelm II expected much of the new king, with no less than an entry of Romania on the side of the Central Powers.

However, anti-Hungarian sentiment ran high in the country because of the Austro-Hungarian policy toward Romanians in Transylvania. Budapest was following a policy of intimidation and domination on the poor Romanians there, and there could be no reconciliation between the two states unless something was done about it.

On the 22nd of October, following pressure from both sides, King Ferdinand again proclaimed the country's neutrality. Behind the halls of power in Bucharest, however, the decision was already taken to join the Entente but to choose an opportune time to do so.

Vrana Royal Palace
October 29th, 1914

"Your Majesty," said General Dimitar Geshov, the King's military adviser. "*Here is, as you requested, the report on the progress of the offensive in Serbia,*" continued the man, giving his monarch a sharp military salute. "*Thank you, General,*" answered the Bulgarian monarch, Ferdinand I.

War had been declared on the 7th of October 1914, followed by the launch of a major offensive on Serbia's eastern border by The Bulgarian First Army under General Kliment Boyadzhiev (comprising the Sixth, Eighth, Ninth, and First Divisions) along with the Bulgarian Second Army commanded by General Georgi Todorov (comprising the Third and Seventh Divisions, a cavalry division).

Bulgaria had decided to join the Central Powers as the fourth country in the alliance following the stellar German victory at the Marne and the subsequent occupation of Paris. The country's military wasn't yet ready, still recuperating from its ordeal in the Second Balkan War in 1913. But an opportunity had risen, and King Ferdinand, who favored Germany and the Central Powers, had decided that the time was ripe for intervention.

From there, things went rapidly, and a treaty was signed with Berlin and Vienna, in addition to an agreement with Turkey, since no Bulgarian King would be so bold as to ally themselves with the hated Ottomans who had occupied Bulgaria for centuries.

Total mobilization was ordered at the beginning of October, even prior to the signing of the agreement, as Ferdinand had already decided to join the conflict. The well-experienced and well-bloodied Bulgarian Army was 600,000 strong and a force to be reckoned with in the Balkans. It also sported a mix of modern and older artillery guns. One-on-one against Serbia, the fight would have been roughly equal. But the Serbs also had to contend with the Austro-Hungarians pushing them hard from the north and already having occupied Belgrade, their capital.

"The cities of Nis and Skopje are now ours, Your Majesty. The Serbs are in full retreat toward Kosovo, and we are beating them hard. Both General Kliment Boyadzhiev and Todorov report heavy casualties, however. The enemy isn't getting beaten easily and, as you know, our forces were not as ready as we would have liked in joining the war so early."

The King tapped the report on the table in front of him with his fingers. Both men were in the Vrana Royal Palace, or more specifically, in the king's office on the fourth floor. The room was a magnificent display of wealth. The floor was made of marble, the wall painted a magnificent red and blue, half-covered in tapestry representing old medieval battles before the Turkish occupation. The desk itself was made of mahogany wood, with golden gildings and decoration on its sides. The king himself was magnificently dressed as he always was, with his full uniform.

"Well, General Geshov, this is satisfactory. When do you think the 1st and 2nd Army will be able to conclude the campaign against the enemy?" "It is believed that within a few weeks, all of Serbia will be under Central Power occupation." The king pondered for a moment. *"That's good, General. Have you also looked into the matter of the rail lines?"* Ferdinand was interested to know when the rail link with Austria-Hungary would be reopened as the Germans had promised military and economic aid in exchange for Bulgaria's entry into the war. The opening of the rail line would mean trains filled with weapons, ammunition, and supplies. Some of it would be bound for the Ottoman Empire, but a decent amount would go to Bulgaria.

"Your Excellency, we estimate that the first train should roll into the country two to three weeks after we smash Serbia. The enemy forces are making a mess of the rails as they retreat, so repairs will need to be done before this happens."

"Very well, General, that will be all," said the king, rising from his chair and walking to the study's window while General Geshov made the military salute before exiting the room. Ferdinand crossed his arms behind his back and lost himself in the magnificent garden view before him, sprinkled with fountains and superb buildings covering the Royal Estate in Vrana.

He wondered where this would all lead him and Bulgaria. He had not taken the decision to go to war lightly. At the same time, he believed in the dream of Greater Bulgaria, and the country needed to expand and recuperate all the lost lands from the Second Balkan War.

Armeeoberkommando (AOK)
Pondering, October 30th, 1914

The Chief of the General Staff for all of the Austro-Hungarian military force, Marshal Conrad von Hotzendorf, sat alone in his office. When all the lights were out, when no one was around and when he was with his own thoughts, he took the time to reflect upon his decision and the war in general. He was located in Vienna, near the Imperial Palace, in the Armeeoberkommando (AOK) building. The organization was the leading body for the Austro-Hungarian forces (K.u.k.), and Conrad was its commander.

The man was a very competent officer. He made great operational plans, had a sound understanding of military affairs, and could lead troops to battle. His main failing (unfortunately for Austria-Hungary and the Central Powers) was that he did not take into account the capabilities of his forces in implementing his brilliantly prepared plans. Had he been a general in the German Army, with its top-notch rail system, command structure, and supply system (not forgetting one unified language for its soldiers), he would probably have gone down as one of the good generals and leaders of the war. But as it was, he constantly failed to apply the knowledge he had of the K.u.k.'s own shortcomings in his grandiose plans.

He looked at the three piles of reports facing him. One was on military intelligence, the second on the Serbian front, and the third on the unfolding disaster that was the Galician campaign.

He picked up the first report and read through the summary on the first page. His face fell as he read the terrible state of his armed forces. Over 30% of the pre-war strength was gone, either killed, maimed, or taken prisoner. Military production was starting to slow down because of the lack of resources (the Allied blockade), and the Romanians were now leaning toward the Entente. At least, the Italians would soon join the Central Powers and that would mean he wouldn't have to send troops he could space anywhere else to the border between the two countries. He dropped the bunch of papers, needing something more positive to cheer him up.

The second report was much more to his liking and spoke of victorious advance and stellar victories against the Serbian Army. Belgrade was occupied (finally), and Conrad felt that the humiliation of the first two failed invasions was washed away. The troops were now at Nis, and some units had even joined up with the Bulgarian troops coming from the East. The enemy forces were now deep into Kosovo and cornered like rats. He smiled, thinking that, at the very least, he would have this bit of great news to present to Emperor Franz Joseph.

He picked up the last pile of papers, and this one he dreaded to read. The situation in the Przemysl fortress was now dire, and it looked like the garrison would surrender soon. If the place fell, there would be nothing standing in front of the Russian armies to spill over into Hungary. If that happened, Conrad didn't know how Budapest would react. Power in the Dual Monarchy was held in Vienna, but the Hungarians had a big say in it, and there was no telling what they would do if hordes of barbarians marched up to the gates of their cities. Politically, there was real danger there, and strategically, Conrad looked at the possible fall of the Empire and the surrender of Austria-Hungary to the Entente.

The Emperor's pleas to Germany had not fallen on deaf ears, and the OHL was railing troops to help his beleaguered forces into the new defensive frontline they were building up in the Carpathians, but for now, it would only be a defensive measure. Lemberg and all of Galicia (except the fortress of Przemysl) were occupied, and that wasn't good for the Empire.

Conrad hoped that the defense would hold in the East while he tried to raise more troops and mop up the Serbs. The Italians had also spoken of sending some troops, but he was skeptical since there was no love between Vienna and Rome because of the border questions and the Italian demands over Austrian territories.

Regardless of the military battles, there was a plethora of other matters he needed to attend to. Ammunition production and allocation, raising new troops, and making sure the imperial military command structure worked.

A sudden knock on the door startled him. *"Yes, what is it?"* *"Sir,"* said the voice on the other side. *"The meeting with the Emperor is about to start, he is waiting for you in the meeting room."* Hotzendorf took a deep breath before answering. *"Very well, tell his Highness that I will be there in a minute."*

Conrad stood up, shuffled the papers in his hand, and stormed out of his office. It was time to give an appraisal of the difficult situation the Empire was in to his master.

Lower Dacha, near Petergof Palace
The overall situation, October 30th, 1914

Nicolas II moved his rifle a little to the left, putting the beast squarely in his sights. *"Now, your Highness,"* said one of his hunters right beside him. Both men were in a camouflaged position under a large tree. Facing them was a large clearing and the animal was milling about in the area, unsure of where to go, squealing in fear. The imperial hunters had herded it into the clearing for the waiting emperor to kill it.

He pulled the trigger, and the rifle recoiled in a cloud of billowing smoke. *"You did it, my Tsar,"* said one of the other hunters on the other side of the clearing. *"The Pig is down!"* Nicolas smiled and finally relaxed somewhat. Hunting was one of his favorite pastimes, and he liked to indulge in it near Petergof Palace (not so far from St-Petersburg), in a place called the Lower Dacha.

The large four-story building made of yellow and red bricks was built on the shore of the Gulf of Finland by Alexander III (Nicola's father) for his son. The nice thing about the Lower Dacha was that it was remote and far enough from Petergof Palace to be isolated from the outside world. This was a place the Emperor came to when he wanted to relax and get away from the craziness of ruling over the largest empire in the world.

Half an hour later, Nicolas exited the car that had brought him back to the Lower Dacha's front yard, where his uncle, Grand Duke Nicolas, waited on the grass, speaking with his wife. *"My Tsar,"* started the Commander-in-Chief of the Russian Army. *"Ah, Grand Duke, I trust the way from the capital to here was uneventful?"* *"All was well, your Excellency."* *"Good,"* continued the Emperor, giving a kiss to his wife followed by a smile. *"My dear, I have some military affairs to attend to, I'll join you for tea later."*

A few minutes after that, both men were sitting down in Nicolas' study, wine glass in hand. *"Dear uncle, what is the news from the front?"* Nicolas already knew of the terrible defeat at Marienburg. He was interested in its aftermath. *"Your Highness, the Germans, under their new commander named General Hindenburg, have started a counter-offensive toward Konigsberg. We believe that Poland is also threatened but that the Germans don't have the troops at the moment. I need to send a lot of reinforcements to General Rennenkampf to make sure he will be able to face the incoming German onslaught."*

"Well," started Nicolas, who, as always, was intimidated by his uncle and unsure of his opinions in front of him. He thus relented. *"Do what you must to stop them, Grand Duke. Do we have the reserves to do that?"* *"Well, I need to pull out some of the troops from Galicia, but given that we have completely beaten the Austro-Hungarians there and are fixated in front of Przemysl, there isn't much action anyway. As you know, we have also defeated the Turks in Sarikamish, and I intend to rail back a corps from that area as well. We also have the newly-raised Northwest and Southwest armies near Moscow that I will move forward. When all is said and done, we should stop the enemy's advance."*

The Northwest and Southwest armies had not yet participated in the war, as they had taken some time to get mobilized. They included the men and military equipment from the Moscow area but also from beyond, like the western Ural region (of cities like Ekaterinburg, Nizhnii Tagil, Chelyabinsk, and Perm). Then from Siberia, and the southern reaches of the Empire (Central Asia). These formations had to be railed through an already overtaxed logistical system, and thus, priority had been given to the units that were needed in the fall offensive in Galicia and Eastern Prussia. They were getting into play only now as a result.

"Very well, Grand Duke," answered Nicolas, taking a sip of his red wine. *"When do you think we will storm Przemysl?"* The Austro-

Hungarian fortress had been holding for two months, encircled and under siege by no less than two full Russian armies, while the other two had started to fight in the Carpathians to try and break into Hungary proper. *"Your majesty, there are reports of enemy reinforcement in the Carpathian frontline. It appears that German Army troops are now arriving in great numbers. The same thing is happening in East Prussia. So, to answer your question about Przemysl, I don't know when, but I am applying pressure on General Brussilov on a daily basis to push him to finish this soon, or we will be in trouble."*

The Tsar laid back on the intricately decorated (with gold lacings) couch. The room they were in was covered with a wooden floor, colorful walls, and several portraits of former Russian emperors and famous battles. Beside them was a large hearth, but no fire burned in it; the day was nice outside. Above the hearth stood a magnificent painting of the Battle of the Nation in Leipzig in 1813, a grand victory against another of Russia's enemies, Napoleonic France.

"I will need to talk to the French and British ambassadors and understand why they aren't pressuring the Germans harder. It would be nice if those troops stayed west." Grand Duke Nicolas didn't answer anything since it wasn't a question, so instead, he took a long drag of his wine, then instantly refilled by one of the very discreet imperial majordomos standing by the walls, wine bottle in hand. He knew the Tsar had a very limited understanding of military strategy and tactics; hence, there wasn't anything to say. The Germans were sending their troops East because they had decided it. It had nothing to do with the Western Allies. And if the OHL moved troops, it was because it could, after soundly defeating the Anglo-French at the Battle of the Marne.

"What of the Caucasus Front and the Black Sea, Grand Duke"" "Well, my Emperor, we are starting to advance into Anatolia as the Ottoman armies before our troops are defeated. But I do not intend to push too hard in that sector since there isn't much to conquer, and we need the troops elsewhere. The Black Sea is under constant attacks by the

Germano-Ottoman fleet roaming freely there since the terrible defeat of our naval forces at the Battle of Cape Sarych." The Tsar also got his glass refilled and then answered. *"Yes, there isn't much we can do but wait for those three new dreadnoughts under construction in Nicolayev." "Indeed, your Excellency,"* answered the Grand Duke as there was nothing much else to say. The Central Powers were complete masters of the Black Sea and could attack at will whenever and wherever they wanted.

"At least we have some positive developments with Romania," continued the Tsar. *"We do?"* answered the Grand Duke. Nicolas smiled. *"We do, Grand Duke. The new king, Ferdinand I, is more inclined to the cause of the Entente than the Central Powers. If we can keep this up against the Austro-Hungarians, our people in Bucharest and our diplomats here, following talks with the Romanian ambassador, believe that the Romanians will join the war. After all, they aren't in love with Austria and want Transylvania back. They are only waiting for the developments in Galicia."* The commander-in-chief of the Russian Imperial Army smiled, thinking. *"This is a very good development, your Excellency. This could mean we could enter the Balkans and try to help Serbia or else attack Bulgaria."*

The two men touched their glasses in quiet anticipation of Romania joining their cause. Things were not going badly for the Empire, and it seemed that if it managed to stop the German offensive, take Konigsberg, and conquer Przemysl, the Russians were in business.

CHAPTER 4

Operation Ares
The attack on Taranto, 11h50 PM, November 9th, 1914

(...) Battleship Marlborough, Royal Navy (...)

"Everything is in place, sir," said Admiral of the Fleet Sir Osmond Brock, David Beatty's Chief of Staff. *"Very well, Admiral Brock. You can tell the signal officers to start sending the execute order. We launch in ten minutes."* *"Yes, sir,"* answered the other man, with an edge to his voice betraying the tension everyone felt at what they were about to do. It was dark outside, as it was the middle of the night.

BRITISH MEDITERRANEAN FLEET (Gibraltar)		
Admiral_____		
BB Malborough	Pre-dread BB Russell (6th battle squ.)	18 DD
BB Ajax	Pre-dread BB Cornwallis (6th battle squ.)	4 CA
BB Conqueror	Pre-dread BB Almermale (6th battle squ.)	4 CL
BB Superb	Pre-dread BB Duncan (6th battle squ.)	
BB Dreadnought	Pre-dread BB Exmouth (6th battle squ.)	
BC Indefatigable	CL Diamond (6th battle squ.)	
BC Invincible	5 DD (6th battle squ.)	

The Anglo-British fleet had sailed three days before from Gibraltar, shrouded in secrecy. They left in the middle of the night, and sailed to the coast of French North Africa to try and avoid sea traffic as much as possible. When they reached the Tunisian coast, they forked south and then sped to the open seas, rejoining Gibraltar on the 8th. They then left the vicinity of the British base and timed their arrival offshore Taranto to arrive in the middle of the night.

Over twenty-seven dreadnoughts and pre-dreadnoughts battleships were about to start a war with a neutral country. The first salvo was going to be one hell of an overwhelming one. No less than twenty-seven dreadnoughts and pre-dreadnoughts battleships, flanked by over a hundred support vessels ranging from cruisers to destroyers, would soon fire in anger at the port of Taranto in Southern Italy.

Furthermore, and compounding the potential disaster for the Italians, they were completely unaware of what the Anglo-French were about to do. Yes, they would soon join the Central Powers, but never in their right mind did they imagine the Entente would be so bold as to do something so ruthless. But it was what it was. If you planned on going to war with the British, you had to be prepared for the gutter-style fighting that had given them an Empire and the World.

FRANCE
French Combined Fleet

Battleships

BB Courbet [Fleet Flagship]	BB France	1 CA
BB Jean-Bart	BB Paris	3 CL

1st Battle Squadron, 1st Division

Pre-Dread BB Diderot	Pre-Dread BB Vergniaud	2 DD
Pre-Dread BB Danton	2 CL	

1st Battle Squadron, 2nd Division

Pre-Dread BB Voltaire	Pre-Dread BB Mirabeau	1 DD
Pre-Dread BB Condorcet	1 CL	

2nd Battle Squadron, 1st Division

Pre-Dread BB Verite	Pre-Dread BB Republique	1 DD
Pre-Dread BB Patrie	1 CL	

2nd Battle Squadron, 2nd Division

Pre-Dread BB Justice [CA]	1 CL	2 DD
Pre-Dread BB Democratie		

The fleet was led by British Admiral David Beatty, one of the Royal Navy's best and most aggressive admirals. Beatty had been commander of the 1st British battlecruiser Squadron before the First Lord of the Admiralty Winston Churchill put him in command of the invasion fleet and was on his way to command the Grand Fleet when Admiral John Jellicoe retired in a few years. Instead, he received a posting for the single most important naval operation to date: Operation Ares.

The idea was to knock the Italian Navy out of the war in one fell swoop and, at the same time, get the Italians to leave the war entirely and stay neutral. By dealing a crippling blow to its fleet and landing in strength, the First Lord of the Admiralty, Winston Churchill, had convinced everyone that this would stun and kill the Italians and that they would not be able to intervene in a time of their own choosing alongside the Central Powers.

If the operation succeeded, then the Italian fleet would be neutralized, making certain the Entente kept naval supremacy in the

Mediterranean. There was a lot of risk involved in the operation, notwithstanding the risk of abject failure in the landings they were about to attempt. Such an attack by sea had never been attempted before in modern times. The risk was increased by where they were about to attack: Taranto was the Regina Marina (Italian Navy's) home port and, thus, bristled with powerful coastal guns and defenses.

"Admiral," said Brock, after a couple of minutes of the ships signaling each other and answering back to the flagship, battleship Marlborough, one of the most powerful units in the Royal Navy at the start of the war. The ship was of the Iron Duke Class, the latest super dreadnought design, with 13.5-inch guns and 29,000 tons of displacement. *"Everything is set. French Admiral Augustin Boue de Lapeyrere also confirmed all ships are ready to execute. Do we have a confirmation of your order?"* "Yes, Admiral Brock. By all means, give the go-ahead order to fire in exactly..." Beatty looked at his pocket watch. "Seven minutes and forty seconds." "Yes, sir."

It was 11h52, and the biggest naval salvo of the war was about to hammer the Italians.

(...) Taranto Harbor (...)

ITALY		
Regina Marina, Admiral Amedeo di Savoia-Aosta		
BB Dante Alighieri	BB Conte di Cavour	BB Andrea Doria
BB Giulio Cesare	BB Leonardo da Vinci	BB Duilio
Pre-Dread BB Regina Elena	Pre-Dread BB Vittorio Emanuele	Pre-Dread BB Venice
Pre-Dread BB Napoli	Pre-Dread BB Benedetto Brin	Pre-Dread BB Saint Bon
Pre-Dread BB Roma	Pre-Dread BB Regina Margherita	Pre-Dread BB Emanuele Filiber

The Italian Navy at Taranto at the time of the Anglo-French attack

Taranto Harbor was the main Italian Naval base and where most of its ships were located. Since the country was still neutral, none of them were at sea that day. During peace, some of them were on patrol and or on cruises, but all had been recalled a few weeks before in preparation for the entry of Italy into the war. Some needed repairs, most needed their coal stores to be filled, and many needed more sailors.

The Regina Marina (the name for the Italian Navy) was a very powerful fleet in the Mediterranean, and it felt protected in Taranto. The city and the harbor had it all. Plenty of steel foundries, coal mines north of it, large naval shipyards and drydocks, and modern defenses for the precious ships it harbored. It had well over a hundred modern guns of all calibers and sizes to defend it. From its position, it could rapidly sail in the Adriatic or the Central Mediterranean.

The Regina Marina was the main reason why the Anglo-French were about to attack. Ranking 7th in the World at the start of the war, the fleet sported six modern dreadnoughts (Dante Alighieri, Giulio Cesare, Conte di Cavour, Da Vinci, Andrea Doria, and Duilio) and nine pre-dreadnought battleships (Elena, Napoli, Roma, Vittorio Emmanuelle, Brin, Margherita, Venice, Saint Bon, and Filiber). With the soon-to-happen Italian entry on the side of the Central powers, these powerful warships could be combined with the also pretty large Austro-Hungarian fleet and thus create a dominant force in the theater. This was something the Anglo-French could not permit, as they had a lot of maritime traffic, convoys, troops, and supplies sailing through it. They were worried so much about it that they removed precious battleships from their Grand Fleet, watching the Germans in the north.

Admiral Amedeo di Savoia-Aosta, the overall commander of the Italian fleet, was sound asleep in his office of the Supermarina (name of Navy HQ), having worked late again and because he'd had too much grappa after his evening meal. In his slumber, he thought he heard lightning and distant thunder. Sentries on the exterior ramparts by the naval guns (the modern section of the defenses) and the ones in the Castello Aragonese, the old fortress at the harbor's entrance, all saw the distant show of light that suddenly appeared over the horizon. Since storms were frequent over the sea, they at first did not see any problem and looked away in indifference. But then the sound traveled to their ears and then they started to register that something was wrong, very wrong.

Seconds later, loud, whistling sounds started to be heard and then became overbearing. It was only then that they understood that an attack was underway. But it was too late; the shells were landing amongst the city, harbors, and on the ships. The Supermarina HQ was severely hit in the first salvo, the building being peppered with no less than five 11-inch shells from the French pre-dreadnoughts, and thus Admiral Savoia-Aosta never woke up.

The big battleship shells slammed almost simultaneously, rocking the ground in a shattering explosion and a blinding light. The blast was so overwhelming and sudden that most Italians in the city were stunned out of their minds by the mindboggling, shattering sound it produced. Then people started dying, ships burst aflame, and the city itself burned.

(…) Battleship Marlborough (…)

"That's one hell of a light show, sir," said Admiral Sir Osmond Brock, commenting on the large orange glow in the distance. The glow grew and then abated, then grew again, as the shells exploded and then more came in. *"Agreed,"* answered Admiral Beatty, as the area was bathed in a faint light despite being ten kilometers from the Italian harbor of Taranto, their target. It meant that an incredibly large fire was burning over the horizon. The two commanders looked through the battleship's bridge viewport, arms crossed behind their backs.

Their nervousness had dropped significantly at the last minute as they achieved their objective. The fleet commander looked at his firing ships and was awed by the display of power by the resounding guns and blast of fire that lit the night. *"From a distance, it must be one hell of a light show as well, although I suspect that the Italians on the receiving end have other things to worry about right now."* Brock laughed softly. *"Indeed, Sir."*

"Are the troops getting ready?" *"Yes, Admiral. The landing ships, destroyers, motor boats, and cutters are gathering for the landings, Sir."* *"Very well, let's do this. Signal the other ships to keep firing until new orders come in. I want to thoroughly smash the enemy before we land our troops."*

(...) Taranto Harbor (...)

Pandemonium erupted everywhere. The Anglo-French shells came in long, obvious, and fiery arcs of fire from the horizon to land in the Italian city and the harbor.

The first ship to get hit was the heavy cruiser Bolzano, smacked by one of Marlborough's 13.5 shells that smashed on its deck and splashed fire and shrapnel on two destroyers nearby. A secondary explosion catapulted some more fire and dark smoke into the sky. The ship was gone an instant later.

The Guilio Cesare took two French shells into its belly as they slashed like a hot knife through butter from its deck to the inside of the ship. The vessel seemed to bend in two like a folding knife and exploded from its center island. Fire sprouted from its side, and a large fire soon engulfed the entire hull.

At almost the same time, the battleship Conte Di Cavour received a combination of five shells from two British battleships (Ajax and Exmouth) and two French ones (Courbet and Danton). The damage done to the ship was extreme, and shrapnel exploded outward, damaging other ships in a showering display of death and destruction.

Soon, the entire harbor area and the water itself were fused together in one raging inferno fed by a continuous rain of fire from the Anglo-French ships offshore.

A wave of shells from battleships and some of the hundreds of support ships peppered the naval ammunition depot in the Mare

Piccolo, one of the two large protected basins inside the harbor. The resulting blast leveled every building within a 300-meter radius and damaged several submarines and destroyers docked near the Andrea Doria. The battleship itself was slammed by a wall of fire and debris, riddling its deck, hull, and guns with metal shards and fire.

The town of Taranto was not spared damage since it lay between one part of the harbor where the majority of ships were docked (the Mare Grande part of Taranto) to the other area (the Mare Piccolo), where many of the Italian heavy cruisers, submarines, and other auxiliary ships rested. Hundreds of shells hit it, and it also was afire by the time the Allies left the area.

Some of the Italian naval defenses fired back, especially the ones on the fixed land defenses, but their counterfire was scattered, and they didn't have the range. The command structure was shattered in the first minute of the attack, and they acted without orders. In the end, their actions were uncoordinated and without any significant results.

When all was said and done, the Regina Marina was completely gutted and shattered. Battleships Guilio Cesare, Conte Di Cavour, and Andrea Doria were completely destroyed. They were sunk in shallow waters, indicating a possible salvage operation, but nothing was certain at that point. The other three dreadnoughts were all crippled and didn't even manage to send one counter-battery salvo. It was fortunate for the Italians that they were moored in docks for some repair and maintenance work as they rested in the shallow waters. The pre-dreadnought battleships were also hit very hard. Elena, Napoli and Roma exploded under the rain of shells as their decks and old armor designs could not withstand the power unleashed on them. The Brin and Margherita were also sunk but to a shallow bottom, thus potentially salvageable. For their part, the last three (Venice, Saint Bon, and Filiberto) were crippled and were out of the fight.

Additionally, twelve cruisers, eighteen destroyers, twelve submarines, and ten torpedo boats were sunk. The rest of the ships were damaged to various degrees, and not one Italian vessel escaped the battle unscathed. The harbor itself was shattered as the Anglo-French shelling continued through the night.

Casualties were enormous, as most Italian sailors had been on leave or in unprotected areas. Admiral Amedeo di Savoia-Aosta was dead, along with most of the Naval staff, as the HQ was destroyed in the first few minutes of the battle. Over five thousand civilians were killed, and over twice that number were injured. Military casualties numbered close to seven thousand.

It was a disaster of epic proportions, one that removed the Italian Navy from play. But at the same time, it pushed Italy into the war, and there would be hell to pay for the Entente as the Italians would soon scream for revenge.

Rome, Berlin, Gibraltar
The next day, November 10th, 1914

(...) Rome (...)

Italian Prime Minister Antonio Salandra was sound asleep and having pleasant dreams when one of his aides came knocking on the door in the middle of the night. *"Sir,"* said the insistent voice. *"I am very sorry I have to wake you up, but something truly appalling has happened,"* continued the obviously frantic and worried voice on the other side of the door. Salandra was still sort of groggy because he'd been in a deep slumber; he stirred out of bed while his wife beside him grumbled. *"Antonio, can't this wait for the morning,"* she said. *"Go back to sleep, dear,"* he answered as he put something on to make sure he was decent.

He opened the door to a very worried and bewildered aide. It was obvious the man had also been woken up in a hurry. *"What is it that can't wait for the morning?" "Sir, there has been an attack on Taranto. It's truly bad, sir."* Then, the Italian Prime Minister went from somewhat awake to fully woken up." *"...What the hell,"* he stammered back. *"Sir, we don't know who's attacking yet, but it's a very powerful attack; the fleet and the city are on fire!"*

"Get me the Minister of the Navy and General Cardona as soon as possible; we need to meet. Also, get the Foreign Affairs Minister; we have to see if someone has declared war on us." "They are all on their way, Prime Minister." "Good," answered Salandra as he, for the first time, wondered if it had been a good idea to declare for the Central Powers. He had a pretty good idea who was attacking, and this wasn't good. It wasn't good at all.

(...) Gibraltar, Wellington Front, right bastion (...)

Wellington Front, named after the late hero of the Napoleonic Wars and First Duke of Wellington, was built in the mid-1800s to replace the old, crumbling Moorish and Spanish walled harbor defenses. It was one of the line walls protecting the Gibraltar waterfront, bristling with heavy guns, casemates, and bunkers.

Since the start of the war, it was also the headquarters for the Gibraltar Defense Force. It was thus naturally where Winston Churchill, the First Lord of the Admiralty, resided as he awaited the news of Operation Ares.

Contrary to the Italian Prime Minister, Churchill was fully awake and in the meeting room with the naval and army commanders on site. They were huddled around a radio set. Wireless radio was still in its primitive infancy in 1914, having been invented in 1913. Telegraph, signal flags, and signal lights were still prevalent in the Royal Navy. But, for this operation, the British had installed a full radio set on Marlborough to make sure news of success or failure could be spread rapidly. Messages were still short and not very detailed, but they didn't need much. They just needed to know if the operation was a success or not.

It was finally midnight, and the following minutes were agonizing to the assembled men in the room. Then, finally, at 12h12, the radio crackled to life. *"Operation Ares a success. Surprise complete. Landing will commence in a few hours."*

The entire room burst into happy cheers and congratulations. While this was all good and well, the First Lord of the Admiralty should have known that this attack would trigger a reaction from a very powerful fleet in the north.

(...) Berlin, joint meeting of the OHL (Heer) and the OKM (Kaiserliche Marine), November 10th, 1914 (...)

A heavy silence hung over the room as the assembled men were a little stunned by the terrible news coming out of Italy. They met at the Imperial Palace in Berlin. Meetings between the Army and the Navy, and the political apparatus of Germany were quite rare, but in this specific case, it was needed because of the terrible Anglo-French dastardly attack on Taranto, the home of the Italian Fleet.

Present at the meeting was the Minister of the Navy, Admiral Alfred von Tirpitz, along with Admiral Hugo von Pohl, the chief of the Admiralty staff and commander of the High Seas Fleet. Also sitting down in the large conference room were the representative of the Army, Chief of the General Staff Helmut von Moltke the Younger and his two usual acolytes, Lieutenant Colonel Richard Hentch (the head of the information division) and chiefs of the Operations Division, Colonel Gerhard Tappen. Politics were represented by German Chancellor Theobald von Bethmann Hollweg, Erich von Falkenkayn (Minister of War), and, of course, the most important of them all, Kaiser Wilhelm II.

They had just heard the details of the damage done during the night on the Italian Fleet by the information division commander, Hentch. *"This is truly appalling,"* started the Kaiser in a wavering tone. He was mad and shocked at the same time. *"Chancellor, had the Italians received any declaration of war?"* Hollweg spoke up. *"Yes, Your Excellency, the German Ambassador to Italy has delivered a note this morning to Prime Minister Salandra." "But.. That is after the attack..."* continued Wilhelm, taken aback by the entire thing. The Italian entry on the site of the Central Powers had been supposed to be a great moment, not... this. *"I know, my Emperor,"* answered the chancellor, powerless to do anything about it.

Von Moltke, more interested in the operational meaning of the entire affair, intervened. *"Lieutenant Colonel Hentch, do you have any information on Italian mobilization or dispositions following this attack? And Colonel von Tappen, can we find any available unit to send to Italy for help?"*

Hentch was the first to speak up. *"As far as my information goes, the Italians were slowly mobilizing in order to avoid alarming the Entente* of its intentions. At this time, the Italian Army was pretty much positioned in the north in anticipation of an offensive against Southern France. There are no major units in the vicinity of Taranto apart from the harbor garrison and the militias in the area." Von Tappen followed suit. "Sir, we can certainly find a couple of divisions and also ask the Austro-Hungarians to get a couple railed quickly to Southern Italy."

Von Moltke sighed heavily. "Well, we'd better since, according to my sources, the enemy has begun its landings in Taranto. We need to nip this in the bud before it goes too far and knocks our newfound allies out of the war."

"Everyone here is missing the real point," said Alfred von Tirpitz. The man was not only the head of the powerful Navy Ministry, but he was also the father of the modern German Navy and thus carried a lot of weight with the Kaiser. Furthermore, he was a very well-respected figure in German leadership circles. "What do you mean, Admiral Tirpitz," said the Kaiser in a tone that was full of hope. "Your Majesty, if this attack has been carried out as it seems to be and with the amount of power it has slammed down on Taranto, I would surmise that the British have sent significant reinforcements to the Mediterranean theater. Although I cannot blame them for this since they could have hardly been excited at the prospect of having Italy join up with the Austro-Hungarian fleet, this represents a major opportunity for us." The Admiral in command of the High Seas Fleet, Hugo von Pohl, stirred expectantly in his seat. The two navy men had already spoken about this. Tirpitz continued since no one spoke up, awaiting what he had to say.

"We now have the French harbors, and as I understand it," he gave a look to Hentch, "they are mostly repaired and ready to receive our ships. I say we sail out of Wilhelmshaven and try to break through the Channel into the Atlantic. If we can position our High Seas Fleet at Brest or any of the Channel ports, we will be in a powerful position to first break the enemy blockade and also seriously threaten the British supply lines." He paused, slamming his fist on the table. "I say we launch now and surprise the Allies. If we are lucky, the bastards have transferred most of the French fleet to the Med, along with a plethora of British battleships that should have stayed in the North Sea to watch for us. Hell, if I were them, this is what I would have done as I contemplated an attack on the Italians in their Taranto stronghold. There is every possibility they transferred major forces in the Med."

From the smile the Kaiser gave Tirpitz, it was obvious to the old navy man that his master liked the idea. Von Pohl was already won over, and then the Army couldn't care less what the Navy did, as long as they didn't impede their own actions. Within ten minutes, the idea was approved, and everything was set in place to implement it the very next day. After all, the German fleet was already ready to sail at a moment's notice to intercept British fleets roaming too close to Germany.

The stage was set for one of the greatest naval battles of the First World War and also one of the most harrowing German operations of the war to date.

Landing and fighting part 1
The 14th French Division attacks Castle Aragonese, November 10th, 1914

The platoon that Philippe Cren and Armand Bonnier were part of (14th French division) was well on its way toward the burning Italian city of Taranto. As they rowed on their small wooden cutter boats, both men thought of the battle to come and what had made them come to this hellish place. Beside them rowed hundreds of other cutters, all going toward the shore to give battle. The sound of battle was overwhelming, dotted with small arms fire and powerful artillery blasts. In the distance, they also heard the rumble of the battleships firing away at the harbor. Once in a while, one bigger-than-usual explosion catapulted fire and what looked like debris (it was hard to say it was still dark), as they would almost be blinded by the constant flashes.

First had come the order to embark on a train and rail to Bordeaux, where the entire division had been picked up by a large fleet of transports escorted by over ten battleships coming down from Great Britain and the two French battleships Courbet and Paris. The trench warfare they'd been involved in had been a slug of mud (it was the fall in the French countryside), death, and boredom, as the Germans had stopped charging their lines while they had done the same.

Following their ride across France to Bordeaux harbor, they embarked on ships and sailed to Gibraltar, where they stayed for a week. They remembered that period of time quite fondly, as they'd been mostly free to roam the island awaiting final embarkation to their unknown destination. They thus were able to visit the entire island and were particularly impressed by St-Michael's cave, rumored to go deep underground and with angels living in it. They had also had run-ins with the famous Gibraltar rock monkeys, but nothing serious.

Finally, the order to get in the transport ships was given, and off they went. It was only at that moment that they learned of their destination, the major Italian harbor of Taranto. They hadn't understood then since the Italians were neutral, but one of their more educated officers explained that the bastards were about (apparently) to join the Central Powers; hence, the decision had been taken to outsmart them and attack first. That had done it both for Armand and Philippe.

Their divisional objective was the so-called Castle Aragonese, a 16th-century castle built on Greek, Roman, Byzantine, and medieval ruins at the entrance of the harbor. The castle was thus reinforced and built upon old following the storming of Taranto by the Ottoman Empire in 1480, clearly showing that its old and thin walls could not withstand more modern gun shells. But by the standards of 1914, it was once more obsolete. Of course, the Italians had garrisoned it and also placed machine guns and several modern naval guns on its walls, but from Armand's point of view, the entire structure was now gutted and dotted with several fiercely burning fires. Furthermore, the front façade of the castle was crumpled down into the sea, creating a large opening into the stone building that the 14th Division's officers clearly intended to use to attack Castle Aragonese.

The cutter bobbed high and low on the waves as the water around them shone bright with the light of the major fire embracing Taranto. Bullets whizzed about and pierced the water around them while heavier caliber shells seemed to blaze above. Other cutters were hit by bullets, and men died, but Armand's boat was unscathed. Looking up, he saw the arcing lights of the Anglo-French fleet going high. He followed their trajectory to the city and harbor, where they exploded, joining into the fire maelstrom, continuously feeding it into an incredible frenzy.

As the boat slammed on the broken rocks below the fallen-down wall and they were rocked forward, small-arms fire swept the British soldiers, many being cut down in bloody gore by the Italian defenders, amazingly still alive after the powerful bombardment. Some of the men jumped from too far from their boats to the shore and sank immediately, burdened by the weight of their equipment. Armand lifted himself up from the unstable cutter and jumped on the pile of crumpled rock. He lost his balance and had to put a knee down to steady himself. That saved his life as a spray of bullets see-sawed just above his head and killed a bunch of his comrades. The men fell in multiple sprays of blood, and he looked worriedly around to see if Philippe was hurt. About a meter to his left, his friend had also fallen, but on his butt, thus he was also alive and well, even if he tumbled back into the water by the cutter boat. *"Quick, Philippe, we need to get up this shit pile!"* And up they went, the rubble-strewn ground sliding beneath their feet. The crumbled wall might have been an opening into the Castle Aragonese; it was hardly a ramp or an easy way in.

The first few minutes were frantic and desperate. British soldiers died in droves, but they were so numerous that their numbers eventually began to tell, and they landed in force. From there on, it was the time for the Italians to die.

(...) Minutes later (...)

"Chaaarrrggge!" yelled Philippe, the now de-facto leader of the small group following the last NCO's death. They all started running toward the bend in the tunnel. They were somewhere inside the Castle Aragonese, but he couldn't tell where, as they were deep inside the structure. There was no time to check the result of their firing and the dead or gravely injured enemies. The tunnel turned to the left for several meters, and it gave way to a large opening where guns protruded to the outside since Armand could see the flashes of explosion dotting the darkness. A few more Italian defenders waited and fired as the rest fled, but they were too few. They hit four French soldiers but then got overwhelmed. They were quickly dispatched with knives, bayonets, and point-blank firing.

Philippe saw the back of an enemy running down the rubble-strewn gallery. It was sloping downward. *"Quick, guys,"* he gestured. *"Follow *the bastards."* Their small group started running in pursuit of the fleeing enemies.

Sometime later, the way was angling down even more as they advanced. *"Look, Bonnier,"* said Cren. *"There is some light over there."* Above them, the battle raged as the castle continuously rumbled with explosions and dust billowing around. The castle was being shaken hard by artillery blasts and it was obvious soldiers fought hard on the other levels as well. They arrived at a large room, what seemed to have been some large room for storage at some time in the past.

And then, shots were fired by the Italians. Several of them had piled up large wooden crates and everything they could find to block the path. Then Armand, Philippe, and the rest of the French attackers bent down reflexively. More shots were fired, answered by Armand and the others. *"Does someone have a grenade?"* said one of the men in the group. One of them did and threw it without adding anything else to the piled-up crates in the large room.

The grenade hit the ground and lodged itself between two loose planks of the makeshift barricade. A moment later, it exploded, the concussion sending the Frenchmen back on their arses. Such an explosion in a confined rock-walled space created a powerful blast wave; hence, no one who had been standing could remain upright.

When they came back to their senses with ears ringing (a few seconds later), the barricade was gone or at least was clouded in a large cloud of dark smoke and billowing dust. Luckily for them, no enemies came through the opening to fire again.

They moved in, bayonets at the ready, and advanced into the smoke. Armand's eyes stung, and he was worried the enemy would fire blindly into the midst, but nothing happened. There was one injured Italian soldier on the ground. Philippe crouched and pulled out his knife to slit the poor sod's throat. Armand put a hand on his shoulder to gesture him not to do it. Cren didn't like to give any quarter to his enemies. His friend gave him a hard look, but he then shrugged his shoulders and left the Italian alone. The man was injured in the stomach, having been pierced by a big shard of wood after the explosion. He gurgled blood from his mouth and soon died. *"You see, Phil, no need to be a killer; he was already dying."*

They were about to move further in when a powerful detonation reverberated across the stone corridor. It was so strong that some of them even fell to the ground, and more dust and debris fell from the walls and ceiling. Then, a wave of dust and smoke burst forth from the corridor they faced, going down from the room they were in.

"The bastards have blown the gallery to stop us from advancing further," said one of the men. They didn't have to go far to confirm what they all thought. The Italians had blown up the corridor they were in to stop them from advancing. Then another explosion was heard, and another. Soon, three more followed. It was the enemy walling them in and stopping them from finding any way inside the fortress.

After a few hours of searching and looking around, they all concluded that there was no more way in for them. Without any officers to give them orders, they decided that it was just as well. They'd done their duty. They had a way out anyway if they walked back to the spot they'd entered. Without any officers or NCO to give them orders, they decided to settle back into one of the tunnels, shared cigarettes, and slept, only bothered by the shaking and the grumbling sound of the siege artillery relentlessly pounding the Castle Aragonese. They knew it wouldn't last, as they'd sent a man back to the cutters to fetch someone who could make decisions, but for that precious moment, they were safe and sound.

Breakout and Pursuit
November 11th, 1914

(...) The German fleet sails, Wilhelmshaven (...)

One of the largest assembled fleets in history was sliding out of Wilhelmshaven under the eyes of German Kaiser Wilhelm II. The man looked at the magnificent scene with a heavy heart, as the fleet was dear to him. It was his creation. Right beside him, Alfred von Tirpitz, the Minister of Marine and the architect of the great fleet, sighed in anticipation. "There goes nothing, your Majesty. The moment for which we have built this great instrument of war is upon us."

"Well, my dear Tirpitz, I hope you are right, for this fleet has cost me a lot of money, and I would hate to lose it. It represents the pinnacle of German power in the world," answered the Kaiser with a long face as he watched the first batch of ships exit the harbor. It was the 1st German battlecruiser squadron under Admiral Frantz von Hipper. The man's job was to clear the way for the fleets that would follow. The two magnificent battlecruisers leading the charge, Seydlitz (the Admiral's flagship) and Von der Tann, gushed dark smoke as their funnels and engines burned the coal inside their big engine room furnaces.

German 1st battlecruiser squadron, Admiral Franz von Hipper		
BC Seydlitz,	CL Strassburg	CL Stralsund
BC Von Der Tann	CL Graudenz	
CA SMS Blüche	CL Kolberg	

"I understand your misgivings, my Emperor. But what is the use of a battle fleet if we keep it in the harbor apart from a threat in the making? We can now make good on the British and the French and sail right into the Atlantic, base our ships where we can hurt them badly, for a change." *"I know, my dear Admiral, I know. I just can't help the fact that I worry about my fleet and I don't want to lose it. These*

ships were built with a lot of work, great sums of money, and superb German engineering. I would hate to see them sent to the bottom."

The High Sea Fleet, Admiral Hugo von Pohl		
1st Battle Squadron, 1st Division (Vice-Admiral Wilhelm von Lans)		
BB Ostfriesland (Flagship)	BB Oldenburg	4 CA
BB Helgoland	BB Thüringen	5 DD
1st Battle Squadron, 2nd Division (Rear-Admiral Friedrich Gädecke)		
BB Posen (Flagship)	BB Rheinland	4 CA
BB Nassau	BB Westfalen	5 DD
2nd Battle Squadron, 3rd Division (Vice-Admiral Reinhard Scheer)		
Pre-Dread BB Preussen (Flagship)	Pre-dread BB Hessen	3 CA
Pre-dread BB Deutschland	Pre-dread BB Lothringen	4 DD
2nd Battle Squadron, 4th Division (Kommodore Franz Mauve)		
Pre-dread BB Hannover (Flagship)	Pre-dread BB Schlesien	4 CA
Pre-dread BB Dantzig	Pre-dread BB Prussia	4 DD
3rd Battle Squadron, 5th Division (Rear-Admiral Felix Funke)		
BB Grosser Kurfürst	BB König	4 CL
BB Markgraf	BB Kronprinz	4 DD
3rd Battle Squadron, 6th Division (Rear-Admiral Carl Schaumann)		
BB Prinzregent Luitpold (Flagship)	BB Sharnhorst	4 CL
BB Kaiser	BB König Albert	4 DD

Just behind the battlecruisers and the escorting light cruisers followed, lost in the morning mist, the High Seas Fleet. Its ships also gushed dark smoke as they raised their steam up to sail into the horizon and to follow von Hipper's squadron. It was a magnificent show of naval sea power, with no less than sixteen superb and pristine new dreadnought battleships closely followed by eight pre-dreadnought battleships.

Then, right behind that was also starting to move the German Battle Squadron, the second part of the High Seas Fleet, with fourteen additional German pre-dreadnought battleships under the command of Rear Admiral Reinhard Sheer.

In total, Germany was sailing out of Wilhelmshaven with a staggering total of thirty-eight battleships, ranging from old (built at the turn of the century) to right off the drydocks (1914). This superb show of firepower was flanked by no less than a hundred escort vessels, from heavy and armored cruisers to destroyers and minelayers, to try and fend off the unavoidable British and French mines surely to await them in the Channel.

Battle squadron Rear Admiral Reinhard Scheer		
4th Battle Squadron, 7th Division (Vice-Admiral Ehrhard Schmidt)		
Pre-Dread BB Wittelsbach (Flagship)	Pre-Dread BB Schwaben	2 CL
Pre-Dread BB Mecklenburg	Pre-Dread BB Wettin	2 DD
5th Battle Squadron, 8th Division (Rear-Admiral Hermann Alberts)		
Pre-Dread BB Braunschweig (Flags)	Pre-Dread BB Zähringen	1 CL
Pre-Dread BB Elsass	1 CA	
5th Battle Squadron, 9th Division (Vice-Admiral Max von Grapow)		
Pre-Dread BB Kaiser Wilhelm II (Fla)	Pre-Dread BB Kaiser Wilhelm der Grosse	3 DD
Pre-Dread BB Kaiser Barbarossa	1 CA	
5th Battle Squadron, 10th Division ((Kommodore Alfred Begas)		
Pre-Dread BB Brandenburg	Pre-Dread BB Kaiser Karl der Grosse	3 CL
Pre-Dread BB Kaiser Friedrich III (Fl)	Pre-Dread BB Wörth	3 DD

"Let's hope we are making the right play, Admiral," added the Kaiser. *"Your excellency, from what I have been able to gather with the Italians so far, the British have heavily gambled on this one. They have at least six or seven dreadnoughts and another six pre-dreadnought battleships that should have been in the North Sea to face us. For the first time since we have envisioned our fleet, my Emperor, we have a shot at defeating the Royal Navy. For the coming battle, well, if the Brits come to it, we'll have the same number of dreadnoughts. They will have more of the pre-dreadnought battleships, but as you know, it might not matter if our ships perform as we hope they will."*

(...) Scapa Flow (...)

"It's confirmed, sir," said the communication officer of the bridge of the battleship Iron Duke, the flagship of the Royal Navy's Grand Fleet. Admiral of the Fleet John Rushworth Jellicoe, 1st Earl Jellicoe, was the commander of the most powerful naval force in the entire world. Although recently weakened (something he had been adamantly against doing) for Operation Ares, it still sported seventeen dreadnought battleships-battlecruisers and over thirty-five pre-dreadnought battleships. It was also supported by well over two

hundred cruisers, light cruisers, destroyers, and other light ships. Its mission was to guard the British Home Islands and the sea lanes against Central Powers depredation. *"Submarine HMS E1 has just reported in that it spotted what looks like the entire German fleet has sailed out of Wilhelmshaven."*

THE GRAND FLEET (BRITISH HOME WATERS)		
1st Battle Squadron		
BB Iron Duke	BB Colossus	BB Vanguard
BB St. Vincent	BB Hercules	CL Bellona
BB Collingwood	BB Neptune	5 DD
2nd Battle Squadron		
BB King George V	BB Monarch	Cl Boadicea
BB Centurion	BB Thunderer	5 DD
BB Audacious	BB Orion	
3rd and 4th Battle Squadron (combined)		
Pre-dread BB King Edward VII	Pre-dread BB Dominion, heavy mortar damage repair Southampton Jan 1915	Pre-dread BB Commonwealth
Pre-dread BB Africa	Pre-dread BB Hindustan, heavy mortar damage repair Southampton Jan 1915	CL Blanche
Pre-dread BB Britannia	Pre-dread BB New Zealand	5 DD
BB Bellopheron	BB Temeraire	CL Blonde
5th Battle Squadron		
Pre-dread BB Agamemnon	Pre-dread BB Venerable	Pre-dread BB Implacable
Pre-dread BB Prince of Wales	Pre-dread BB Queen	CL Topaze
Pre-dread BB Bulwark	Pre-dread BB Formidable	5 DD
Pre-dread BB London	Pre-dread BB Irresistible	
7th Battle Squadron		
Pre-dread BB Prince George	Pre-dread BB Jupiter	CL Sapphire
Pre-dread BB Caesar	Pre-dread BB Majestic	
8th Battle Squadron		
Pre-dread BB Albion	Pre-dread BB Vengeance	CL Proserpine
Pre-dread BB Canopus	Pre-dread BB Goliath	5 DD
Pre-dread BB Glory	Pre-dread BB Ocean	
9th Battle Squadron		
Pre-dread BB Hannibal	Pre-dread BB Mars	Pre-dread BB Magnificent
Pre-dread BB Illustrious	Pre-dread BB Victorious	
1st and 2nd Battlecruiser Squadron (combined)		
BC Lion	BC Princess Royal	13 CA
BC New Zealand	BC Invincible	10 DD
Channel Fleet		
Pre Dread BB Lord Nelson	4 CA	3 CL
		7 DD
Cruiser Force C (Seventh Cruiser Squadron)		
Euryalus (Rear-Admiral Christian)	Southampton (Commodore Goodenough)	
CA Bacchante	CL Birmingham	CA Aboukir
CA Cressy	CL Falmouth	CA Amethyst
CA Hogue	CL Nottingham	
CL Liverpool	CL Lowestoft	
Destroyer flotilla (combined)		
45 DD	32 DD	

Jellicoe answered his communication officer with a face. The fleet was ready to sail at a moment's notice because he'd expected the Germans to try and break out of the North Sea the moment they realized just how many heavy units the Entente had sent to the Taranto attack. Jellicoe wondered what Churchill now thought since the man had once said that he (Jellicoe) was the only man in the world who could lose the war in one day. The First Lord of the Admiralty referred to the possibility of a major naval defeat at the hands of the Germans. Admiral Jellicoe now wondered if Churchill thought the same thing, now that the Germans were out and he didn't have any superiority in dreadnoughts but a rough parity.

But Jellicoe was made of the same vein as the great admirals of the past and harbored the same aggressive spirit that men like Lord Nelson had displayed in the Napoleonic Wars. It didn't matter to him if he didn't have overwhelming superiority anymore. He would race to battle.

"Very well, Vice Admiral. Order all ships to raise steam and for the ones already at sea to link up with the grand fleet near our pre-determined coordinates for this scenario. All ships are to go at best speed." "Yes, Admiral." The British Royal Navy had several operational contingency plans for when and if the German High Seas Fleet tried to sortie. All these plans involved some way of combining its overwhelming forces into one gigantic fleet. In the case of the Germans trying to cross the Channel, they were to rendezvous off the coast of Southern England, ten miles off the small city of Margate. Once assembled, they were then to proceed to the Channel and give battle to the Germans.

A titanic clash was in the works.

(...) Gibraltar and London (...)

Down south in Gibraltar, First Lord of the Admiralty Winston Churchill was sipping his morning tea when the news was relayed to him the German High Seas Fleet was on the move. "So soon," was the only thing he said. While the attack on Taranto was going well and the Italian Fleet was already mostly gone, he'd dreaded a fast reaction from the Germans. And there it was. A cold chill ran down his spine, thinking of the fact that Jellicoe would now have to fight the bastards with roughly equal force, rendering the outcome of the fight a lot more random.

Prime Minister Herbert Henry Asquith was also busy with his morning tea when the dreadful news broke out that the Germans were on the loose and in force in the North Sea. A special meeting of the War Cabinet was called at 10 am, and the King attended. Everyone in England held their breath, and soon, the news of the impending battle spread like wildfire all across the British Isles. Every Englishman then wondered what the future would hold for their country and prayed to God for a victory.

113th Royal Field Artillery, 25th RFA Brigade
Somewhere south of Taranto, November 11th, 1914

"Be careful, you dimwit," said Lance Bombardier Stimms, as one of the men manhandling the gun did a false move, breaking one of the steel bars supposed to hold the gun, almost dropping it into the sea. The 18-pounder was rolling on the precarious harbor planking and threatened to fall into the churning sea below.

The 113th battery of the 25th Brigade's RFA was trying to land its gun to position itself to be able to support the advancing troops across the city of Taranto. A day after the initial landings, most of the harbor area and half the city were now under Anglo-French control, but Italian resistance was stiffening. They were opposite the now-destroyed Castle Aragonese and moving to an area where some of the infantry units got busy clearing a path through the rubble and enough space for the guns to unlimber.

While the landings had been met with success, it was obvious the enemy forces would soon be strong enough to counter-attack and that artillery would be needed. A few hundred feet down, where Archibald Tottenkam toiled hard to get his weapon across the planking, two more transport ships were busy disgorging French 75mm field cannons.

About a thousand yards toward the inside of the city. Archie could see the battle was raging between the Entente and the Italians. News from there was good, and it seemed that the Anglo-French had more troops in the area and were thus continuously advancing.

When the gun was finally rolled onto the dock, they were directed to their horses, already landed, and a traffic sergeant sent them to their assigned sector about seventy yards further down into the city, in a small-town square. An hour later, they finally unlimbered the gun into their assigned firing position. By mid-afternoon, they were at last ready to fire their first shells.

"*Fire,*" ordered Lance-Bombardier Stimms. And the gunner pulled the cord, and the gun blasted away, recoiling backward in a cloud of billowing smoke. "*Reload,*" continued Stimms. Archibald knew this was going to be a long day, as the frontline battle was apparently stiffening, and the Italians were pouring a lot of reinforcements.

The Dover Barrage
Minefield, November 11th, 1914

"Sir, the minesweepers in front report that this is a very heavy minefield," said the flag officer to the commander of the German 1st Battlecruiser Squadron, Admiral von Hipper. The Admiral watched over the plot and saw that they were near Dover. He reflected that he would have done the same if he had been in the British shoes. He wondered how deep this minefield was.

As if the mines themselves wanted to give the German commander confirmation or an answer, a powerful explosion rocked the heavy cruiser Blucher, positioned on the Seydlitz's port side. A powerful fireball expanded across the ship's hull, and a high column of water catapulted into the air. A few seconds later, light cruiser Stralsund and Gaudenz were also hit by mines. Gaudenz listed heavily to starboard, while Stralsund's engine room was on fire and flooding. The was not an auspicious start. *"Order all ships to stop and get the destroyers and minesweepers in front. We need to clear this minefield for the main fleet. "Also, send a radio signal to Admiral von Pohl to slow down; we don't want his precious dreadnoughts hit by mines." "Yes, Sir."*

The Dover Barrage was laid deep at over eighteen miles, with mines placed at regular intervals. Underwater cables and other mines were also laid to stop German submarines from crossing into the Channel. The Barrage was by no means impenetrable as the British did not have enough mines to block such a large area, but it was big enough to act as a major deterrent to any major fleet wanting to sail by. The idea was to get the German fleets to slow down long enough for the Grand Fleet to sail down from Scapa Flow at full speed and intercept them, hopefully engaging in the naval battle to sink the High Seas Fleet and end the German naval threat once and for all.

Fleet Admiral Hugo von Pohl thus had to slow down his ships and hovered near Calais, outside of what the Germans figured was the extent of the large British minefield, while the minelayers and destroyers of the Battlecruiser Squadron cleared a path through it. Imperial naval intelligence figured that the British would take at least a day and a half to muster their ships and come down to give battle, and thus, Pohl figured he would have a lot of time to pass before the Grand Fleet arrived.

As it happened, he didn't have that much time since British Admiral Jellicoe was already only half a day away.

Somewhere north of Versailles
German frontline, 2nd Army, 4th Division, November 11th 1914

"Hey, you recruit," said Oskar to one of the new soldiers gallivanting above the sandbags on the trench. "You shouldn't stick your head out..." His words were cut mid-sentence by that same young (and stupid) soldier's head exploding like a ripe melon. The next words he wanted to say died in his open mouth as he watched one more new guy getting his head blown off by an enemy sniper.

The freaking French had some hotshot shooter in the area, and the bastard had already claimed over twenty kills. He wondered what would be done about the guy. They needed their own sniper to counter the man.

Oskar stirred from his makeshift seat (he had been sitting on a pile of sandbags fallen from the back wall of the trench, and shook his boots, trying to remove the mud from them. It had rained again last night, and the entire trench was now a quagmire and a water puddle. The entire area stank of unwashed men, piss, and dead corpses. Not that he minded anymore. He was used to the terrible smell and dismal living conditions. He'd heard through the grapevine that some of the German Imperial Engineers were doing wonders north of their position and building real accommodation in the trenches, like below-the-earth bunker systems with sleeping cots and other more humane facilities, like kitchens and spots to rest.

But the worst was the enemy artillery, just like the German artillery for the Allies. It pounded the trenches relentlessly (more often than not at night) and impeded everyone from sleeping. Oskar, like the others, had also gotten used to catching sleep whenever possible and longed for the day they would be sent on leave in the rear. Then, he figured he would sleep for two days straight without pause.

At least they weren't attacking anymore, Army High Command having sent a ton of reinforcements to the East, making any attacks in the

West futile and forcing German to go on the defensive. He was completely fine with that, as this meant he would not be exposed to the direct machine gun fire and the withering shrapnel and artillery once they got over the protected area of the trench.

Two medics walked by to see if the poor lad who had just been shot could be saved, but seeing that he was missing a head, they just shrugged their shoulders and put him up on a stretcher for burial in the rear.

Oskar decided to try and forget that it happened, and lit himself a cigarette. He had picked up the habit since he started fighting, and he found it soothing. Some said it was bad for health and also gave bad lungs, but he didn't care. He could die in the next minute anyway if a shell landed in the trench where he was, or else the damned officers could order an attack. OR even worse, he could be facing yet another French offensive. The enemy was quiet, but you never knew with the Frenchies. They were unpredictable, and their British allies were super aggressive.

The Naval battle of Cape Griz Nez, Part 1
November 11th, 1914

As the German minesweepers busied themselves into clearing a safe channel for the German High Seas Fleet through the Dover Barrage, the British Grand Fleet barreled down from Scapa Flow and made good time to the Dover Strait, where the Germans hovered a little too long.

By 12:46 in the early afternoon, the first British ships were sighted by Kaiserliche Marine destroyer S139, acting as a screen and early-warning detection picket line north of the High Seas Fleet. The ship was shelled by British battlecruiser Lion, Admiral Beatty's (now commander of the Combined Mediterranean Fleet shelling Taranto) former flagship. The big ship's double salvos bracketed the big destroyer, also called *"large torpedo boat"* by the official German classification. Miraculously unscathed and continuously dodging, it turned south and made top speed to rejoin the fleet and warn Pohl (by signal flags since it didn't have a wireless radio) of the impending disaster. For there was no mistake about it. The German ships wanted to avoid a direct confrontation with the Royal Navy's superior numbers.

Seeing that he was now discovered and that he was probably near the main body of the enemy fleet, Admiral Jellicoe ordered his vessels to assume battle formation and to spread to get ready for battle. He then sent a radio message to London that he was engaging the enemy.

About twenty minutes later, the news of the sudden appearance of the British Grand Fleet right on his doorstep sent a cold chill down Pohl's spine. It wasn't that the man was afraid of battle, he just knew that the challenge for which Germany had been preparing herself for the last fifteen years was at hand.

He was faced with one of two decisions. Spread his ships and order his battleline to ready itself to receive the Royal Navy, or double down on the previous gameplan (follow his sets of orders) and sail his ships through the Dover Barrage even if the way wasn't clear, thus risking that some of his precious warships could hit mines.

"Admiral," said his chief of staff, right beside him on battleship Ostfriesland, the flagship of the fleet. *"Orders, sir,"* continued Vice-Admiral Henning von Holtzendorff, an old but willy naval commander who had come out of retirement as war was declared.

Pohl lifted his hand in annoyance and to stall his right-hand man. *"A moment, Vice Admiral,"* he answered finally. He wondered if the British had sailed with their entire fleet. If they had, then the best play was to slice through the mines and try to avoid full battle. If not, then he had the entirety of the High Seas Fleet with him; thus, he would be in a position to destroy the English ships, significantly changing the course of the war. German intelligence (the Information Division under the command of Lieutenant Colonel Richard Hentsch) had estimated the British had sent at least six to seven dreadnought battleships and or battlecruisers in the Mediterranean for its ongoing Italian Operation.

Either way, he had options. *"Vice Admiral von Holtzendorff, what is your opinion,"* he finally said. It was never bad to have someone to brainstorm with. *"Well, sir, I know what you are thinking, and I believe the right play is to continue with our mission to rebase in Brest. Regardless of whether we can give battle and win (or lose), the idea is to spread the Royal Navy with our forces based in Atlantic ports so we can raid their supply lines."* He paused, crossing his arms behind his back. Holtzendorff was an old man with a long beard, but Pohl valued his opinion. Furthermore, he was in favor with the Emperor; thus, it was never bad to heed his advice. And then he took his decision.

(...) An hour later (...)

The German High Seas Fleet engaged at full speed into the Dover Barrage, and soon explosions were reported, while the first salvos started to be fired because the British were in range. Dreadnought battleship Helgoland slammed on a mine, and a powerful blast opened its hull to water, greatly reducing its speed. Battleship Nassau was also soon hit by a mine in its midsection, causing a large fire in the engine room and greatly reducing its speed. Then, in quick succession, the following ships were hit as well, while the German sped through the minefield like there was nothing there: pre-dreadnought Mecklenburg (Stern damage), Kaiser Barbarossa (aft magazine, crew quarters) and Brandenburg (waterline and armor belt), and five cruisers were also damaged seriously. Seven torpedo boat-destroyers were also completely destroyed as they opened the way (under orders) for the big battleships.

All the while, the gunnery exchange was in full swing. Jellicoe's fleet arrived on the scene and opened up with all guns blazing on the fleeing Germans, who also responded with all they had. Soon, more ships started to burst afire, and sailors died. Because of its superior numbers, the Royal Navy rapidly took advantage, and the German fleet started to buckle under the heaviest gunnery demonstration in history. Over fifty battleships rained down fire on them while they responded with about thirty-five on their side.

The battle was then in full swing half an hour later, just offshore Cape Griz Nez. The spot was the closest to Southern England and, where the German minesweeper and destroyers had concentrated their work and where the German battleline snaked its way across. All the while, the decks of the German ships were burning, and they fired their guns as if their survival depended on it.

The returning German fire was able to hit some British ships as well, killing a heavy cruiser and damage on the following ships: BB Centurion, stern, forecastle damage, BB Audacious, got smashed on the #1 turret (destroyed), pre-dreadnought Africa was sunk because of a hit on the main magazine that blew off, pre-dreadnought BB Agamemnon, received heavy water line damage and gutted deck, following two armor-piercing shells hits. Finally, the pre-dreadnought

BB Bulkwark had its engine room burst on fire following a hit in one of its main funnels.

The Grand Fleet also gave a lot of damage back to its enemies, with some of their shells even igniting some mines, compounding further damage to the Germans. Pre-dreadnought BB Lothringen was hit and received heavy rudder, stern, and with #2 main turret damage. Pre-dreadnought BB Rheinland was hit (critically) on the bridge (and its captain was killed) and also received boiler damage. Two heavy cruisers were sunk with multiple hits, and seven destroyers were sunk. The pre-dreadnought BB Schwaben was unlucky enough to hit a mine; at the same time, a shell slammed on the waterline, gutting it and opening it to water so it sunk in less than a minute.

After almost an hour of fighting and with his fleet still engaging as fast as possible through the minefield, Pohl had to make a dreadful decision and sacrifice some of his ships to save the rest.

Landing and fighting part 2
The 14th French Division in action at Taranto, November 10th, 1914

(...) Three O'clock in the morning (...)

Private Armand Bonnier took another sip of his water canteen. He was parched, and no amount of drinking seemed to quench his thirst. Combat and rifle fire did that to a man. The cordite and the rifle smoke ran a man's throat dry like nothing else did. Looking at his cards, he saw he had three aces, and there was still one card to go on the draw. He tried to keep the best composure he could and as straight a face as possible. Three aces were very rare. Another private with a bloody face continued dealing the cards. One to Philippe, another one to Armand, to one more man in the makeshift group, and then one to himself. Armand flipped the last card and felt a surge of excitement. He drew a fourth ace!

This was very rare indeed. He flickered a glance toward the pile of cigarettes in the middle of the makeshift table (it was a piece of broken column). This hand was going to be a great haul. Cigarettes were handy merchandise for trades, and there was no telling when they would get more.

The worn French soldiers were in a weird moment. It wasn't time to play cards, but they needed to take their minds away from what they'd been through and what they were about to receive again the next day. Hunkered down in the ruins of the Castle Aragonese, they were trying to relax before they were sent back into the mayhem of battle. It was late in the night or early in the morning, as Armand thought he could see flickers of the sun coming up on the horizon.

"One," said one of the soldiers whom Armand couldn't recall his name The man kept a straight face, dropping another smoke into the pile. *"Call,"* answered Philippe, following with his own cigarette. It was then Armand's turn. He wanted to reel them in and continue to bet so he could get the biggest pot of the evening. *"Call, and up one*

more," he said, trying to stay casual. The other soldier in the game (the dealer) folded with a disgusted face. His luck had been bad since they'd started playing. He instead took a long sip of his water canteen.

They were sitting on the rough ground in their makeshift hiding place facing the Italian positions. They could barely stand up in it even if the height had been supplemented with whatever they had found. *"Call,"* said Philippe and then other nameless soldier. It was their third turn. He decided it was time. *"Five,"* he said, pushing his remaining stash into the pile in the middle. The remaining three players gasped at the sight of the thing. *"You're bluffing, you asshole,"* said Philippe with a smile, looking at him suspiciously, trying to decipher his unreadable face. He put five more in to call. Having a hard time controlling his emotions, Armand took another sip of his water canteen. Nameless soldier called as well, and they dropped their cards at the same time. Nameless showed two pairs, Philippe a triple, and then Armand showed his cards. *"Damn you, Bonnier!"* Cren just grumbled and lifted himself up from the ground, leaving the game. He was broke; he didn't have any more cigarettes.

"It's a wrap for me, too," said nameless with a yawn, leaving Philippe shrugging his shoulders. *"I guess it's over, hey, my friend?"* Armand just smiled and brought one of the cigarettes to his mouth to light it and enjoy his victory.

He figured that it would not be a bad idea to try and catch some sleep. Dawn was going to arrive sooner than later, and the silent battlefield would soon light up with fire and destruction. He didn't know why the battleships weren't firing (they'd stopped an hour ago), but he felt it was great because he would not have been able to sleep otherwise.

An all-out attack was planned at dawn, one that promised to be intense. He wondered if he would survive the coming day. Everyone in the 14th Division knew that the Italians were far from beaten and would fight like the devil. After all, it was their city. His eyes closed without him even noticing he was falling asleep.

(...) The assault (...)

He ran and ran. He was winded, zipping through swirling smoke. The ground rocked, and it wasn't easy to keep his balance. For a moment, he thought he saw Philippe running through the dust storm near him. Intellectually, Armand knew that many of his comrades ran beside him, but the sound of battle was so loud and the smoke so heavy that he felt alone. His ears ringed, the acrid air stung at his eyes watered. His lungs were on fire from the sprinting and bad air, and his legs were burning from exertion.

The general attack order had been given the moment dawn broke over the horizon. The night before, the 14th Division had completed the conquest of the Castle Aragonese, and they'd been able to catch a few moments of sleep as the battleships stopped firing for about an hour before they resumed their shelling of Italian positions. They'd jumped out of their hiding holes just as gigantic explosions blossomed on the rock and its vicinity. The enemy, unfortunately for the landing Anglo-French forces, finally brought some artillery to bear, or maybe it was the ships in the harbor; Armand didn't know.

Bullets raced from one side to the other, the French forces stopping their advance to aim and fire their rifles while Italian defenders fired from the half-demolished buildings facing the backside of Castle Aragonese. The assault was going well, and for the first time, they reached the fortifications themselves. It was difficult to advance on the broken, uneven ground. The place had been bombed hard. It was pockmarked by giant craters and broken rock pieces ranging from pebbles to human-sized boulders.

He finally made it to a large, broken piece of the castle and was able to shelter behind it. The thing had been cracked open like an egg, and fire still spewed out from it. He decided that it had just been hit by one of the battleship guns since the destruction looked fresh. More and more of his comrades just seemed to appear out of the thick muck along with several other soldiers and put their backs on the broken wall of the bunker. A sergeant led the group they were part of. *"We are almost there, men. We need to spring out in this open area,"* the NCO pointed at a large town square between the castle and the demolished buildings where the Italians were firing from.

The men, including Armand and Philippe, a few feet away, stirred out of their prone positions and started to advance again, but this time, they ran to avoid being killed by the withering fire facing them. The bullets zipping around his ears sounded like bees flying around him. Further down and in the middle of the town square, he again found a place to hide, this time behind the fallen giant statue of some Italian general on a horse. The thing was lying prone on the ground and was large enough for a man to crouch behind it. It was mayhem. Philippe and several other men joined him a few moments later, dropping to the stone-paved ground as if their lives depended on it.

Their makeshift reprieve didn't last long, as they were called back to the action by a passing Lieutenant. *"Men, get up; we've got a city to conquer,"* he yelled as he stopped in front of them, apparently oblivious to the enemy bullets blazing by. Armand and his comrades did, and they started running again. *"Charrrrrge!!!!"*

The death ride
Battle of Cape Griz-Nez Part 2, November 11th, 1914

(...) Bridge of dreadnought battleship Ostfriesland (...)

"And finish the message with, May God be with You," said Admiral Pohl, disgusted about what he'd just ordered. The High Seas Fleet wasn't going to make it; the British were tightening the noose, and the fact that they had the plans to the minefield and knew of the channels to go through. In short, the enemy was going a lot faster than his own ships, and they were winning the battle with their superior firepower.

After conferring with his Chief of staff, Vice-Admiral Henning von Holtzendorff, he'd decided. The 5th Battle Squadron, composed of the two pre-dreadnought battleships and reinforced by battleship Worth and three light cruisers, was given the job of turning around and fighting the British to the end to give enough time for the remainder of the High Seas Fleet to escape.

Vice-Admiral Max von Grapow was the commander of the 9th Division, 5th Battle Squadron, and led four pre-dreadnought battleships, three destroyers, and three light cruisers. His job was to die for the Empire, and Fleet Admiral von Pohl was not proud of what he'd done. "Sir," said von Holtzendorff, "There is no choice; the main body of the fleet needs to survive." Somehow, the old naval commander's words didn't soothe Pohl in the least.

(...) Battleship Iron Duke (...)

"Well, well," said Admiral Jellicoe, crossing his arms on his chest and smiling. *"Little German bully wants to escape,"* he continued, laughing softly. *"Sir, said his chief of staff. Some of the enemy ships are turning to give battle." "Yes, Vice Admiral, I can see that. Well, if they are looking for a fight to die into a blaze of glory, let's oblige the brave chaps."*

(...) Battleship Kaiser Wilhelm II (...)

On board the pre-dreadnought battleship that bore the name of the Emperor, the mood was heavy and solemn. Vice-Admiral Max von Grapow, the commander of the 9th Division of the 5th German Battle Squadron, decided to take a moment to speak to his men as the ships turned to cross the "T" on the British, presenting their full broadsides to maximize the damage they would do. In doing so, the damage to his ships would be increased as they would present a larger target, but alas, it could not be helped.

"Gentlemen, it has been an honor serving with you all. I suppose the name of this ship was pre-destined to die in a blaze of glory. Make one final prayer, and then let's fight." The sailors and officers on the bridge all responded with a solemn head nod. *"Signal the other ships to fire at will. The longer we stay afloat and fighting, the longer the High Seas Fleet survives."*

(...) The Death Ride (...)

5th Battle Squadron, 9th Division (Vice-Admiral Max von Grapow)		
Pre-Dread BB Kaiser Wilhelm II (Flagship)	Pre-Dread BB Kaiser Wilhelm der Grosse	3 DD
Pre-Dread BB Kaiser Barbarossa mine damage aft magazine, crew quarters	Pre-Dread BB Wörth	3 CL

The unequal fight started well for Grapow's ships since both Kaiser Barbarossa and Worth lodged four hits each on the dreadnought battleship Thunderer, with a major fire, destroyed boiler, magazine damage, waterline, and hull damage, leaving the ship crippled and dead in the water.

The three destroyers turned about and charged at full speed, all torpedo's blazing. They died each in a powerful explosion, but not before launching their weapons that slammed each on dreadnought battleship Bellopheron, reducing its speed by half and taking in water, crippling the pre-dreadnought BB London, which would need to be towed out of the zone after the fight. Finally, another twin set of torpedo's sank the light cruiser Topaze.

The aging German battleships scored some more hits, but then the Hammer of God landed on them, and then they started dying in a catastrophic maelstrom of fire. Well over forty-five battleships and a hundred-plus cruisers and support vessels fired on them at roughly the same time.

At first, the entire sea seemed to lift in the air, peppered by mines exploding from shells hitting them. Then, the water was sprinkled with expanding fireballs and towering columns of fire. The next minute, shrapnel debris showered the water's surface, and then when the water geysers finally abated, what was left were sinking, flaming warships. Kaiser Wilhelm was hit on his two boilers, igniting an explosion that gutted the bridge (killing von Grapow) and half the crew. Kaiser Barbarossa wasn't even there, replaced by a cloud of sinking debris on the water. Kaiser Wilhelm Der Grosse was sinking rapidly from the stern, and the Worth was like a large, burning, bright fireball without anyone alive inside. The three light cruisers were also gone or sinking. It was a massacre.

EPILOGUE

The fall of Taranto
The Entente storms the Italian Harbor November 13th, 1914

By November 14th, Taranto was completely occupied by the Entente, and more troops were brought in. By November 16th, the entire area of Apulia, or else the heel of the Italian boot, was mastered by the Anglo-French forces.

Italian troops were brought in the hundreds of thousands, while the Allies entrenched themselves in an intricate network of field fortifications supported by numerous artillery units. With their strong battleship force, they were able to repulse everything the new Central Power member threw at them.

The entire Italian Fleet was thus destroyed and or captured. This was a strategic disaster of epic proportions for the Central Powers.

At the same time, the Anglo-French launched an ill-fated offensive against the western border of Italy at a town called Ventimiglia just east of Monaco. All were repulsed by strong Italian fortifications and well-equipped troops. By November 18th, the entire frontline was fixated in trench warfare, much like the Western front south of Paris and at Verdun-Belfort.

The Entente was successful in its endeavor to eliminate the Regina Marina, but the Italians added three million soldiers to the Central Powers. While these fresh troops might not have a major impact on the Franco-Italian border, they would do wonders on the Eastern front. Discussion on this very aspect started to be discussed by the middle of November since the Germans would take any, and all help they could get to master the Russian Juggernaut.

The fall of Serbia
King Ferdinand backstabs Serbia, November 1914

Once October morphed into November, the fight was over for the Serbs. As they retreated in Kosovo, there had been talks of evacuating the Serbian Army through Montenegro to Corfu via the Entente Combined Mediterranean Fleet, now towering as masters in Taranto.

A week later, the commander of Serbian forces, Marshall Putnik, dropped the towel and decided that there was no hope of beating the invaders and that his only option was to move across the mountains to the Adriatic.

The Serbs were thus trapped in Kosovo, facing a choice between a fight to the death or a retreat across the mountains. The 300,000 or so remaining soldiers moved into the mountains. The weather was terrible, the roads filled with snow, with far-below freezing temperatures. Tens of thousands died during the trek because of the weather, hunger, and simple exhaustion. Furthermore, and compounding the problem, Albanian warlords took the Serbs for invaders. They were forced to do so as their neighbors were mortal enemies by religion and also because they had hated each other since time immemorial. The survivors reached the Adriatic coast after about three weeks. From there, the same transport ships that landed the now twelve divisions in Apulia (around Taranto) picked them up to bring them into the Allied perimeter and bolster the Entente forces there.

Taranto soon became the seat of the Serbian government-in-exile, complete with parliament. Much of the Serbian army thus enlisted to fight for the Allies against the Italians in exchange for future help in regaining their country.

Brest, German-occupied France
The High Seas Fleet arrives in port November 12th, 1914

(...) Battleship Ostfriesland (...)

It was a fleet in shambles that arrived in Brest in the early hours of the morning. Fleet Admiral Hugo von Pohl's High Seas Fleet had survived the breakout attempt into the Channel, but not without heavy losses. Most of his ships were damaged to varying degrees, ranging from critical to esthetic, and the operation had so far cost four battleships and fifteen other support ships (cruisers, destroyers, minesweepers). It was not a good tally, but Pohl figured it had to be expected.

The Royal Navy was far from stupid, and they'd prepared for such an attempt by the Kaiserliche Marine. *"Admiral, would you want a motorboat sent to the ship for you to go to land and speak with the authorities there,"* said von Holtzendorff, as the man knew there was much work to do. Ships needed coal repairs and had many injured sailors. The Kaiser and the OKM (Navy High Command) would also require a full report on the action at the Battle of Cape Griz Nez and the crossing of the Dover Barrage. "Yes, thank you, Vice Admiral," he answered wearily. He was so very tired; it had been a very long two days.

(...) Battleship Iron Duke (...)

Admiral John Jellicoe, the commander of the British Grand Fleet, was sitting alone in his office, listening to the low hum of the ship's engines. The battle was over for now, and the fleet headed for Southampton, Plymouth, and Portsmouth, all located in Southern England.

For the Grand Fleet, there would be no return to the Scapa Flow base since the Germans were now in Brest. While Jellicoe felt satisfied with his major tactical victory at the Battle of Cape Griz Nez, he knew that the British Empire was now in a whole new world of trouble with such a German Fleet resting in Brest. From there, the enemy could send its fleet south, west, or north, intercept convoys, and execute many raids across the entire British coastline.

But at least he hadn't *"lost the war in one day,"* as that pompous bastard Churchill had said of him. No, he'd beaten the Germans bloody and promised to himself he would do so again the moment the bastards decided to sortie out of their new lair.

THE STORY WILL CONTINUE IN BOOK 2 OF THE WW1 ALTERNATE SERIES:

1915 ALTERNATE

Thank you very much for reading my work.

I HAVE A NEW FACEBOOK PAGE! PLEASE GO AND VISIT: https://www.facebook.com/profile.php?id=61558770082344

*** Please review my book(s) on Amazon and Goodreads.com and try not to be a troll.
.

*** Send me an email at souvorov@hotmail.com if you feel like chatting with me. I respond to every email.

www.maxlamirande.com

THE GREAT WAR ALTERNATE SERIES
BY MAX LAMIRANDE

Book 1: *Schlieffen Alternate*
Book 2: *Great War Alternate (Summer-Fall 2024)*
Book 3:
Book 4:
Book 5:
Book 6:

THE BLACK DEATH SERIES

Book 1: *Space War*
Book 2: *Invasion (TBD)*

THE BLITZKRIEG ALTERNATE SERIES
BY MAX LAMIRANDE

Book 1: Blitzkrieg Europa
Book 2: Battle Europa
Book 3: Struggle Europa
Book 4: Fortress Europa
Book 5: Stalemate Europa
Book 6: Staggering Europa
Book 7: Faltering Europa
Book 8: Crumbling Europa
Book 9: Falling Europa
Book 10: Soviet Europa
Book 11: Red Europa
Book 12: Climax Europa
Book 13: The Walder Chronicles Part 1
Book 14: The Walder Chronicles Part 2
Book 15: The Walder Chronicles Part 3

THE PACIFIC ALTERNATE SERIES
BY MAX LAMIRANDE

Book 1: Blitzkrieg Pacific
Book 2: Battle Pacific
Book 3: Struggle Pacific
Book 4: Staggering Pacific
Book 5: Burning Pacific
Book 6: Sallying Pacific
Book 7: Siege Pacific
Book 8: Faltering Pacific
Book 9 Crumbling Pacific
Book 10: Collapsing Pacific (June-July 2024)

THE NAPOLEONIC ALTERNATE SERIES
BY MAX LAMIRANDE

Book 1: *Austerlitz Alternate*
Book 2: *Friedland Alternate*
Book 3: *1809 Alternate Summer-Fall 2024*

THE AXIS ALTERNATE SERIES
BY MAX LAMIRANDE

Book 1: The Bear and the Swastika
Book 2: World War
Book 3: Axis Triumphant
Book 4: Axis Victorious
Book 5: Axis overwhelming
Book 6: Stalemate
Book 7: Axis resurging (summer 2024)

Also, from the same author:

BLITZKRIEG PACIFIC
Book 1 of the Pacific Alternate Series

The year is 1942.

The world is at war. Almost every major nation has declared support for the Allies or the Axis. The Third Reich occupies Europe, and the British Islands have been invaded and conquered by the Germans. Metropolitan France has fallen, along with its North African colonies. Spain and Turkey have joined the Axis. The Middle East is Axis. The USA and Soviet Russia are also at war with the Third Reich.

Only one major power is still on the sideline. Imperial Japan, already busy in its war of conquest in China, dawns on the idea of conquering the Pacific and Southeast Asia following German successes in Europe and the subsequent weakening of the resource-rich Franco-British and Dutch colonies.

The United States, following Japan's occupation of the French colony of French Indochina in 1940, froze all of Tokyo's assets, stopped scrap metal deliveries, and was just about to stop delivering oil to the hungry Japanese military machine, a move that is certain to trigger a reaction from the warmongers in Tokyo.

President Roosevelt's decision to do so is about to have dire consequences for America. The Imperial Navy has set its sights on the main US base in the Pacific, Pearl Harbor. And all across the Japanese-held islands of the Pacific, the forces of the Rising Sun prepare for a full-scale invasion that they hope will give them control over the resources the country needs to continue on its expansion.

This is the story of the War in the Pacific.

Also, from the same author:

THE BEAR AND THE SWASTIKA
Book 1 of the Axis Alternate Series

The year is 1939.

The world rocks with the news of the signing of the Germano-Soviet pact. A dark veil soon falls on Europe as Poland is invaded and destroyed by the overwhelming forces of the Wehrmacht and the Red Army.

France and the United Kingdom can only sit by and watch the two military juggernauts obliterate the Polish state. No one believes the two totalitarian regimes can agree in the long term as their ideologies completely contradict each other.

Russia wants influence in the Balkans, has eyes on Finland, and wants an opening to the Mediterranean. Germany needs Romanian oil to keep its war machine operational, and Hitler is adamant about not letting the Bolsheviks gain another inch of ground in Europe. At least not more than he has already given out in the treaty of non-aggression signed before the Polish campaign.

The year is 1940.

The French campaign then unfolds with a disaster for the Allies, and the Germans win an incredible victory over the combined forces of the United Kingdom and France. British forces narrowly escape to their island with the remnants of their armies, and France surrenders. Half of the country is occupied by the Germans. It seems that the swastika will conquer the world, especially with the Russian bear watching its back.

Germano-Soviet Axis talks were organized in October 1940 concerning the Soviet Union's potential entry as a fourth Axis Power during World War II. The negotiations include a two-day conference in Berlin between Soviet Foreign Minister Vyacheslav Molotov, Adolf Hitler, and German Foreign Minister Joachim von Ribbentrop. The two powers will try to agree on a formal alliance to divide the world.

The fate of liberty hangs in the balance.

Also, from the same author:

BLITZKRIEG EUROPA
Book 1 of the Blitzkrieg Alternate Series

September 1st, 1939.

Germany invades Poland, igniting a major European war. A few months later the French are also invaded, and the allied armies are utterly defeated. Then the Dunkirk disaster happens, and the United Kingdom loses most of its land army.

Soon, the British Isles are also attacked, and the British are hard-pressed with a serious German invasion. The French struggle to resist the Axis forces bent on conquering all of their mainland home country and the Western African Colonies.

America, watching from its safe shores, cannot stay still while Western Europe and all of the Mediterranean fall to the forces of the Axis. And when the Afrika Korps plunges over the Suez and invades the Middle East, the Soviet Union finally decides to join in.

This is the story of the Second World War.

Also, from the same author:

SPACE WAR
Book 1 of the Black Death Series

The Empire built by Haakon the Great is no more. It's 4124, and the Human race has spread to the stars in four different star clusters by achieving the speed of light and wormholes. A civil war has broken out between the different human enclaves to see who the next emperor of humanity will be.

The Ptolemy and Hadesian Star Nations are invading Elysium, allied with New America from the Alpha Perseis Cluster. Large battles are being fought in star systems between former comrades of the Imperial Fleet. In space, battleships unload their powerful weapons at each other while giant battle mechas fight for control of the ground.

The opportunity is too great for the evil Cybernetic forces in the Caldwell 14 Star Cluster. Having fought – and lost – a terrible war against the Empire two hundred years ago, they are gathering for a return engagement against humanity.

A thousand years ago, Haakon dreamed and foresaw a terrible time for humanity. The Black Death is coming to consume all, and his Empire will not be there to fight it.

Also from the same author:

AUSTERLITZ ALTERNATE
Book 1 of the Napoleonic Alternate Series

DECEMBER 2ND, 1805

The War of the Third Coalition rages in Europe. Battles have been fought, and Napoleon Bonaparte's Grande Armée sweeps everything before it. After a big victory over an Austrian Army in Ulm, the French occupied Vienna, the capital of the Austrian Empire.

The Russians entered Austria to come to the help of their Allies and under pressure from the British. The Austro-Russians and the French are about to clash in a small, unknown town called Austerlitz.

And then everything changes. The French stop trying to retake the Pratzen Heights, and the day's battle ends in a stalemate for both armies. Kutusov, the allied army's leader in the absence of young Tsar Alexander (who fell ill and is still somewhere in Galicia), decides to retire the army northward with the Austrian Emperor's approval.
The news galvanizes the Revolution's enemies and of the Empire, jealous of Napoleon's success and wanting him gone. The Prussians decide to join the war and move their troops into Austria to link their forces with the two other powers. The German states and other countries like Naples rethink their stances in the conflict. And the French Emperor's internal enemies, ever wishing the old regime's return, start plotting to overthrow the government in Paris.

All the while, the Ottoman Empire, convinced by the French several months earlier to enter the war, has decided to intervene in favor of Bonaparte and invade southern Hungary with an Army. Austria is on the brink of annihilation, but Napoleon's Grande Armée also has a big challenge ahead since it now needs to defeat three major powers simultaneously.

Everything will come down to either Napoleon's genius to overcome the odds and win regardless of the troops arrayed against him, or his defeat and the end of the French Empire.

This is the story of the Napoleonic Wars.

www.ingramcontent.com/pod-product-compliance
Lightning Source LLC
Chambersburg PA
CBHW070731020526
44118CB00035B/1181